PERSONAL FINANCE

AT YOUR FINGERTIPS

Ken Little

ALPHA

A member of Penguin Group (USA) Inc.

This book is dedicated to my wife, Cyndy, and our cabin in the woods.

ALPHA BOOKS

Published by the Penguin Group

Penguin Group (USA) Inc., 375 Hudson Street, New York, New York 10014, USA

Penguin Group (Canada), 90 Eglinton Avenue East, Suite 700, Toronto, Ontario M4P 2Y3, Canada (a division of Pearson Penguin Canada Inc.)

Pentuin Books Ltd., 80 Strand, London WC2R 0RL, England

Penguin Ireland, 25 St. Stephen's Green, Dublin 2, Ireland (a division of Penguin Books Ltd.)

Penguin Group (Australia), 250 Camberwell Road, Camberwell, Victoria 3124, Australia (a division of Pearson Australia Group Pty. Ltd.)

Penguin Books India Pvt. Ltd., 11 Community Centre, Panchsheel Park, New Delhi—110 017, India

Penguin Group (NZ), 67 Apollo Drive, Rosedale, North Shore, Auckland 1311, New Zealand (a division of Pearson New Zealand Ltd.)

Penguin Books (South Africa) (Pty.) Ltd., 24 Sturdee Avenue, Rosebank, Johannesburg 2196, South Africa

Penguin Books Ltd., Registered Offices: 80 Strand, London WC2R 0RL, England

International Standard Book Number: 978-1-59257-644-9
Special Markets Edition: ISBN 978-1-61564-116-1
Library of Congress Catalog Card Number: 2006920578

 3   5   7   9   10   8   6   4   2

Interpretation of the printing code: The rightmost number of the first series of numbers is the year of the book's printing: the rightmost number of the second series of numbers is the number of the book's printing. For example, a printing code of 07-1 shows that the first printing occurred in 2007.

Printed in the United States of America

Note: This publication contains the opinions and ideas of its author. It is intended to provide helpful and informative material on the subject matter covered. It is sold with the understanding that the author and publisher are not engaged in rendering professional services in the book. If the reader requires personal assistance or advice, a competent professional should be consulted.

The author and publisher specifically disclaim any responsibility for any liability, loss, or risk, personal or otherwise, which is incurred as a consequence, directly or indirectly, of the use and application of any of the contents of this book.

Most Alpha books are available at special quantity discounts for bulk purchases for sales promotions, premiums, fundraising, or educational use. Special books, or book excerpts, can also be creaed to fit specific needs.

For details, write: Special Markets, Alpha Books, 375 Hudson Street, New York, NY 10014.

Publisher: **Marie Butler-Knight**

Editorial Director/Acquisitions Editor: **Mike Sanders**

Managing Editor: **Billy Fields**

Senior Development Editor: **Phil Kitchel**

Senior Production Editor: **Janette Lynn**

Cover/Book Designer: **Kurt Owens**

Indexer: **Brad Herriman**

Layout: **Brian Massey**

Proofreader: **Aaron Black**

CONTENTS

INTRODUCTION

Personal Finance At Your Fingertips is a reference book of a different type. We have organized and formatted this book to bring you the important information you need about personal finance topics, but not every single detail and tiny bit of information.

The chapters focus on the most important things you need to know about personal finance without bogging you down in needless detail. You'll find the information you want on a personal finance topic quickly without reading the book cover-to-cover.

The topics all fit together because personal finance is a comprehensive subject, but you can find the piece of information you are looking for by going directly to that subject. The goal is to get you to your information by the most direct route possible. If the information you need is in Chapter 4 and concerns credit card debt, you can go directly there and get your question answered. Handy "SEE ALSO" arrows tell you exactly where to go:

◁ *SEE ALSO 4.6, "Repairing Your Credit"* ▷

In addition to the SEE ALSO pointers, you'll also find a sidebar titled, "Words to Go." This sidebar defines terms you'll find in the surrounding text.

WORDS TO GO . . . *WORDS TO GO . . . WORDS TO GO*

Words to Go are quick definitions of financial terms discussed within the chapter. These definitions are provided to enhance your understanding of the material covered.

Each chapter contains these pointers, which direct you to other areas in the book for additional information on a topic mentioned in the preceding paragraph.

The topics are presented in a logical order, progressing from the general to the more specific. The broad overview of financial planning moves through budgeting and money management to more complicated areas such as insurance, taxes, investing, estates, and so on.

Many people have a personal financial issue right in front of them that occupies most of their attention. It might be financing a college education for their children, planning a comfortable retirement, or an investment question. These major topics are compartmentalized for rapid access and focused attention. Jumping around in this book is no problem—that's the way we designed it, to be responsive to those questions and concerns that you need to know about right now.

Here is a general overview of the book's structure:

Chapter 1, "Personal Financial Planning": This chapter defines financial planning and covers goal setting and working with a professional planner.

Chapter 2, "Budgeting": The budgeting process is defined and you are shown how to create a spending and savings plans that addresses your financial goals. The use of personal financial software is reviewed along with how to set up an emergency cash reserve.

Chapter 3, "Banking": Financial institutions, bank products, services, fees, and regulations are covered in this chapter, along with the time value of money and identity theft.

Chapter 4, "Credit and Debt": What is good debt and bad debt? How much is too much debt? Managing your credit and debt is covered in this chapter, which includes credit cards, credit rating, repairing your credit, and bankruptcy.

Chapter 5, "Housing": This chapter looks at the benefits and drawbacks of owning versus renting your house, how to buy and sell your home, working with a real estate agent, selling your home yourself, building a home, and the details of renting and leasing.

Chapter 6, "Automobiles": Should you buy a new or used car? What is the true cost of leasing? This chapter discusses the details of buying, leasing, and financing an automobile.

Chapter 7, "Insurance": This chapter covers the important aspects of life, auto, renters, health, disability, and long-term care insurance.

Chapter 8, "Taxes": Federal income taxes are discussed and explained along with tax saving strategies, the alternative minimum tax, and audits.

Chapter 9, "College Financing": The costs of college, including the various forms of financial aid, tuition plans, and other sources of financing are discussed in this chapter.

Chapter 10, "Investment Planning and Management": This chapter defines investment objectives and options, along with examining the risk/reward relationship. Return on investments and using asset allocation are examined. Trading through a broker and online are compared.

Chapter 11, "Investing in Mutual Funds and Exchange Traded Funds": This chapter looks at the mechanics and different types of mutual funds and exchange traded funds. Expenses and how to find good investments are covered.

Chapter 12, "Investing in Stocks": The basics of stocks and stock markets are covered along with the different types of stocks, finding good stocks, employee stock options, and calculating your return on investment.

Chapter 13, "Investing in Bonds": This chapter covers the sometimes complex world of buying and selling bonds. Different types of bonds—U.S. Treasury, agency, municipal, and corporate—are examined along with the risk of investing in bonds.

Chapter 14, "Retirement Planning": This chapter covers aspects of retirement planning from goal setting to planning. Also examined are Social Security and Medicare benefits, along with private pension and retirement plans.

Chapter 15, "Retirement Accounts": The various retirement accounts that help you reach your goals are discussed including IRAs, 401(k), 403(b), and others.

Chapter 16, "Estate Planning": Planning your estate is discussed along with such topics as probate, wills, trusts, and so on.

Appendix A, "Words to Go Glossary": A comprehensive glossary of personal financial planning terms for your reference.

Appendix B, "Resources": A list of helpful websites and other references.

Acknowledgments

Thank you to Alpha Books, Mike Sanders, and Phil Kitchel in particular for seeing this project through. Alpha Books has brought out another series of useful books and I hope this one will be a resource for people wanting help understanding their personal finances.

1
PERSONAL FINANCE PLANNING

1.1 PERSONAL FINANCIAL PLANNING

Financial Planning Defined

The First Step in Planning

The Purpose of Setting Goals

Financial planning is an active, ongoing process that looks at your total financial picture. In this subchapter, you'll see where the process starts and why setting specific, yet exciting goals is the key to making them happen.

Financial Planning Defined

Personal financial planning is the process of organizing and planning your income, expenses, and savings to accomplish significant long-term goals. The two largest financial goals most people face are funding their retirement and financing a college education for their children. Financial planning can make it possible to achieve both of these goals.

Personal financial planning encompasses every aspect of your financial life, including how you spend and invest your money and protect your assets. It is a **holistic approach** to money management that goes beyond investing and savings accounts. A working financial plan is a fluid document that adapts to new life circumstances such as new children, divorce and remarriage, medical conditions, college decisions, and career changes.

WORDS TO GO . . . *WORDS TO GO . . . WORDS TO GO*

A **holistic approach** to financial planning looks at every aspect of your life and considers what will work and won't work based on your lifestyle.

Depending on the complexity of your financial situation and your life, your financial plan may be a formal document that a professional prepares or a simpler budget that captures all the necessary information, along with some mutually agreed upon goals.

For a financial plan to be useful, no matter the format, it must be realistic, clear in its goals and intentions and, most important, have the emotional support of all the participants. Support is important because there will inevitably be conflicts as differing goals compete for limited resources. Most families will find it difficult to fully fund a retirement plan and save adequately for college expenses at the same time, for example. In addition to major long-range goals, other short-term goals and needs will also require resources.

A personal financial plan that is too rigid will fail because it does not recognize that life is fluid and changeable. Personal financial planning keeps you focused on the major goals, while allowing some flexibility for events and needs that may require short-term or immediate action.

For example, if you need a new car, there are several ways to finance the purchase—which one makes the most sense? You should check the numbers, but it always makes more sense to keep your interest costs down. If that means a large down payment (money that could have gone into the college fund), you are still better off keeping financing costs low. Your personal financial plan should allow for this type of short-term goal and the adjustments to other goals.

◁ *SEE ALSO 6.4, "The Auto Loan"* ▶

The First Step in Planning

The preliminary step in building a personal financial plan is to make an honest assessment of where you are right now, financially and emotionally, in terms of committing to a disciplined plan.

The financial assessment should include a net worth statement (covered in subsequent sections of this chapter) and a realistic projection of your family's earnings potential. If you're just starting out in the work world, you may not have a good idea of your earnings potential, so make an estimate. If you see your income growing 3 percent per year, that's a good place to start. That's not far off the recent rate of inflation and is equal to the "**cost of living**" increases that many companies hand out.

WORDS TO GO . . . WORDS TO GO . . . WORDS TO GO

Cost of living is a generic phrase used to describe the general increase in the cost of goods and services. It comes from the Labor Department's Consumer Price Index, which is also known as the rate of inflation.

If you and your partner plan to work full time, factor both incomes into the projection. If one of you plans to take off to start a family temporarily or to become a full-time at home parent, that changes your future income picture.

If one partner is the sole bookkeeper, the other needs to become a participating partner as soon as possible. You both will find it difficult to agree on goals if only one has a firm understanding of the financial situation.

Couples must also face another financial reality: an understanding that money matters may not have the same significance for one partner that they do for another. One partner may be a saver, nervous if the savings account is not growing at a steady rate, while the other partner may not feel the same need. Conflicts arise when a spender and a saver try to work out a financial plan because their priorities are different.

Establishing a starting point, which begins with a net worth statement, is the beginning of a basis for agreement: "Here is where we are. Where do we want to be in x number of years?"

The Purpose of Setting Goals

The purpose of setting financial goals in your plan is to interject discipline in the process and give you a sense of accomplishment as you reach or approach the goals. Major financial goals such as retirement and college funding usually require years of effort to achieve. Funding your retirement is a goal that begins with the first job you take as an adult. Staying motivated for a goal that is years, maybe decades, in the future may be hard for some people. The key is to set interim goals that are shorter in term and will give you a sense of accomplishment. Set short-term goals of one year or less to get you motivated to act now. For example, a short-term goal may be to increase participation on your 401(k) plan another percentage point.

Mid-term goals are one to three years. These goals should require more effort and are something you build to reach. An example might be replacing maturing bank CDs with mutual funds, if that is appropriate for your situation.

Long-term goals extend beyond three years. Your retirement goal may be much further out than that, but it's easier to plan a task over the next 5 years than it is one over the next 20 years. Too many variables make long range planning difficult and the distant payoff is unrewarding. Break long-term goals into more manageable pieces and it will be easier to accomplish them and, equally important, keep yourself motivated to do the next step.

1.2 FINANCIAL GOALS

Retirement

College

Financial Independence

Preparing for retirement is the single most important financial goal we all will set, because it is the most expensive. A college education for our children comes next for many families. Others may define financial independence as one of the top three financial goals. However you sort these goals, they will get most of the attention in your financial plan. This subchapter explains why.

Retirement

Thanks to advances in medicine, people are enjoying long, healthy retirements. This is good news for the millions of people who retire each year, but it's an example of the law of unintended consequences. The unintended consequence in this case is that people are outliving the money they set aside for retirement.

Setting a dollar amount goal for retirement is challenging because it is difficult to predict how long it will have to last. Most people reaching retirement age in the first part of this decade began careers when life expectancy was lower than it is now. The result is retirement plans that might have been adequate for people several generations ago may no longer provide enough money for the length and style of life today's retired people want to enjoy. People must either increase their retirement plan funding or supplement their retirement plan with another source of funding.

◁ *SEE ALSO 14.2, "Determining Financial Needs"* ▷

Social Security, which was never meant to replace private retirement plans, is under tremendous pressure to meet the needs of its participants. As baby boomers retire over the next 20 years, pressure on Social Security and Medicare will only increase as more people draw benefits out of the system and fewer people pay taxes into it.

◁ *SEE ALSO 14.4, "Social Security and Medicare"* ▷

Many private companies have switched much of the responsibility for retirement savings to the employee by changing their retirement programs from **defined**

benefit plans to defined contribution plans. Defined benefit retirement plans are the traditional pensions that most companies offered until the shift began in the 1980s. These plans defined your retirement benefit based on your salary and your number of years of employment. The plans were also very expensive for companies to offer, especially as retired workers lived longer and drew on the fund for benefits longer.

The switch to a defined contribution plan has put more responsibility on the employee. Now, only the contribution to the plan is defined, but the ultimate retirement benefit is unknown. These plans, the 401(k) and companion 403(b), require employees to decide how much, if any, to save for retirement and how the money is invested. The employee's contribution is invested in one of several mutual funds or other investments offered with the plan.

◀ *SEE ALSO 15.1, "Types of Accounts"* ▶

WORDS TO GO . . .WORDS TO GO . . .WORDS TO GO

Defined benefit plans calculate retirement benefits using a formula that applies a percentage to an average salary (usually the last five years or the best five years of compensation) and adds in a longevity bonus for the number of years worked. This gives employees a monthly benefit for the rest of their life.

Defined contribution plans provide the employee an opportunity to invest pre-tax money deducted on a regular basis in a group of mutual funds and other investments. The employer may match part of the employee contribution, but is not required to by law. The employee will only know how much is contributed to the plan. The ultimate benefit at retirement will depend on how well the employee's choices of investments performed.

The defined contribution plan offers the opportunity to accumulate more in a retirement fund than you might have had under a traditional pension. However, there is no guarantee the plan will provide any benefit—no guarantee that the money you invest in mutual funds will grow or not suffer a severe loss just at the time you need it.

◀ *SEE ALSO 14.1, "Setting Retirement Goals"* ▶

Obviously, setting a goal for retirement becomes more challenging when it is difficult to know the ultimate value of your investments. It will be easier to stay focused on your retirement goal if you quantify it in some way other than a general "financially secure." Identify a place you want to retire (condo on a golf course), an activity you want to pursue (sailing to the Bahamas), or some other way of visualizing your retirement. Make it emotionally appealing and you'll find the sacrifices easier to make.

College

You can measure the value of a college education in dollars and cents when you compare the earning power of a typical college graduate with that of a high school graduate. By some estimates, a college graduate will earn three times more than a high school graduate over a lifetime.

Funding a college education is usually a cost-effective investment in the future. There are other reasons to get a college education, of course, but this is a book on financial planning, so we'll stick to the financial aspects. Parents may (and should) start saving for college when their child is still very young. You may not know whether your child will want to go to college or even have the academic skills, but it's best to assume the best and begin saving.

Setting a goal for college funding while your child is still very young has the advantage of establishing that priority in your budget. You can use a variety of funding mechanisms and let compounding work for you. There are several mechanisms for saving for college, including a traditional savings account of some type, a trust account, or one of the state-sponsored college education funds. In some cases, parents will choose all three as a way to beat the high cost of a higher education.

◁ SEE ALSO 9.4, *"Tax-Free College Savings Plans"* ▶

College costs have been growing faster than the rate of inflation. Depending on which state you live in and whether you consider a state-supported school or a private institution, costs have increased by 8 percent or more most years this decade.

It is not necessary to set a goal of 100 percent funding of college for your children. Even though the cost of college is high and climbing, there are numerous sources of assistance, including scholarships, grants, financial aid, and other loans that will ease the actual cost of college.

◁ SEE ALSO 9.2, *"College Financial Aid"* ▶

Financial Independence

A personal financial plan can help you achieve financial independence however you define it. **Financial independence** may mean becoming debt-free or at least free from high-interest credit card or other consumer debt. It may mean paying off the mortgage. For some couples, it may mean one partner is able to stay home full-time with the children.

WORDS TO GO . . .WORDS TO GO . . .WORDS TO GO

Financial independence is a goal that may mean different things to different people, but it is a valid goal nevertheless. If you can visualize what financial independence means to you and put it into a financial perspective (debt-free, own your on business, and so on), you can plan for it.

Whatever financial independence means to you, it won't happen without setting goals and building a plan to achieve those goals. Your financial plan sets your priorities. Those priorities are used in making financial decisions. With priorities in place, you have standards to measure whether your decisions advance those priorities or hinder them.

For example, if your financial plan calls for saving to buy a house in three years, every purchase that is not in the plan (your budget) will make it take that much longer to reach the amount you need. Buy a $4 coffee drink every day, and in three years you have put your goal off $3,000.

Achieving financial independence or any financial goal is an equation of time and investment. The more time you have, the smaller investment you must make; the less time you have, the larger the investment required.

◀ SEE ALSO 3.7, *"Time Value of Money"* ▶

Mitigating this equation is the level of risk you are willing to take with your investment. The less risk you are willing to take, the longer it will take to achieve your goal. If you accept more risk, you may reduce the length of time required to achieve the goal—but there is less certainty and you may lose some or all of your investment.

◀ SEE ALSO 10.3, *"Risk and Reward Relationship"* ▶

A financial plan not only states the goal, but provides the means of achieving it, whether through saving, investing, or most likely a combination of both. It also sets out a plan for spending and controlling expenses (budgeting) that prevents unnecessary expenditures from sabotaging the goals.

Set short and mid-term goals for financial independence so your progress is measured and rewarded. As these goals are attained, create new ones that advance the plan toward the long-term goal(s).

1.3   PERSONAL FINANCIAL PLAN

Components

Annual Review

Planning Math

This subchapter looks at the basic components of a financial plan, the annual review, and the math involved in building a plan.

Components

Personal financial plans can be as simple or complicated as they need to be for individual situations. The number and type of assets you have may require a lengthy and detailed financial plan weighing the interaction between assets owned, tax and estate implications, and your own personal risk tolerances. Your plan must consider all these variables along with your primary goals to arrive at the right strategies.

For most people, the process isn't so complicated, but it still has to be comprehensive. The financial plan addresses four very broad questions:

▶ Where are you now?

▶ Where do you want to be?

▶ What resources do you have to commit to the goals?

▶ How much time do you have to meet the goals?

Each of these broad questions have detailed questions that provide the overall answer.

Where Are You Now?

Before the financial planning process can begin, there must be a clear, quantified starting point. This starting point includes financial information, as well as some check-offs regarding necessary steps to protect assets and income.

The financial information is a net worth statement, a listing of all that you own minus all that you owe. The balance is your net worth, or what would be left if you sold everything and paid off all your debts. Your net worth statement is a key indicator of your financial health. Lenders will want to see a version of it before making loans. It is an important part of your financial plan and serves as one marker of progress, because you can update it annually or as often as you want or need.

Additionally, it is necessary to catalog insurance policies on each partner. If one or both of you are without life insurance policies and disability insurance, part of your financial plan must include adding that coverage. For people over the age of 55, the consideration of long-term care insurance is also an issue for the financial plan.

Adequate insurance for all assets (home, furnishings, vehicles, and so on) is also included in this part of the financial plan.

◀ *SEE ALSO Chapter 7, "Insurance"* ▶

Where Do You Want to Be?

Setting financial goals, both long-term and otherwise, will put your financial plans in motion by providing motivation for executing the plans. These should be a mixture of short-, mid-, and long-term goals, related to something or someplace that gives you a sense of emotional excitement and adds energy to the plan.

Goals should be specific in dates and amounts along with the "cabin in the woods" emotional goal. What cabin? Which woods? How much does a cabin cost? What will it take to make this happen? When you attach action items to goals, concrete steps come next. Now you have put your plan into motion.

What Resources Do You Have to Commit to the Goals?

A careful examination of your saving and spending habits, along with a current assessment of what you are currently contributing to financial goals (retirement plans, for example), is necessary to identify additional money you can use to fund your goals.

An integral part of this process is a spending budget or spending plan. Establishing a spending budget is the way to control expenses, and controlling expenses is the way to recover money for investing in your goals.

◀ *SEE ALSO 2.3, "Spending Plan"* ▶

How Much Time Do You Have to Meet Your Goal?

Time is a critical part of a financial plan. If you have 30 years to fund your retirement, a regular investment program and the **time value of money** can accomplish a great deal. On the other hand, if your retirement is 10 years away, your plan will have to accelerate the level of investment, because you have less time for compound growth to work its magic on your account.

The **time value of money** addresses the concept that a dollar today is better than a dollar tomorrow. You can invest a dollar today and it will earn interest. A dollar tomorrow is worth less than a dollar today thanks to inflation.

For short and mid-term goals, the plan will define the proper investment products to meet those needs. The purpose of categorizing goals by time frame is to match appropriate investment products.

Stocks are not appropriate investment vehicles for short-term goals. Although stocks historically offer the highest potential rate of return, they can be volatile over short periods. You wouldn't want to have your stock investment take a downward swing just when it was time to cash in for a short-term goal. Bank certificates of deposit (CDs) or a money market mutual fund are more appropriate for short-term goals, because these investments are relatively secure.

Mid-term goals of two to five years have more flexibility, but are still too short for pure stock investments. A mutual fund that paid high dividends and maintained a fairly stable price could be a choice, as could a long-term bank CD or U.S. Treasury Note because of their safety and higher yield over short-term saving instruments.

Goals that are more than five years out are candidates for stock investments, whether in individual stocks or aggressive stock mutual funds, such as growth funds. In either case, as your goal nears, watch performance and consider switching out of stock investments and into a more conservative choice like bank CDs.

Annual Review

A personal financial plan is not a document that you finish, file, and never see again. You should review it at least annually, and more often if something important changes in your life (marriage, divorce, children, and so on). The annual review is important to avoid slippage that occurs with inattention. Some sections of the plan, such as the spending plan, may become part of your everyday financial life—at least at first. It is a good idea to do the review at about the same time every year so the results cover a comparable period. In January or February for the previous year is a convenient time because you will be assembling financial documents to file tax returns during that period.

The first part of the review is a recalculation of your **net worth statement.** If you compare the new statement with the previous one, you should see that you've made progress in improving your financial life. Note whether your debt has dropped (if this was one of your goals) and how your assets have increased. Check insurance coverage and amounts for correct levels, and make sure the beneficiaries to all policies are as you want them. The same goes for your wills and trusts.

WORDS TO GO . . .WORDS TO GO . . .WORDS TO GO

A **net worth statement** is a listing of all you own and all you owe—your assets and liabilities. When you subtract your liabilities from your assets, the remainder is your net worth.

If you belong to a company-sponsored retirement plan, ask yourself if this is a good time to increase the amount of your contribution. If you're self-funding your retirement and are not maxed out, consider increasing your contribution.

Unless you have had a dramatic change in your life, you shouldn't need to redo your personal financial plan each year. You should, however, update it with new amounts for contributions and checks of new coverages for dependents.

Short-term goals may be ending and some mid-term goals may become short-term. Watch investment products for these goals to match the appropriate product with goal. As mid- and long-term goals come closer to the end of their period, begin the process of switching out of more risky investment products and into ones that are more conservative.

Planning Math

There is no difficult math in personal financial planning. There are two main calculations that you should do annually: your net worth statement and checking your debt-to-income ratio.

Preparing your net worth statement is more of an exercise in gathering information than in doing math. The net worth statement, however, is key to measuring your progress. You can measure progress toward specific goals, but the net worth statement measures your overall financial health.

If you use personal financial software such as Quicken or Microsoft Money, it will produce the net worth statement for you after you enter the information. But completing a net worth statement does not require a computer or software. There are numerous models to follow—here's one:

Category	Current Value
Assets:	
Cash	$_____
Savings accounts	$_____
Checking accounts	$_____
Certificates of deposit (CDs)	$_____
Money market accounts	$_____
Money owed to me (utility deposits, etc.)	$_____
Life insurance (cash value)	$_____
Stocks	$_____
Bonds	$_____
Mutual funds	$_____
Other investments	$_____
Individual retirement accounts (IRAs)	$_____
SEP—IRA accounts	$_____
Keogh accounts	$_____
401(k) or 403(b) accounts	$_____
Other retirement accounts	$_____
Market value of your home	$_____
Market value of other real estate	$_____
Cars and trucks (blue book value)	$_____
Other vehicles	$_____
Jewelry and collectibles	$_____
Personal property	$_____
Other misc. assets	$_____
Total assets	$_____
Liabilities:	
Mortgages	$_____
Auto loans	$_____
Credit card balances	$_____
Home equity loans	$_____
Student loans	$_____
Other loans	$_____

continues

continued

Real estate taxes	$_____
Income taxes	$_____
Other taxes	$_____
Other misc. debt	$_____
Total liabilities	$_____
Net worth **(total assets minus total liabilities)**	$_____

Don't overstate the value of your assets or understate the extent of your liabilities. This is an exercise in honest assessment, even if the news is not what you hoped it would be. When you do the addition and subtraction, you may find you have a negative net worth, meaning you owe more than you own. This can easily happen if you have high levels of credit card debt or bought a home with a low or no money down loan and find that the current market price is below what you owe. The same is true for an auto loan. It is guaranteed that if you finance a car with little or nothing down, the moment you drive it off the lot, you owe about 15 to 20 percent more than the car is worth, because new cars depreciate that much almost instantly.

The net worth statement has two components: **assets** and **liabilities.** To make the statement meaningful, it is important to assign a current value to each item on the statement. Obviously, you won't own or owe all the items on this sample.

WORDS TO GO . . .WORDS TO GO . . .WORDS TO GO

Assets are physical items and financial accounts you own that can be converted to cash.

Liabilities are ongoing debts you owe. They are not monthly bills for services, but obligations that will follow you, even if you moved to another location.

Your net worth statement is a snapshot of a point in time, so pick a day when you have access to the financial information you need to complete the assets portion of the statement, and fill in the accounts with the balances on this day.

For real estate and other less easily valued assets, you may have to do some research to arrive at realistic figures. Ask your realtor for comparables to your house, if possible, so you have an idea of what it might sell for on the open market.

For jewelry and collectibles, make your best estimate if you have a modest amount. However, if you own heirloom jewelry or significant modern jewelry, an insurance appraisal of market value might do. For collectibles that have more than sentimental value, an appraisal from an expert may be in order. In either case, for the net worth statement, it is better to underestimate the value than overestimate. You may be planning to sell the jewelry or collectible in the future to fund a goal, but both categories are notoriously unpredictable when estimating future value.

The **debt-to-income ratio** tells you if you are carrying too much debt. This is the same ratio lenders use when considering whether you are creditworthy of a mortgage loan.

WORDS TO GO . . . WORDS TO GO . . . WORDS TO GO

Debt-to-income ratio is a measurement of how much consumer debt you are carrying relative to your income. It is an important ratio to judge your financial health, used by lenders to decide if you are financially strong enough to take on more debt.

The debt-to-income ratio is another annual review check that helps keep your debt in line with your income. It doesn't presume that all debt is bad, but measures how large of an impact debt has on your income and therefore your financial health. If debt is a large percentage of your income, your financial health is in jeopardy. Here is a worksheet to help you calculate your debt-to-income ratio:

Debt-to-Income Ratio Calculation	
Monthly Debt Payments	
Mortgage payment or rent	$_____
Home equity line of credit or loan payment	$_____
Car payments	$_____
Student loan payments	$_____
Minimum credit card payments times two	$_____
Other monthly loan amounts	$_____
Child support payments	$_____
Total Monthly Debt Payments	$_____

continues

continued

Monthly Income

Take home pay	$_____
Other monthly income	$_____
Other annual income, divided by 12	$_____
Total Monthly Income	$_____

Debt-to-Income Ratio

Total Monthly Debt Payments/Total Monthly Income $_____

Notice that debts are ongoing obligations, not one-time bills. Don't include the telephone bill because you can cancel service anytime you want and eliminate the expense. Do include credit cards and any other consumer debt that will follow you even if you move. Income only includes steady sources such as your paycheck. Don't include gifts, bonuses, and one-time windfalls. If you work on commission, make the best estimation you can or use an average of the last six months.

There are ranges to determine if your ratio is good or bad. If you go to a bank for a loan, they will consider these ranges:

▶ 30 percent or less is considered excellent.

▶ 30 to 36 percent is a good ratio and should not cause any problems.

▶ 36 to 40 percent is pushing the limits and lenders are going to want a good reason why it is this high. They will also want strong numbers in other areas of your personal financial statement to offset this borderline ratio.

▶ 40 percent or more, for many lenders, is too high. It tells them you are already far in debt and may have trouble if a problem develops with your finances.

You should have the same perspective as professional lenders. Maintaining a good to excellent debt-to-income ratio is a form of financial security. It protects you in the event of a financial emergency because you are not living on the edge where a missed car or house payment is possible.

1.4 **USING A FINANCIAL PLANNER**

What Planners Do

Fee-Based Planners

Commission-Based Planners

In this subchapter, you'll learn about professional financial planners and what services they provide. You will also learn about the two main types of planners: fee-based and commission-based.

What Planners Do

Professional financial planners facilitate the planning process and add value by providing advice on how to best achieve your goals. Financial planners spend time gathering information, most of which comes from extensive questionnaires that probe every aspect of your financial life. Many planners use computer-based systems that do most of the calculations for the plan, including the standard net worth statements, debt-to-income ratios, and much more.

Most planners will examine your life insurance coverage to see if it is adequate for your family situation and recommend appropriate levels. They will go through the questionnaire you completed and note whether you have a will, if you have a durable power of attorney to make medical decisions, and so on. All of these areas will be addressed in your plan.

The plan will note your financial goals, such as retiring at age 62, and detail a course of action to accomplish that goal based on the resources you have available (if possible). You will get recommendations on how to invest your money to meet your major goals of college for the kids and retirement for you.

Depending on the type of planner you use, you may be handed a plan with recommended courses of action or you may work with the planner to implement the action items, including buying investment and/or insurance products through the planner.

Be aware that anyone can call themselves a financial planner. In most states, it requires no license unless they sell security or insurance products along with planning services. If you are going to use a financial planner, selecting one with a professional designation is the best way to ensure quality work and service. Look for one that is certified by one of the following organizations.

▶ **Certified Financial Planner (CFP):** This is the top professional designation for financial planners. CFPs have knowledge of investments, estate and retirement planning, insurance and taxes, and must complete extensive coursework and pass qualifying exams.

▶ **Chartered Financial Consultant (ChFC):** These planners must complete coursework and pass exams on financial planning, investing, insurance, taxes, and estate planning in addition to completing three years of work experience in financial planning.

▶ **Certified Public Accountant and Personal Financial Specialist (CPA and PFS):** These are CPAs who have taken additional coursework specializing in financial planning.

▶ **Charter Life Underwriter (CLU):** These professionals work for life insurance companies and study the same financial planning topics as the ChFC designation.

There are two fundamental types of financial planners and they split along how they are compensated by clients: fee-only financial planners and commission-based financial planners.

Fee-Based Financial Planners

Fee-based financial planners produce a financial plan complete with recommendations and advice. They will counsel you on strategies to achieve your goals, but they don't provide any products or sell anything other than the plan and their expertise. It is up to you to buy the recommended products to implement the plan.

Fee-based financial planners maintain that they serve the client best, because they only serve the client and make no commissions from the sale of any other products or services. This leaves them free to recommend what is best for the client without regards to product commissions as a source of compensation. These plans are the most expensive, because this is the planner's total package. Fee-based planners also tend to produce the more comprehensive plans, although this is not an absolute.

If you have a complicated financial life and the initiative to follow though on a fee-based planner's recommendations, this type of planner is worth considering.

Commission-Based Planners

Commission-based financial planners perform the same basic services as their fee-based counterparts, but follow the plan with an implementation schedule.

These planners may charge a small fee to produce the plan, but earn most of their compensation by recommending and selling financial products to implement the plan—these would include mutual funds, insurance products, and so on.

Commission-based financial planners note that without their guidance, many clients would not fully implement the plan. Their ongoing relationship means it is more likely the client will stick to the plan. Notions of conflicts of interest are dismissed with the observation that inappropriate product recommendations could result in sanctions from regulatory agencies—and a bad reputation.

2

BUDGETING

2.1 CREATING A BUDGET

Why Budget

Defining Income and Expenses

Accounting for Other Income

Budget Model

Budgets are not about restraining spending so much as bringing a sense of order to it. In this section, we look at the positive reasons for budgeting and why it makes sense to match income and expenses to your real world experience.

Why Budget

Budgets provide a structure that recognizes financial goals and organizes spending to meet those goals. Living expenses account for the largest portion of most people's budget, with smaller amounts set aside for financial goals such as retirement and college expenses.

Without a structure to handling money, many people find they have nothing left at the end of the month to invest toward their financial goals, but have a difficult time explaining where they spent their money. It is often not the large purchases that defeat savings promises, but rather many smaller buys that add up to large dollar amounts.

Budgets plan for spending as well as saving and investing. A spending plan will accommodate the occasional indulgence or luxury as well as the steady investment program in future goals. This prevents incurring high-interest credit card or consumer debt for items that, while nice to have, get you no closer to your most important goals. Budgets prevent you from financing consumables (food, clothing, and such) with credit card debt that you'll have to pay back with (high) interest.

The most important function of a budget is to assign a portion of your income to major financial goals. This process of "paying yourself first" means you'll be funding your financial goals each and every month—not just those lucky months when you have something left over after you paid all the other bills.

Defining Income and Expenses

Preparing a budget begins with defining income and expenses. For many people, "income" is simply their paycheck. For others, especially people working mainly for commission or tips, defining and projecting income becomes more challenging. For your budget to work, you must assign income to the months in which it occurs. If you work for a paycheck, this is usually the same amount each month. Retail workers on commission may have a higher income in the holiday months, which should be reflected in their budget. Likewise, any seasonal work should reflect higher income in those months.

Unless your paycheck is the same every month, don't take your annual income and divide it by 12 to get a monthly figure. This is important because your budget needs to match your **cash flow.** If your income is lower in some months, your spending should be adjusted to reflect that decrease.

WORDS TO GO . . . *WORDS TO GO . . .WORDS TO GO*

Cash flow in the context of a personal budget refers to when and how much money is received in your bank account. Some people get a paycheck every week or two weeks; others may be on commission and get paid some time after orders are booked, for example.

The same process works for expenses. Your mortgage or rent will probably stay the same for 12 months and you can budget accordingly. However, if you live in the north, your utility bill will be much higher in the winter months, while residents of the south will have higher bills in the summer months. You can't take your total utility expenses for a year and average them for a monthly cost. They will be off almost every month. In climates of extreme heat and cold, utility costs can spike several months out of the year and your budget should anticipate those expenses.

Don't budget bonuses! They may not happen next year, even if they've always happened in the past. Anticipate salary increases, but be realistic. It is better to underestimate than be overly optimistic.

The purpose of identifying and slotting income and expenses is to note months when the relationship is out of the ordinary, especially when expenses are high and/or income is low.

Accounting for Other Income

People who work in sales often earn bonuses or higher commissions for surpassing sales goals. While these bonuses are important parts of their income, they aren't certain or guaranteed, so this income should not go into the budget.

However, people who have been in the same jobs or with the same company for some time have some confidence in their ability to meet quotas and earn bonuses. Not accounting for this potential income discounts a significant part of the family's annual income. One way to handle this income is to account for it after the fact and adjust the budget when the bonus is earned. This has the benefit of not counting something that may not happen and lets you budget actual dollars rather than estimates. You can budget the money over several months or as a lump sum contribution to one of the financial goals for the year.

Your budget should reflect your life, and in most cases real-life annual income and expenses aren't neatly divide into 12 easy pieces.

Budget Model

Write down your budget or put it on your computer. Don't try to budget in your head—it won't work. After you have worked with your budget for some time, you'll develop shortcuts that can reduce the paperwork or computer time, but starting out, record every number and detail.

A basic budget lists your income and expenses for the upcoming months. Some people do an annual budget, while others work six months in advance. If you have a reliable paycheck, you should be able to do an annual budget; people who work on commission or are self-employed may find six months works better. In either case, your budget isn't written in stone. You can adjust it if circumstances warrant—however, changing your budget because you have failed to live by it is not acceptable!

Use this example as a guide on which to model your own budget; eliminate those items that don't apply to you and add others that do apply.

Category	Monthly Budget Amount	Monthly Actual Amount	Difference
	Income		
Salaries	_____	_____	_____
Bonuses, commissions, etc.	_____	_____	_____
Interest income	_____	_____	_____
Investment income	_____	_____	_____
Miscellaneous income	_____	_____	_____
Income subtotal	_____	_____	_____

continues

continued

Fixed expenses

Mortgage or rent	____	____	____
Homeowners/ renters insurance	____	____	____
Property taxes	____	____	____
Other taxes	____	____	____
Car payments	____	____	____
Auto insurance	____	____	____
Credit cards	____	____	____
Student loans	____	____	____
Other loans	____	____	____
401(k) or IRA	____	____	____
Stocks, bonds, mutual funds	____	____	____
College fund	____	____	____
Savings	____	____	____
Bill paying fund	____	____	____
Emergency fund	____	____	____
Insurance (medical, dental, vision)	____	____	____
Child support	____	____	____
Alimony	____	____	____
Fixed expenses subtotal	____	____	____

Nonfixed expenses

Electricity	____	____	____
Water and sewer	____	____	____
Natural gas or oil	____	____	____
Telephone (land line, cell)	____	____	____
Groceries	____	____	____
Day care, babysitting	____	____	____
Unreimbursed medical expenses, co-pays	____	____	____
Gasoline, oil	____	____	____

continues

BUDGETING

continued

Category	Monthly Budget Amount	Monthly Actual Amount	Difference
Auto repairs, maintenance, fees	_____	_____	_____
Other transportation, (tolls, bus, subway, taxis)	_____	_____	_____
Nonfixed subtotal	_____	_____	_____

Discretionary expenses

Category	Monthly Budget Amount	Monthly Actual Amount	Difference
Cable TV, videos, movies	_____	_____	_____
Eating out, lunches, snacks	_____	_____	_____
Computer expense	_____	_____	_____
Fitness (yoga, massage, gym)	_____	_____	_____
Hobbies	_____	_____	_____
Subscriptions and dues	_____	_____	_____
Vacations	_____	_____	_____
Pet food	_____	_____	_____
Pet grooming, boarding, vet	_____	_____	_____
Toiletries, household products	_____	_____	_____
Gifts, donations	_____	_____	_____
Grooming (hair, make-up, other)	_____	_____	_____
Dry cleaning, laundry	_____	_____	_____
New clothes	_____	_____	_____
Pocket money	_____	_____	_____
Discretionary expenses subtotal	_____	_____	_____
Total monthly expenses (add all subtotals)	_____	_____	_____
Your balance (subtract expenses from income)	_____	_____	_____

There are three categories of expenses: fixed, nonfixed, and discretionary. You'll have entries in all three categories. **Fixed expenses,** such as your rent or mortgage, don't change from month to month. Nonfixed expenses, also called **variable expenses,** do change in amount from month-to-month. Some may not occur every month. **Discretionary expenses** fall in the "nice to have" category, but are not necessary for daily living. Some might argue that if you have a pet, then food for the animal is not discretionary. That is true, but you chose to have a pet; it is not a necessity.

WORDS TO GO . . .WORDS TO GO . . .WORDS TO GO

Fixed expenses remain the same regardless of any activity during the month. These expenses include such items as the mortgage or rent, fixed-rate auto loans, and so on.

Nonfixed expenses or **variable expenses** change from one month to the next, often because of some action on your part. A credit card bill will change based on any payment or additional charges you make during the month.

Discretionary expenses cover items and services that aren't necessary for maintaining your home or life. They may include items or services that are important to your career, such as haircuts and clothes, but are matters of personal choice.

Your budget should have an amount for each item you anticipate an expense for that month. At the end of the month, you can add up your actual expenses to see how well you did against your budget. Steps in the next section will help you fill out the expense items in your budget.

2.2 TRACKING EXPENSES

Capturing Expenses

Seasonal Distribution of Expenses

Using Budget Payment Plans

One of the main reasons most small businesses fail is they do not control their expenses. Your family is similar to a small business, and it's just as important for you to control expenses. The first step is capturing how much you are spending and on what.

Capturing Expenses

Do you know—without looking—how much it costs to operate your household each month? Within $100? How about $250?

Building a budget begins with understanding where your money goes each month. Many people cannot tell you where they spent their money during the past month. Hundreds of dollars in expenses are "lost," because they have no way of tracking the outflow, and no idea whether the money went for necessary or frivolous expenses.

One way to understand where your money is going is to write down every penny you spend during the week: actual cash, credit cards, checks, and debit card transactions. Don't count your normal bill-paying expenses, such as rent or utilities. Count only those items or services you purchase out of your pocket. Carry a small note pad in your pocket or purse and write down every time you spend any money, no matter how little. Do this for several weeks, or however long it takes you to get a representative sampling of your routine out-of-pocket spending.

When you're ready, make a spreadsheet on your computer or just use a sheet of paper, and put each expenditure into a category. The categories can be broad, but narrow enough to show specifically where your out-of-pocket money is going. For example, the category "snacks" could include coffee on the way to work, a soda from the machine in the lunchroom, and so on.

When you've accounted for everything you have spent in the time you recorded your expenses, you may be shocked at how much money you spent—and how much of it was on frivolous items. Identifying exactly where your money is going and what it is going for is the second part of preparation to build a budget.

Seasonal Distribution of Expenses

As noted in the section on income, expenses don't fall into tidy 12-month increments in real life. Some months certain expenses will be higher or lower than other months. You can count on expenses being higher during the holiday season, when school starts in the fall, at some point during vacation season, and so on. Your personal experience may be different, but almost everyone can count on there being times during the year when one or more of their expenses are higher than normal.

It is important to your budget to identify these seasonal expenses and plan for them, especially if your income is not consistent during all 12 months of the year. If you have one or more months of high seasonal expenses and the same or lower income expectations, your budget needs to plan for a potential cash short-fall during those months and either cut back other expenses or plan to save some money from other months to cover the lower income.

Using Budget Payment Plans

One way to help you plan your expenses is to use the budget payment plan that some vendors offer. Utilities can be very helpful, because many offer a budget payment that makes planning easier.

Although it may be slightly different in your community, here's how most budget payment plans work for utilities. The utility will look at your consumption over a peak period (winter in the north or summer in the south) and come up with an average bill. You will pay this amount each month regardless of your actual usage. During months when usage is below the budgeted amount, you build a credit; in months when usage is over the budgeted amount, your account may show a negative balance.

Every six months, the utility will look at your usage and payment amount to see if any adjustments need to be made. If there has been a significant change in your usage or the cost of fuel to the utility, your budgeted amount may be raised. However, if your account is running a positive balance (you're paying more than you're using), the utility may reduce your monthly payment for the next six-month period.

Any other tools you can use to take the guesswork out of budgeting expenses will make your budget a more accurate instrument.

2.3 SPENDING PLAN

Plan Expenses

Manipulate Expenses for Unexpected Opportunities

Budgeting is a process that matches spending with financial responsibilities and goals. A spending plan provides for those responsibilities and goals, while building in flexibility to accommodate the things that bring joy to your life.

Plan Expenses

A spending plan is as simple as it sounds, yet it is very important to your personal financial success. Without a plan for expenses, you have no way to control how much of your income is going to which expenses. The key benefit of an expense plan is that you control how your money is spent rather than paying all your bills at the end of the month and wondering where the money went.

If you captured your expenses in the previous section, you have a good idea where your money is going. You know where the big bills come from: mortgage or rent, utilities, food, and so on. In addition, you'll have captured other expenses such as clothing, gas, haircuts, and so on.

Your spending plan is a dynamic version of your budget that can be as simple or sophisticated as you want or need it to be. For the first few months, just get it all down on paper or your computer so you can see how it works. If you can follow it without a formal plan after that, fine, but you may find that a formal spending plan gives you more freedom than you think to accomplish important financial goals and make room for some fun.

Plan out your weekly spending to include those items you know you must pay (bills) and those items that come around only so often (haircuts). Match your income to the expenses by week so you will not be caught short of cash. Include as a "must pay," contributions to those important long-term financial goals.

◀ *SEE ALSO 1.2, "Financial Goals"* ▶

With your expenses planned out, you can see where your money is going. If an unexpected expense such as an auto repair comes up, you may be able to shift some of your discretionary spending to another month to find the money for all or part of the repair. The advantage here is you don't necessarily have to go into debt and put the repair on a high-interest credit card. Even if the bill is too big to pay in one month, you can put it on a credit card and pay it off in two or three months by shifting or deferring discretionary spending. Without a spending plan, you might not have enough information to know how to pay for the repair in such a short time, and you could end up paying a huge amount of interest.

If you know your income is going to be lower than normal for the next month or two, you can reduce your expenses and/or delay your discretionary spending until your income increases. Having a working spending plan that tracks your expenses precisely gives you the information to make informed decisions.

Manipulate Expenses for Unexpected Opportunities

Spending plans are not all about preparing for financial disasters. They also allow you to take advantage of an unexpected opportunity to enjoy yourself—in a financially responsible way, of course.

A group of friends decides to head for the ski slopes and invites you along. If you have a spending plan, you may be able to juggle your spending so that the trip doesn't put you in credit card debt or drain your emergency cash reserve. When you know what you spend money on and when you spend it, you have a powerful tool to help you not only meet financial goals, but also take advantage of opportunities to enjoy life without hating yourself Monday morning. However, if you don't know where your money goes, you have no control over your financial life and the fun things in life tend to just put you farther in debt—and farther away from your goals.

2.4 SAVING PLAN

The 90 Percent Rule

Short-Term Savings Options

For many people, saving money is a struggle. There never seems to be money left at the end of the month for saving or investing. A change in attitude can make a big difference in whether you have a savings and investment plan or continue to struggle month to month and year to year.

The 90 Percent Rule

Have you struggled in the past to find enough money in your monthly budget to save toward your long-term financial goals? The problem for most people is that they let their finances control them, rather than the other way around. It may seem like an impossible switch to make, but if you are ever going to achieve personal financial success, you must be in control. One way to take control is to set limits on expenses.

There is a good example from the world of business that works like magic in personal finance. Most people know the basic profit formula:

revenue – expenses = profits

The problem with this formula is that profits are just what's left over, not what the business owner planned. A better formula is:

revenue – profits = expenses

See how this formula puts profits first and makes expenses a by-product? To make this formula work, the business owner must be able to control expenses, because the money to pay them is limited.

We can adapt the same formula for a family budget. If the goal is to save 10 percent of the take-home income, then the family must plan to live on 90 percent of the take-home income for expenses. This is how you build your budget and your spending plan. That 10 percent is not available for living expenses. It has another purpose—to fund your long-term financial goals. There's nothing magic about saving 10 percent, but it's a good number to shoot for if you're just starting out, and a base to build on if you're already developing saving habits.

You can make this painless in a number of ways. Most mutual funds will set up an automatic debit from your checking or savings account on a monthly basis, so the money comes out automatically as long as you make sure there's enough in the account when the debit is made. If you participate in an employer-sponsored retirement program, contributions will be taken out of your paycheck before you ever receive it.

◀ *SEE ALSO 11.1, "Mutual Fund Basics"* ▶

You should consider the money you are saving for a long-term financial goal sacred. Only in the direst of emergencies (to avoid foreclosure, for example) should you withdraw any money from these savings.

Short-Term Savings Options

Invest money for long-term financial goals in the investment products appropriate for your situation. However, you will still need short-term savings, because most investments (stocks, stock mutual funds, and so on) are not suitable for holding cash on a short-term basis. The risk factor for these investments is quite high over the short term, so you will want to avoid them for your savings needs that are less than three years in the future.

Most families need a ready supply of cash to pay bills and meet short-term needs, especially in between paychecks. Interest-bearing bank accounts are a safe place for this type of savings need.

◀ *SEE ALSO 3.3, "Savings Accounts"* ▶

You may also have short-term financial goals that you want to save toward. Most investment options are not suitable for any goal that is less than three years away. However, you can look to products such as mutual fund money market accounts, which pay competitive interest rates and have the flexibility of offering a check-writing option.

◀ *SEE ALSO 11.2, "Types of Mutual Funds"* ▶

2.5 PERSONAL FINANCIAL SOFTWARE

Building a Budget

Track Expenses and Income

Prepare for Taxes

Choosing the Best Personal Financial Software

If you're comfortable with computers, personal financial software makes keeping your money organized much easier. The major products offer user-friendly interfaces that make learning the basics quick and easy.

Building a Budget

The two leading brands of personal finance software, Quicken and Microsoft Money, have excellent tools that help you build and maintain a budget, as well as manage your daily finances and investments. Both brands are built around the "check register" concept. Income and expenses are assigned to an account as you enter deposits and expenses (checks, credit card transactions, debit cards transactions, cash transactions). The programs assign entries in the check register to the income and expense categories you have setup.

The nice feature of the software is that you only need to enter information once, and the program builds a variety of reports off the same data. One of the reports it will generate for you is a budget based on your spending habits. It helps to have several months' worth of data already in the system before it tries to build or validate the information. Both systems allow you to download information from your bank, so a quick way to get started is to use this feature to get several months' worth of information into your system. Most banks allow you to download financial records, but check with your financial institution to make sure. You will have to clean up some of the downloaded information, because it may not have all the data you need (the payee, for example). Even with cleaning up the missing information on some transactions, which should be in your paper check register, it is much quicker than entering past information manually.

◀ *SEE ALSO 3.2, "Checking Accounts"* ▶

When you are ready, the system will spit out a budget based on your spending and income patterns. You are free to edit the budget to reflect new goals or spending habits you would like to break. The software will show you an annual budget with charts and graphs that will help you analyze your spending. As you enter information, your budget is updated automatically, which can help you monitor your spending by categories. If appropriate, you can reduce spending in a category that approaches its limit early in the month so you won't bust your budget.

The graphing capabilities of both programs are helpful in identifying areas where your spending patterns do not reflect your important financial goals. You can see how much money is going to consumables (snack food, eating out at lunch, frivolous purchases, gas for unnecessary trips, and so on) that don't add much to your true quality of life and nothing to your long-term financial goals.

Track Expenses and Income

Personal financial software serves several purposes. Some people use it strictly for budgeting and planning purposes, but most people find it becomes their sole or main check register and the place to record all their financial transactions.

Unlike a paper check register, you can track credit card transactions as well as bank and cash purchases. Most credit card vendors will let you view your transaction records online and many will let you download the information. Like your check register, if you stay on top of your credit transactions, there will be no nasty surprises when the bills come.

More importantly, you can assign credit card transactions to the same categories as your other purchases, so they easily integrate into your budget.

Both Quicken and Microsoft Money have a check-writing function. You can order special checks that print out on your home computer or print out a paper version of the check and then write out a regular check out of your checkbook. You can also use an online bill-paying service that lets you skip paper checks altogether. Most major banks also offer an online bill-paying service.

◯ *SEE ALSO 3.4, "Other Banking Services"* ▶

There are two ways to use the software to capture your transactions. The method you choose is a matter of personal preference.

The first method is to enter each transaction into the system manually. Every check you write, each debit card transaction or ATM cash withdrawal, each credit card charge, and any cash withdrawal at the bank would go into the register. Ideally, you would do this every day or several times a week. This method depends on your keeping good records in your paper register or by some other means. If you forget a transaction, you can go online to your bank and find the information.

The second method involves downloading your transactions into your program on a regular basis—every couple of days. You may still have the issues with some data not coming through, so you'll still need to keep records on transactions. If you always have enough cash to cover your expenses, this method is safe enough. However, if you periodically run short of cash, you could risk bouncing checks if you are not on top of your account balance. You should also check with your financial institution to make sure it has no limits on downloads or security issues with frequent downloads.

Prepare for Taxes

One of the biggest hassles in doing taxes is getting all of your information together. Both Quicken and Microsoft Money flag items that may be potential items for tax consideration, such as medical expenses, charitable donations, and so on.

For tax preparation, Quicken has the edge over Microsoft Money, in part because the same company (Intuit) produces TurboTax, the best-selling personal tax preparation software package. Quicken alerts you to potential deductions during the year and helps prepare withholding tax estimates.

Quicken also prepares running copies of tax schedules A, B, and D, so you can see where you are as the year progresses and make plans accordingly. **Schedule A** is the form for itemized deductions and **Schedule B** is where you report interest and ordinary dividends. **Schedule D** is the form for reporting capital gains and losses.

WORDS TO GO . . . WORDS TO GO . . . WORDS TO GO

Schedule A is found on your IRS form 1040, also known as the long form, and it is where you list your itemized deductions such as unreimbursed medical expenses, charitable contributions, and so on.

Schedule B is also found on your IRS form 1040 and it is for reporting ordinary dividends (from stocks or mutual funds, for example) and interest income.

Schedule D is attached to your IRS form 1040 and it is for reporting short and long-term capital gains or losses.

Schedule A is particularly important because it will determine whether you have enough deductions to itemize or whether taking the standard deduction is a better tax decision. If you know you are close to the tipping point between the two (and an updated Schedule A will help you determine that, along with Schedules

B and D), you may want to take some actions late in the year to create more tax deductions. These might include prepaying charitable contributions, selling an unprofitable asset for a loss, and so on.

◀ *SEE ALSO 8.1, "Income Tax"* ▶

Both Quicken and Microsoft Money export tax information to popular tax preparation software.

Choosing the Best Personal Financial Software

Which personal financial software product is the best choice, Quicken or Microsoft Money? In terms of functionality, you won't go wrong with either product. Both come from obvious top-notch companies and are well respected. There are some differences, but more in the interface (how it works with you and you with it) than substance.

Quicken Is the Leader

Quicken is the market leader in personal financial software and has been for a number of years. The company (Intuit) has stretched the product line from a simple, easy to use personal check register to a sister product that does accounting and payroll for small businesses (QuickBooks). In addition, Intuit offers the clear leader in personal tax preparation software, TurboTax.

Quicken offers three levels of its personal financial software and several add-ons. Even the entry level is sophisticated enough for people looking for an electronic check register and organizer. Other levels add bells and whistles that make the product a sophisticated financial manager that handles not only your checkbook but your investments, too. Acknowledging that many people run small businesses either full time or as a side to their full time job, the company has a product that integrates business and personal accounting.

Quicken is easy to use and most people can begin working with the software almost right out of the box. The familiar look of the check register-like screen is inviting and intuitive.

Microsoft Money has the "Look"

Microsoft Money, like virtually all Microsoft products, looks very familiar the minute it opens up. The menus across the top look like other Microsoft products, which makes navigating easy.

Microsoft Money makes greater use of the Internet than Quicken to deliver content to the product. This is particularly helpful for financial, tax, and investment information, which the product offers. Microsoft Money will update your investments every day and alert you to news concerning your holdings (with an Internet connection).

You can use a web-based version of Microsoft Money, meaning the software resides on the Internet and you can access your information from any computer with an Internet connection. This has real advantages for people who are on the road a lot and don't carry a computer with their financial records.

The Choice Is Yours

Quicken is the market leader in this field, but Microsoft Money offers an equally functional product. If you are concerned about learning a new piece of software and are comfortable with Microsoft products, Microsoft Money will be very familiar. If you are looking for slightly more depth, especially in the tax preparation area, Quicken may be the better choice.

In either case, you can try both products risk free, either through a money-back guarantee or free-trial download. You can also take a virtual tour of the products at their websites to get a feel for how they look and act.

The Quicken Intuit website is: www.quicken.intuit.com.

The Microsoft Money website is: www.microsoft.com/money.

2.6 EMERGENCY FUNDS

Rules for Emergency Reserve

Where to Place Emergency Funds

Every family needs a cash reserve for emergencies. This reserve should be in place before you begin putting away money for other financial goals.

Rules for Emergency Reserve

Emergencies, by definition, come when we don't expect them. Sometimes they are small emergencies that need immediate attention but have no long-term consequences. Other emergencies are more serious and have long-term consequences— a breadwinner is laid off or their employer closes the business. What will the family do until that income can be replaced? What if that was the sole income for the family? This is a true emergency and it will have serious long-term consequences. You can add other emergencies to this list such as a serious illness or disability that prevents a breadwinner from working, a fire, or some other disaster that destroys the home and so on.

To weather these emergencies, families need an **emergency cash reserve** that will carry them for a period until they can reasonably expect the emergency will pass. There are two questions to resolve about your emergency fund:

1. What should it replace?

2. How long should it last?

WORDS TO GO . . . WORDS TO GO . . . WORDS TO GO

Emergency cash reserve is a ready supply of cash in bank products or a money market mutual fund that you can tap in a hurry in the event of an emergency such as the loss of a job, a big uninsured medical expense, or some other financial crisis. You should have enough to keep your household running for six months.

Each family will answer these questions differently. The first task is to determine your absolute living expenses. These are the expenses for "keeping the doors open and a roof over your head." They include the mortgage or rent, utilities, food, and other essential expenses. Cable television, club memberships, and other "nice to haves" are not included in these expenses.

Once you come up with your essential living expenses, you'll have an idea of what your monthly needs are to stay in your house and keep your children in school. This monthly figure will be what you whittle your expenses down to if you or your partner loses your job(s). If your income is severely reduced, don't wait for things to get bad before you begin reducing expenses. Assume that things aren't going to get better soon and begin cutting expenses immediately. Some of the cuts may take time to appear in your budget because of notices you have to give to terminate services.

Cash is your most important asset right now, so hoard it. Although it is normally a bad idea, only pay the minimum on credit cards and any other debt you have to preserve cash. Put a halt to almost all discretionary spending.

Take the figure you determined was your monthly essential expense and multiply it by six. That is your cash reserve: the minimum cash you should have on hand for an emergency. A safer reserve is six months worth of your current take-home pay. If you cut your expenses to the essentials and had six months of take-home pay in reserve, you could stretch that to perhaps eight months if needed.

When you are living on your emergency cash reserve, avoid any unnecessary expenses, because you don't know how long it will take to replace your old income. Consider taking a part-time job while looking for a new position. This could be with a temporary employment agency or perhaps a night position to leave your days free to job hunt. Any money, even if it is much less than you were used to making, will help extend your emergency cash reserve.

Where to Place Emergency Funds

You should invest your emergency reserve funds where they will always be immediately available to you. Don't invest the funds in the stock market because short-term fluctuations make stocks too risky for this purpose.

SEE ALSO 10.2, "Investment Objectives"

Bank products that don't lock in your money are appropriate, including money market accounts and savings accounts, but not certificates of deposit because of the penalty for early withdrawal.

SEE ALSO 3.2, "Checking Accounts"

Another place to park money at a possibly higher rate of interest is a money market mutual fund. You have quick access to your funds and most offer a check-writing feature.

◀ *SEE ALSO 11.2, "Types of Mutual Funds"* ▶

Wherever you deposit your emergency cash reserve, remember it must be quickly accessible (within a few days) and safe. You're not looking for the highest return possible, just a safe place to park the funds so you'll know they'll be available when you need them.

3

BANKING

3.1 CHOOSING A BANK

Traditional vs. Online

Savings and Loans and Savings Banks

Credit Unions

Choosing the Best Financial Institution

You have more choices now about how and where you bank than ever before. This section will help you sort through your options.

Traditional vs. Online

Not too many years ago, different financial institutions had well-defined roles. Banks had checking accounts and did business loans, savings and loans lent money to buy homes and did other consumer lending, and credit unions were sources of small personal loans and car loans for employees of a business or governmental entity. Now, thanks to deregulation, the lines between financial institutions have blurred so that it is almost impossible to distinguish them based on products.

A traditional bank is a misnomer in the sense that no bank offers just "traditional" banking services anymore. Even smaller independent banks are able, through partnerships and alliances, to offer insurance, investment services, and a host of other financial products. Larger banks offer these products and services through vast networks of nationwide branches.

So your choice in banks is not so much one of services as of delivery. Pushing that front has been the growth of strictly online or net banks. These are not online branches of existing brick and mortar banks, but rather banks that started as Internet-based institutions and intend to stay that way.

Internet banks offer most of the same services as regular banks, but in many cases are able to pay higher interest rates because they do not carry the overhead of a physical structure. Net banks have been around long enough to push most regular banks into offering their own version of online banking. By forming partnerships with **ATM networks,** the net banks have overcome initial problems such as making deposits and retrieving cash that physical banks don't have to worry so much about. These networks string together thousands of machines so consumers' access cards will work in many locations.

The people who find net banks attractive are the early adapters who are hooked on technology and jump at anything that will make their life easier. People who travel a great deal enjoy the convenience of the online banks, since they can do their banking from anywhere there is an Internet connection. Many physical banks offer the same services with their online offerings, but haven't always matched the interest rates and fees the net banks offered.

If you value the contact of a person when conducting your business, a net bank is probably not for you. Many of the conveniences offered on pure net banks—online bill paying, for example—are available to customers of regular banks, especially those with larger multistate facilities such as Bank of America, Wells Fargo, and others.

Savings and Loans and Savings Banks

Aggressive S&Ls, as savings and loans are known, offer most if not all of the same products and services as retail banks. They can be active lenders not only in residential markets but in other types of businesses. The S&L industry almost didn't survive deregulation in the 1980s, due to a scandal led by institutions in Texas that swept the market. However, thanks to regulatory reorganization (S&Ls are now under the insurance arm of the FDIC), the industry is back on its feet and very active in many markets. An S&L has no structural advantage over a bank. They're still not regulated exactly the same, but little of this has anything to do with consumers.

Savings banks are a hybrid financial organization that falls somewhere between a regular bank and an S&L. There are some advantages for the owners of a savings bank, but little to distinguish one from a regular bank or an S&L.

Credit Unions

Credit unions once were limited to people with a common employer; however, they now have much broader membership criteria. Credit unions offer many of the same financial services as banks and other financial institutions. Credit unions are still member-owned, which means they return profits to the depositors in the form of lower rates on loan products and higher rates on deposit instruments.

While they are always very competitive, credit unions are not always the best deal when it comes to loans. Always check rates at other lenders. Lending is a very competitive market, which depends on what institutions are paying for the capital they lend. The more they pay out in interest on deposit products, the harder it is to keep loan rates low.

A downside to credit unions is they are typically confined to a small geographic area. Unlike multistate banks, if you move to a different state, it is unlikely you'll find the same credit union to serve you.

Choosing the Best Financial Institution

Which is the best financial institution for you: a regular bank, an online bank, a credit union, an S&L, or a savings bank? From a product point of view, you can probably get every financial need met at any of these institutions. Your decision is as much about your lifestyle as it is about the products.

Most people want their banking services to be as convenient and hassle-free as possible. Other factors such as fees and services are important and we'll discuss them in the coming sections. The answer, then, is not to dwell on the name on the building or the website, but focus on the combination of convenience (however you define that), products, services, and fees that makes the most sense for you. The only absolute is that the bank must be insured by the FDIC. If it does not have this coverage, look elsewhere for your banking services.

The Federal Deposit Insurance Corp. (FDIC) protects bank and S&L accounts. The FDIC protects individual accounts up to $100,000 against the bank failing, but not all products and services offered by banks are covered. FDIC covers checking and savings accounts, along with certificates of deposit. The insurance covers individual accounts for up to $100,000 against the failure of the bank. If you have a joint account, in which either person has right of access, the FDIC insures it up to $200,000 because each person's portion would be recognized as $100,000. It is always a good idea to check with a bank official if you have questions about FDIC coverage.

It is important to know that the FDIC insurance only protects you in case the bank fails (goes into bankruptcy). It does not protect you from theft or embezzlement. Most financial institutions carry separate insurance and bonds that provide some protection from these losses.

If you buy insurance products, annuities, mutual funds, or stocks through your bank, those are not covered by the FDIC insurance. The FDIC also does not cover credit union accounts. This is not a major problem because the National Credit Union Administration protects credit union accounts up to $100,000.

3.1

3.2 CHECKING ACCOUNTS

Demand Deposit Checking Accounts

Interest-Bearing Accounts

Money Market Accounts

Online Checking Accounts

In this section, we'll look at basic checking accounts offered by banks and others. If it's been awhile since you opened a new checking account, this section may clear some of the clutter.

Demand Deposit Checking Accounts

A **demand deposit** checking account is one that you have access to anytime without penalty for withdrawal. Demand deposit also applies to savings accounts, which you have access to anytime the bank or financial institution is open. When used in the context of a checking account, we are talking about your basic account.

WORDS TO GO . . . WORDS TO GO . . . WORDS TO GO

A **demand deposit** account is an account at a financial institution with no strings attached, that is no penalties for early withdrawal or minimum wait for withdrawals. It's your money and you can have it when you want it. You will usually pay for this convenience with a low rate of interest.

Banks will call it by their own marketing name, but it is usually the starter account for people who don't write many checks or have many deposits each month. Some banks charge a fee for this type of account—either a flat fee per month, a per item charge, or a combination of both. Other banks may waive the fee if you keep your balance above a certain minimum. If the account does pay interest, it is usually a very small amount.

These accounts may be fine for students or seniors if their check and deposit volume is under the maximum allowed and assuming the fee is not too high. Most of these accounts offer an ATM card/debit/credit card combination to people with adequate credit ratings.

Interest-Bearing Accounts

Many consumers find they qualify for an interest-bearing checking account, which is a concept the credit unions pioneered in some parts of the country. You will want to study the terms of interest-bearing accounts carefully so that you understand what conditions must be met to earn the interest. The bank may (and probably does) require a minimum balance. It is important to understand how this minimum balance is computed. Some banks take an average balance for the month and if that number is above the required amount, you earn the interest. Other banks look at your balance each day and if it falls below the minimum on any one day, you don't earn interest for the whole month. To make matters worse, you may also have to pay a fee for that one day the balance fell below the minimum. Read the fine print!

The interest paid on these checking accounts is very low, but it's more than your money is earning just sitting in a regular checking account. It is important you weigh the value of that interest payment with the likelihood you will meet the requirements on a regular basis. If you're unlikely to consistently meet the requirement to earn interest, you might want to consider a different type of account.

Money Market Accounts

Bank money market accounts are not the same as money market mutual funds. Money market accounts are demand accounts that pay a higher rate of interest than other accounts. However, you usually have to maintain a much higher balance to earn this high rate of interest.

In addition, money market accounts place restrictions on the number of transactions you can make in the account each month (three deposits and three withdrawals, for example). You write checks from the account, but there is usually not an ATM or debit card associated with the account.

These accounts are great places to park emergency funds or to hold money for payments that you make only periodically—college tuition, for example.

◄ *SEE ALSO 2.6, "Emergency Funds"* ►

Online Checking Accounts

Online checking accounts come in the same types as most regular accounts. You get paper checks and ATM and/or debit cards to use just like at physical banks. Thanks to debit cards, you can avoid most of the problems of businesses accepting online checks (since they are "out of town" checks). People attracted to online banks find electronic bill paying an important feature, so paper checks are not an issue.

The most difficult logistical obstacle to overcome is how to accept deposits when there is no "physical" bank. Several online banks have developed relationships with ATM networks to accept deposits for them. If you can have your paycheck direct-deposited by your employer, that's the best solution. Before you sign on with an online bank, make sure they handle deposits in a way that will work for you.

3.3 SAVINGS ACCOUNTS

Passbook Savings

Certificates of Deposit

The Best CD Strategy

3.3

There are two strictly savings products offered by financial institutions. Savings accounts pay almost nothing in interest, but give you immediate access to your money. Certificates of deposit pay much more in interest, but you have to commit to locking in your money for a set period.

Passbook Savings

The basic savings account at most financial institutions is the passbook savings account or statement savings account, although it may go by another marketing name. It evolved from the days when the customer literally brought in a small passbook with each deposit or withdrawal. Bank or savings and loan personnel put the passbook into a special printer that recorded the transaction and printed the new balance including any new interest the account had earned.

Some smaller financial institutions use this system, but most have switched to a computerized passbook that prints your balance on the deposit verification slip. At the end of the month or quarter, depending on the account and amount of activity, you will get a printed statement showing all the transactions and earned interest. These accounts often have limits on the number of transactions allowed each month. Why? Because they are not profitable for banks and the more activity there is, the less profitable they are. Banks want the money to stay in the account and be available for lending.

What use are these accounts that pay minimal interest and place limits on transactions? Well, they're great accounts to start kids out on for savings. Have them put some part of their birthday or holiday money in the account and show them how it grows, even if it is very slowly.

You can use the accounts to park a small amount of your emergency reserve fund, where it can do double duty as the backup for your overdraft protection. This protection, which the bank offers for a small fee, allows the bank to transfer money out of your savings account to cover any checks that would normally be overdrawn because you did not have enough money in your account. You pay for this service, but the fee is much less than the fee for bouncing a check. There is more information on overdraft protection in Section 3.5.

Savings accounts are not as benign as they may seem. Some require a minimum balance or they may charge a quarterly or annual fee. Due to the low interest they pay, you won't make any money on these accounts, but you don't want to lose money because of fees, either. There are limits on transactions for most savings accounts, usually six per month, so check with the bank for their policy.

Certificates of Deposit

Bank certificates of deposit (CDs) offer the highest interest rates (for longer maturities) of any bank product. Those high rates come with the catch that your money is locked up for a set period. For most CDs, you will pay a penalty of up to 10 percent if you withdraw your money before maturity. Law does not set the penalty and banks can charge what they want as long as the policy is disclosed before you buy the CD. It is possible, especially on short-term CDs, to lose not only all of your earned interest, but also some of your principal if you withdraw funds prematurely. Understand the penalty policy before you buy a bank CD, and be certain you won't need the funds before the CD matures. There are circumstances where a bank will waive the penalty, including death or permanent disability of the owner, if the owner is declared mentally incompetent, or if the CD is in an IRA or 401(k) plan and the owner is age 59½ or older. These aren't universal exclusions, so check your bank's policy.

CDs are relatively safe because of the FDIC insurance on accounts up to $100,000, and they're a convenient place to park money for short periods. The interest rates paid by CDs are tied to short-term bank rates set by the Federal Reserve Board and influenced by market competition for funds. Banks "borrow" money when you purchase a CD. It is the equivalent of a loan that the bank must pay interest on and, at some point in the future, return the principal to you. The bank makes money by lending out that same money at a higher interest rate. The difference between the two interest rates is the **spread.**

WORDS TO GO . . .WORDS TO GO . . .WORDS TO GO

The **spread** is a financial term that describes the difference between two interest rates—one the bank pays and the other the bank collects. It is also used to describe other financial arrangements where there is a difference in price or interest rates. The difference or gap is the spread. Sports betting enthusiasts will also recognize the term as the difference in points between what one team is expected to score over another.

There is a relationship between interest rate paid and length of maturity. The longer the maturity of the CD, the higher the interest rate you should expect. The reason for this relationship is that the longer your money is committed at one interest rate, the greater the chance that market interest rates will change. If interest rates rise during this time, your money will not earn the highest rate available because it is locked into the CD at a fixed rate.

CDs with shorter maturities can take advantage of new interest rates, but pay lower rates initially.

CDs come in a variety of maturities ranging from six months to five years or more. Banks have great flexibility in designing their CD products. You can choose from several different varieties of CDs, and new ones come on the market regularly. The CD market is very competitive and banks frequently add new products and new features to existing products. The following are general product descriptions—consult your local bank for specific product features and additional products.

The Basic CD

The basic CD is a time deposit ranging from six months to five years. The bank offers a different rate for the number of years to maturity. The longer it is until maturity, the higher the interest rate. Most CDs automatically rollover for another equal term at whatever the current interest rate is when it matures, unless you elect to cash it in or do something different.

Many banks allow you to deposit more money into the CD when it rolls over to a new CD. You may also have the option of receiving your interest payments on a semi-annual basis during the life of the CD. If you don't choose one of these options, when your CD matures you'll receive the original principal and any interest the CD earned during the period.

Increased Rate CD

One of the problems with a CD is that while you own one, interest rates may rise and you will be stuck with a lower rate. Some banks offer a CD that lets you increase or bump up your interest rate to the new, higher rate. Sometimes called a bump-up CD, these accounts let you take advantage of higher interest rates. Most allow you one rate increase during the term of the CD. The catch is you start off with an interest rate that is lower than the current market rate. If interest rates don't increase, you will lose the interest income that is the difference between a regular CD and the bump-up CD's lower rate.

Flexible CD

The flexible CD lets you withdraw money from your account without penalty. The bank may allow only one or two withdrawals without penalties during the term of the flexible or liquid CD. Flexible CDs have a lower interest rate than comparable regular CDs. You may also have to maintain a certain account balance or the rate will drop even further. This is the basic structure; however, your bank, if it even offers this product, may have different requirements.

If **liquidity** is important, there may be other ways and other products that will accomplish your goal. Talk to your banker about other choices that may meet your needs without the restrictions. The brokerage CD also offers liquidity.

WORDS TO GO . . .WORDS TO GO . . .WORDS TO GO

Liquidity refers to how easily and quickly you can convert an asset to cash. Stocks and mutual funds are liquid because you can sell and get cash easily. Bank accounts, such as savings and checking are liquid. Real estate is not liquid at all, since it could take some time to find a buyer and close the deal to get your money.

Callable CDs

The bump-up CD is an option if you believe interest rates are going to rise. However, if interest rates fall, it is the bank, not you, that is in the bad position. Banks would prefer to call in high-interest CDs and replace them with ones at a lower interest rate. One way they can do that is by selling you a **callable CD,** which gives the bank the right to redeem the CD before the maturity date.

WORDS TO GO . . .WORDS TO GO . . .WORDS TO GO

A **callable CD** allows the financial institution to call or redeem the CD after a certain period, typically six months. This means you bear the interest rate risk. If rates fall, the bank can call your CD once the protection period ends. You get your principal and interest to-date, but lose the higher paying CD and must reinvest your money at the now lower rate.

Banks must usually wait six months or some period before they can call a CD and, if they call your CD, you receive your full principal and any earned interest. The incentive for you to take the risk that the bank would call your CD is a higher interest rate.

Callable CDs pay more than regular CDs—not a lot more, but enough that it may be worth the risk. Your risk is that the bank will call your CD at a higher interest rate and you will have to reinvest your money at the now lower market rate.

No-Interest CDs

No-interest or zero-coupon CDs pay no periodic interest, but are sold at a deep discount off face value. When the CD matures, you redeem it for full face value and the difference is the interest. For example, you might buy a zero-coupon CD earning 6 percent for $890 and redeem it in two years for $1,000. The $110 difference is the interest you earned. **Coupon** refers to the interest payment of the CD.

WORDS TO GO . . . *WORDS TO GO . . . WORDS TO GO*

The term **coupon** comes from the bond markets where, years ago, bond investors had to clip coupons off the actual paper bond and send them in to receive their interest payment. Thus, the term "coupon clippers" was given to bond investors.

This simple example shows the math. The reality is most zero-coupon CDs are for at least 10 years. Although you don't receive any interest payments until the CD matures, the IRS says you owe money every year on the interest as if you received it. Your tax bill is not spread evenly over the term of the CD. It builds each year, so the largest tax bite comes at the end of the term. Before you buy a zero-coupon CD, check the tax consequences with a competent advisor.

The zero-coupon CD is almost identical to the zero-coupon bond in terms of tax treatment.

SEE ALSO 13.2, "Types of Bonds"

Variable-Rate CDs

As the name says, these CDs have interest rates that change. The bank usually ties the rate to a common interest rate index or to certain U.S. Treasury rates. The risk here is the fluctuation in interest rates. If rates go up, the CD's rate can adjust upward; however, if rates drop, the CD's rate will fall also. Banks may cap the number of times a rate can change. You may also have account balance minimums to meet.

Brokerage CDs

Some banks use stockbrokers to market their CDs nationwide, and there is an active market for buying and selling CDs. This provides a degree of liquidity that is not present with regular CDs, since owners can sell the account without a penalty for early withdrawal on the open market.

This convenience comes with the risk that you could lose money in the open market if you decide to sell the CD before maturity. In many cases, the bank pays the commission to the broker, not you, but always check to see that this is the case.

Here's how you can lose money by selling your CD: if interest rates rise, the CD you own becomes worth less money because new CDs pay higher interest rates. In order to sell your CD, you will have to discount the face value, so that the interest rate gives the owner a yield equal to the new CDs.

Likewise, if you want to buy a brokerage CD in the secondary market that has a higher rate of interest, you may pay a premium over the face value of the CD. Either way, have your broker figure out what the net to you is before buying or selling CDs on the open market.

Despite the potential risks, selling your CD in the secondary market may be less expensive than paying an early withdrawal charge on a regular CD.

There are some advantages to buying CDs through brokers, especially if you plan to hold them until maturity. You can accumulate more than $100,000 in CDs in one brokerage account by buying multiple CDs from different banks. This eliminates the paperwork of opening an account at each bank. Each CD of $100,000 or less is protected by the FDIC because the accounts are at different banks and the insurance is on the bank not the account.

Brokers offer many different types of CDs including those discussed in this section and some that may be unique to their firm. Be aware that one type of CD favored by many brokers is the callable CD. The broker should disclose to you if the CD has a call provision.

The Best CD Strategy

Bank CDs are very competitive products and it pays to shop for the best rates. One place to start is www.bankrate.com, which lists the best rates by geographic area for CDs. This will give you bargaining information. Your local bank may not want or be able to match the best rate available, but they may be willing to increase the interest over their advertised rate. You can also check with your stockbroker if you are interested in a brokerage CD—most major firms, including discount and online brokers, offer them.

One of the risks of investing in CDs is that to get the best rates, you must take the longer maturities. However, longer maturities (more than two years, for example) expose you to the potential that interest rates will rise and you will be locked into a CD paying a lower rate. Two strategies address this problem: laddering and focused CD buying.

Laddering CDs

People with laddering CDs recognize interest rates will change, but don't try to guess when. This strategy places your money in the best position to take advantage of current high, long-term rates and provide for the liquidity of short-term maturities. Here's how it works:

If you want to invest $25,000 under the best terms both now and in the future, rather than buying one CD now, divide the money into five $5,000 units and invest it this ways:

- ▶ $5,000 one-year CD
- ▶ $5,000 two-year CD
- ▶ $5,000 three-year CD
- ▶ $5,000 four-year CD
- ▶ $5,000 five-year CD

At the end of the first year, take the $5,000 from the maturing one-year CD and buy a new five-year CD. The next year when the two-year CD matures, buy another new five-year CD. After four years, all of the CDs in your ladder have five-year maturities. With this strategy, you are buying the highest paying CD each year with the maturing old five-year CD.

Tell the bank that you don't want the first four CDs to roll over for the same term or it will ruin your ladder. Once you cycle through the ladder, the CDs will all renew for five-year terms. You can build your ladder for any number of years you want, although beyond five years gets into an investment period that might be more appropriate for stocks or mutual funds.

This same laddering strategy works for bonds as well.

◀ *SEE ALSO 13.6, "Buying and Selling Bonds"* ▶

Focused CD Buying

This strategy for buying CDs looks forward toward a financial goal, such as college tuition or a down payment on a house. You have a date when you need the money, so you buy CDs with the same maturity date (when you will need the money), but at different times This provides you with a chance to buy some CDs when rates are better than at other times.

CD Buying Guidelines

If you aren't going to use laddering or a focused strategy, remember these two bank CD buying tips:

▶ When interest rates are trending up, buy shorter-term CDs so you can take advantage of new, higher rates.

▶ When interest rates are trending down, buy longer-term CDs to lock in higher rates before they fall farther.

▶ If there is no trend or you are unsure which way interest rates may go, stick with CDs of two to three year terms.

3.4 OTHER BANKING SERVICES

ATMs

Overdraft Protection

Online Banking

In this section, we'll cover several services that make banking more convenient.

ATMs

ATMs or automatic teller machines, if anyone remembers what the acronym stands for anymore, have come a long way since the days of simply dispensing cash. Many banks have relied on them to become minibranches, especially in large urban areas where maintaining a network of physical branches is expensive.

Most bank accounts will offer you an ATM access card. Often this card is also a debit card, but if you choose not to have a debit card or don't qualify, the card simply accesses the bank's ATMs and the bank's chosen ATM network.

All ATM cards require you to use a personal identification number (PIN) to access your account. Some banks let you choose your own number, while others assign you a PIN. With the card and the PIN, anyone can access your account, so guard your PIN (don't write it on the card, for example).

Modern ATMs offer a wide variety of services. You'll find the most services available at the bank's own ATMs and usually fewer services available at other ATMs. Bank ATMs allow you to:

- ▶ Withdraw cash
- ▶ Make deposits
- ▶ Make loan payments
- ▶ Transfer money between accounts
- ▶ Check balances
- ▶ Buy other products such as phone cards, stamps, and so on

In most cases, if you use your bank's ATM, you will not be charged a fee. However, that is not universal, so check your bank's policy on ATM usage and fees. When you use an ATM in a network other than your bank's, you may pay a fee for the privilege; in fact you may pay two fees: one to the company that owns the ATM and one to your bank. So avoid using ATMs that are not owned by your bank, if possible. A $2 fee on a $20 withdrawal is a huge (10 percent) fee to pay for the convenience of getting some cash. If you must use an ATM that is going to charge you a fee, take out enough cash for the whole week, rather than just enough to get by for a day. The reason is most fees are flat charges, so the more you withdraw, the less it costs you on a percentage basis.

ATMs are places where people get cash and that can lead to security issues. Always be aware of your surroundings and if an area around an ATM doesn't look secure (particularly walkup ATMs), find another location.

If your card isn't returned (some machines retain the card during the transaction) or is stolen, contact your bank immediately. Your liability may be limited to $50 if your card is used without your permission if you notify the bank within two business days. After that, your liability goes up dramatically. Your bank should provide you with specific information on your liability and responsibility in the event your card is lost or stolen.

If you use your debit card as an ATM card, other conditions may apply.

◀ *SEE ALSO 4.3, "Debit Cards"* ▶

Overdraft Protection

Bank fees can eat into your balance, and one of the largest fees you can pay is an overdraft charge for writing a check when there was not enough money to cover it. Fees for overdrafts as the bank calls them can be $35 or more per check. In addition, the merchant will likely hit you with a bad check fee also.

To avoid all of these fees, banks offer an overdraft protection service. The protection ties your checking and savings accounts and gives the bank permission to transfer money out of savings to cover bad checks without notifying you in advance. There is a fee for overdraft protection, but it is much less than paying the overdraft penalties and having bounced checks show up on your credit report.

You will have to maintain a savings account with sufficient balance to cover possible overdrafts—your bank may have a minimum account balance requirement.

Overdraft protection is worth the money for people who don't have a steady or reliable source of income, for example the self-employed or people paid only on commission. For people with a steady paycheck, it may not be worth the cost. If you bounce checks more than once a year, you should look at your spending and/ or record-keeping habits to determine why this is happening.

Online Banking

Online banking services are available from most banks. Larger banks offer a comprehensive range of services online, including viewing account transactions to see what checks, debits, deposits have cleared; transferring money between accounts; paying bills; applying for loans; buying certificates of deposit; and opening other savings accounts.

Thanks to debit cards, which act like checks and take money directly out of your checking account, it is easier to get behind in your check register if you fail to note every time you use the card. Accessing your account several times a week to check debits, checks, and other charges against your check register will keep you current with your account balance. Before this information was available, customers had to hope that all the items were entered into the check register and that they were entered correctly. A mistake might mean a check was written for more than the balance of the account. With daily access to your account, you can know the balance more precisely than waiting a week or ten days after the end of the month to receive a bank statement.

If you use electronic bill paying, automatic debit for investments, or other charges, it is important that you remember to enter these charges each month in your register. Viewing your account online reminds you to do this at the appropriate time of month.

3.5 BANKING FEES

Account Maintenance

Minimum Balances

Transaction Fees

Banks make a substantial portion of their income from fees they charge for various services and penalties for failures to comply with account requirements. In this section, we'll look at how these work and what you can do about them.

Account Maintenance

Banks often charge fees to simply maintain various accounts. These fees may be a flat charge for the privilege of having an account at the bank. Often checking accounts that don't require a minimum balance require an account maintenance fee. Savings accounts frequently require at least an annual fee to cover the administration of the account.

You can avoid some of these fees by being careful about the accounts you choose or watching account balances (see the next section). Other fees for account maintenance or administration are unavoidable; however, the bank should disclose all fees upfront before you open an account. Don't let bank personnel off the hook when they say, "All the fees are explained in the brochure." Insist that they explain the fees to you or go over the brochure, including the fine print, so you know under what circumstances your account may be charged a maintenance or administration fee.

Minimum Balances

The minimum balance requirement on bank accounts is a source of confusion for many consumers. The reason is banks can compute the minimum balance a number of different ways, and how they make the computation will determine if you owe a fee or not. This is another case where bank personnel need to be very clear about policy so you know what the rules are for your account.

The bank may charge you a fee if the balance in your account drops below a minimum amount—but, how is that minimum computed? There are two basic methods:

▶ The single low balance method will charge you the fee if your balance falls below the minimum even for one day of the month.

▶ The average daily balance computes the average daily balance for the whole month and if it is below the minimum, you pay the fee. This is the best method for the consumer, because it allows for those days in the month when several big checks or debits clear at the same time. Otherwise you will have to maintain a large balance in the account, which may not be the best use of your excess cash, even if the account is paying a small amount of interest.

3.5

Transaction Fees

The other way banks make money is on accounts and services that they charge transaction fees. For example, certain checking accounts may offer the first 25 transactions (checks and deposits) for free and then put a transaction fee on each one after that. These accounts are designed for people with very few trans-actions each month and, if you keep activity low, are good arrangements.

Due to the rising cost of operating and maintaining physical branches, some banks have accounts that charge you a fee if you use one of their personnel to conduct your business. The account might be set up so that in each month you get three transactions with a teller (either inside the bank or drive up) and after that, each time you use a teller, there is a fee associated with the transaction. Banks want to encourage customers to use electronic deposit, ATMs, online banking, or any method that reduces the number of humans they must employ.

3.6 BANKING REGULATIONS

Holding Deposits

Electronic Processing—No Float

The days of writing a check on Wednesday knowing you're going to deposit a paycheck on Friday are gone. Thanks to technology and banking regulations, you shouldn't rely on float. Regulations guide how long banks can hold deposits before crediting them to your account and it is in your best interest to know the rules.

Holding Deposits

Making a deposit doesn't mean the money is automatically available for you to spend. Regulation CC, which is part of the law that governs banking, sets down rules on how long banks can hold certain deposits before crediting them to your account. The law is to protect banks from bad deposits and to allow consumers access to their money in a reasonable time.

When you make a deposit, you may notice the deposit slip has two balances—the account balance and the available balance. The difference between the two is what the bank is holding back for some period. How long the bank will hold the deposit or portion of the deposit depends on the type of deposit.

Funds from checks drawn on local banks are usually available the second business day, but checks from out-of-town banks may not be available for five business days. These deposits must be available the next business day:

- ▶ Cash deposited in person
- ▶ U.S. Treasury checks
- ▶ Electronic payments
- ▶ Federal Reserve Bank or Federal Home Loan bank checks
- ▶ State or local government checks deposited in person
- ▶ Cashiers or certified checks

Banks may hold deposits made at ATMs until the second business day.

If you have just opened the account or have a history of overdrafts, expect longer holds on deposits. Banks have some discretion in how long they hold deposits, although holds beyond the ordinary periods should have some justification.

Understanding these rules can save you overdrafts and headaches. If you have an out-of-town check you need sooner than the normal hold, ask an officer of the bank if it can be expedited. Do this before you deposit the check. If you are a good customer, the bank may be willing to work something out for you.

Electronic Processing—No Float

Many vendors are now "swiping" your check through an electronic reader that converts your check to an electronic funds transfer and the money is debited from your account within one or two businesses days. This effectively eliminates the float that some people relied on to get them through to the next payday. This process speeds up the collection of funds for the retailer, which increases the speed of cash flow. For the consumer, it is important to know that writing a check may mean the funds are coming out of your account very soon.

One of the biggest revolutions in the banking industry is the move away from retaining and processing paper checks. The industry and regulators realize the tremendous cost and potential for error in processing the billions of checks that are written each year. Over half of all banks no longer return cancelled checks with monthly statements now and that number is growing. The Federal Reserve Board enacted a regulation in October 2004 called Check 21 that has set the stage for the eventual elimination of retaining canceled checks. Instead, electronic versions (images) of canceled checks will be retained. Some bank customers currently receive a printed version of these electronic images instead of the actual checks.

These substitute checks have the front and back image of the original check and can be used as proof of payment the same as the original check. Customers of some banks that don't receive copies of their canceled checks may be able to see them online. If you need proof of payment, there is a procedure for ordering a substitute check. Other customers will receive copies of the checks printed in smaller form on sheets called image statements. Image statements show several checks per page.

It doesn't matter whether you receive substitute checks, image statements, or no canceled checks with your statement; you are still protected by the same laws that govern checks and check writing.

3.7 TIME VALUE OF MONEY

Compound Interest

APR and APY

Inflation and Purchasing Power

Interest and time combine to make your money grow in a savings account through the mathematical magic of compounding. Compounding is a powerful tool when it works for you and an awful foe when inflation uses it against you. In this section, you'll learn how compounding works for you and against you.

Compound Interest

Compound interest is the single most important mathematical principal in understanding your personal finances. Once you understand compounding, the rest of the important math concepts make sense. At its essence, compounding is your principal earning interest, and that combined principal and interest earning interest, and so on. It has been described as interest earning interest. While it seems simple, the effect is dramatic when you add time to the equation.

The more time compounding is allowed to work, the more dramatic the effect. Consider that $10,000 invested at 4 percent and compounded monthly grows to $10,407 in one year. However, if you leave the money in the account for 25 years untouched it grows to $27,138.

When you put money in bank deposit products that earn interest, you are counting on the power of compounding to help your earnings. How much compounding helps will, in part, be determined by how often it occurs. Some bank products compound monthly, while others may only compound quarterly or annually. This can make a difference over a period. Here's why:

DIFFERENT COMPOUNDING PERIODS FOR $10,000 AT 4 PERCENT FOR ONE YEAR

Annually	Semiannually	Quarterly	Monthly	Daily
$10,400	$10,404	$10,406	$10,407	$10,408

The difference is not extreme for one year, however if you follow this sequence out 10 years or more, the gap between what you would earn on daily compounding versus annual compounding would be significant.

Compounded annually: $14,802

Compounded daily: $18,220

Difference: $3,418

It pays to pick a savings product that compounds with the greatest frequency.

APR and APY

Most consumers are familiar with the Annual Percentage Rate (APR) that they see on advertisements for all loan products. The Consumer Protection Act of 1968 attempted to provide consumers with the information they needed to compare the true costs of loans. The APR was to include all costs of the loan so consumers would know exactly how much the loan was costing when fees and other expenses were added. Unfortunately, the law, also known as Truth in Lending, didn't work out the way it was hoped.

The problems arise when it comes to home mortgages, unfortunately the largest loan commitment most people make. Mortgages are quoted with two numbers: the interest rate and the APR. The APR is supposed to include all the other fees and expenses of the mortgage so consumers can compare two loans. Problems arise because there is no one way expenses are figured into the loans, so one company may include a charge that another company does not. The calculation is so complicated that specialized software is required.

The APR for mortgages was built on some faulty assumptions, which accounts for some of the confusion. For example, fees and charges are amortized over the life of a 30-year note, although most mortgages are paid off through a sale long before then. Some lenders include certain charges while other lenders don't include the charges.

You are better off ignoring the APR on home mortgages and focusing on the actual interest rate of the mortgage—this is what payments will be based on. Deciding on a loan package is a complicated decision that very seldom rests on one number. There are points, fees, and other considerations. Reducing the decision to a single number is simplistic and likely to produce a bad decision.

◁ *SEE ALSO 5.4, "Financing and Refinancing"* ▷

While the regulators didn't get it right on APR, they did get it right on APY or Annual Percentage Yield. APY is a way to compare deposit products to see which is the better deal even if they have different compounding periods but the same term. The APY lets you accurately compare deposit products by computing annual figures that are comparable. Whichever product has the highest APY is the better deal for you.

You should note that the APY may or may not represent an actual yield. For example, deposit products with a six-month term also have an APY, but that doesn't mean that's what you will earn. It is just for comparison purposes.

Inflation and Purchasing Power

Just as compounding works to build your savings, it can work to destroy them through the erosion of purchasing power by inflation. Inflation is the loss of purchasing power due to the decline in value of the dollar. Stated another way, inflation is the general rise in prices with no corresponding increase in value. Inflation has been called the "silent tax," because it takes value from your savings and investments.

Here's an example, using statistics from the U.S. Bureau of Labor Statistics, which calculates the rate of inflation, if you bought $1,000 worth of goods in 2000 those exact same goods would cost $1,110.54 in 2005. This was a period marked by very low inflation, yet your purchasing power effectively fell $110 because the same goods cost that much more in 2005.

This erosion of purchasing power is dangerous because it compounds and, over the years, even a low rate of inflation can eat substantial pieces of your savings. Consider if you are earning 4 percent on your savings and inflation is 2.5 percent that you are really netting (before taxes on the full 4 percent) 1.5 percent each year.

This erosion of savings is why you should consider other investments besides bank products for part of your nest egg. Stocks and mutual funds offer the possibility of returns that exceed those offered by bank deposit products.

◀ *SEE ALSO 10.4, "Asset Allocation"* ▶

3.8 IDENTITY THEFT

Guarding Against Identity Theft

It is hard to turn on the television or read a popular news publication without seeing something about identity theft. Thanks to computer networks, it is possible for people with evil intentions to become an electronic version of you and open credit card accounts, buy real estate, borrow money—in short do financially anything your good credit will let them do. This section discusses how you can protect yourself.

Guarding Against Identity Theft

Identity theft happens to millions of people each year. A thief can get your identity many ways:

▶ They can steal it out of your garbage from old bank statements or bills

▶ They can steal your mail and get personal information

▶ You can give it to them when they pose as legitimate businesses

▶ They can buy it from legal and illegal sources

You can do much to protect yourself. One of the most important pieces of information to protect is your Social Security number. With this number and a few other pieces of information, crooks will have no trouble creating a new you that can run up big credit card bills and other financial problems.

There are only a few cases where your Social Security number is required. Never give it to a stranger over the phone or by e-mail, even if the person contacting you claims to represent your bank or some other official sounding organization. If someone wants your Social Security number, ask why. In most cases, to open a bank or financial services account, you will have to provide it. However, the grocery store doesn't need it and anyone else who wants it should provide some legal reason for needing it. Don't accept their word that "it's required," find out for yourself if you legally need to provide it.

You should check your credit report at the reporting agencies (contact information is in Appendix B) at least three or four times a year or subscribe to a service that checks for you. This is one way to determine if anyone is opening accounts in your name.

There are steps to take to reclaim your identity:

▶ Contact the three credit bureaus by phone first and follow up with an immediate letter asking to put a fraud alert in your file. This lets creditors checking your file know that something may be wrong and requests they contact you before changing your account or opening a new account in your name. Get a copy of your report and look for unauthorized charges in the "Inquiries" section. You will need to contact any tampered with or phony accounts and close them. Also, ask the credit bureaus to remove inquiries from the phony accounts from your report.

▶ File a report with the police to have a record of reporting the crime.

▶ If the identity thief is using your credit cards, you are liable for only the first $50 if you contact the card issuers immediately.

▶ Contact every bank or other financial institution and alert them to the theft. If you suspect the thief may have access to your account information, immediately close all accounts and open new accounts with different passwords and so on.

▶ Find any creditors listed on the credit report who opened accounts for the thief under your name. Send them a certified letter swearing you are not the person who opened the account and ask them to clear your name from the fraud on the account with the credit bureaus and get a copy of their statement. If they refuse to clear your name, demand a copy of the application they accepted to open the account—they have to send you a copy. Point out the false information on the application.

▶ If creditors or their collection agencies offer to settle on an account, refuse because this will stay on your credit report for up to seven years.

▶ If there is a substantial sum in dispute, consider hiring an attorney to help you resolve the matter, but don't accept a settlement—you did nothing wrong.

4

CREDIT AND DEBT

4.1 DEBT MANAGEMENT

Good Debt vs. Bad Debt
Benchmarks for Debt Management

Managing your personal finances is the process of controlling expenses and investing for the future. The most critical expense you must control is your debt. Not all debt is bad, but bad debt can destroy your financial plans and defeat your goals. In this section, we examine the difference between "good" debt and "bad" debt.

Good Debt vs. Bad Debt

Some debt is worth incurring and other debt is not. Debt that buys you an asset that appreciates or holds some value is not the same as financing a **consumable** (food, clothing, gasoline, and so on). Learning to make smart debt decisions is an important step to good money management. When you understand the relationship between the cost of **financing** any purchase and its long-term value, you can make better decisions about how to use debt.

> **WORDS TO GO . . .** WORDS TO GO . . . WORDS TO GO
>
> **Consumable,** in the context of consumer finance, means any good or service that is used immediately and provides no lasting value. Financing consumables is a poor personal finance decision because you use and/or dispose of the goods or service, but continue to pay interest on the charges.
>
> **Financing** is borrowing money to purchase goods or services. If you charge something on a credit card and don't pay the balance in full when the bill arrives, you are incurring a debt and paying interest on the money you borrowed.

Good Debt

The key to identifying "good debt" is two-fold:

▶ Good debt buys an asset that appreciates or holds some value, or is some intangible that permanently improves your quality of life.

▶ You can purchase good debt at a reasonable interest rate and for a term that suits the purchase and your financial situation.

Most of us need to borrow the money required to buy a first house. A house will usually not depreciate and, in many cases, it will appreciate over time. If you can afford the monthly payments and all the other expenses associated with owning a home, it is usually a good investment, both financially and emotionally. In addition to providing shelter and a home for your family, residential real estate has historically been a good long-term investment. Unless you go overboard and buy more house than you can afford, it definitely falls into the good debt column.

As you pay down a home mortgage, you build **equity** in the property—that is, you owe less money and the value of the house rises or, presumably, doesn't fall.

WORDS TO GO . . .WORDS TO GO . . .WORDS TO GO

Equity in a loan context is the difference between an asset's value and what you owe on the asset. If you sell the asset and pay off the loan, what remains for you to keep is the equity.

Financing automobiles becomes slightly more complicated. Most people will have to borrow some money to afford a new or late-model used car. If you opt for sensible transportation and plan on keeping the same vehicle for five or more years, it can be good debt, too. On the other hand, people who fall in love with the latest model every year or two and trade up will find themselves paying an exorbitant amount of interest and, in the end, much more than the vehicle is worth.

Good debt can also buy intangibles like a college education or classes to update your job skills.

Even the important items like houses and vehicles that would normally be considered good debt must meet the financial as well as the needs qualifications. A mortgage on a house at an exorbitant rate is not good debt and can put you into financial trouble that is difficult to shake. One of the more troubling areas where people should be using good debt is financing vehicles; however, they often make poor debt choices, which result in paying much more than necessary.

Bad Debt

"Bad" debt may be harder for many people to avoid because of spending habits that have developed over many years. Our consumer-spending driven economy has made it very easy to finance almost anything, from a multimillion dollar house to a hamburger, fries, and a soda. Most abuse of debt is done with credit cards, although there are many other opportunities such as in-store charge cards, "factory" financing of vehicles and major appliances, and so on.

Debt at any level becomes a serious problem when there is a disconnect between the act of buying an item on credit and the understanding that the money must be paid back, often with interest. When this happens, people often are surprised each month at the balance on their credit card bills and can't remember where or what they spent the money on.

People often fall into bad debt by not understanding the terms and implications of the debt they incur. Financing vehicles is a good example of how not under-standing the process can get you in deep trouble. It is tempting to use one of the low- or no-money-down financing plans to get into a new or late-model car. Unfortunately, the excitement soon wears off and some people are ready to trade in for a newer vehicle. There are dealers who will accommodate them up to a point. What the buyers don't realize is they are signing a note for more than the vehicle is worth. They rolled the high remaining balance of the previous note into the new note after the trade-in. This can happen once or twice before the next lender says you owe too much and you'll have to pay down the note before you can trade in the vehicle you have.

◀ *SEE ALSO 6.4, "The Auto Loan"* ▶

Automobile manufacturers, lenders, and dealers have tried to work around this by pushing the leasing of vehicles as the "inexpensive" way to own a new vehicle every two or three years. The truth is that leasing is a very expensive way to own a vehicle. If you don't know how to negotiate a good lease, it can be a financial problem.

◀ *SEE ALSO 6.5, "The Auto Lease"* ▶

The same situation can happen in real estate. Although most people think resi-dential real estate always goes up, that's not always the case. If you have a no- or low-money-down note and there's a decline in values (or you overpay), you can end up "**upside down**" in your note, meaning you owe more than the property is worth.

WORDS TO GO . . . WORDS TO GO . . . WORDS TO GO

Upside down in a loan, whether for a home or a vehicle, means you owe more than the asset is worth. This can happen because the asset depreciates in price or you paid too much in the first place. In either case, you may have to pay down the note to get out of it.

The big examples of bad debt may be easy to spot, but it's the smaller, everyday charges that often do the most ongoing damage to people's personal finances. The biggest mistake people make with credit cards or in-store charge cards is charging consumable items like food, clothing, gasoline, and such to their cards and not paying off the balance each month.

There is nothing wrong with charging dinner with friends, but don't do it unless you know you can pay off the entire credit card bill at the end of the month. Credit cards are examined in more detail in the next section, but at 18 percent interest for some cards, the cost of financing rises rapidly.

Use debt wisely to finance assets that appreciate or improve your quality of life and avoid financing consumables.

Benchmarks for Debt Management

Lenders measure the amount of debt you carry as a sign of financial well-being. You can and should do calculations yourself on an annual basis or anytime you are contemplating taking on more debt. This ratio tells you if your debt is where it should be or too high. You can't argue with the numbers—and you shouldn't, because if you apply for a loan, the lender will look at the same ratio.

The primary ratio is your debt-to-income ratio, which tells you and lenders how much of your income is going towards your consumer debt. The higher the number, the greater danger you will not be able to make all your debt payments if some other financial problems arose—a large medical bill, or one partner is laid off or loses their job, for example.

You calculate your debt-to-income ratio by adding up your loan commitments and dividing by your take-home pay. Don't include your mortgage or rent payments— you want to focus on all your other consumer debt. Here's what to include:

- ▶ Car loan or lease payments
- ▶ Credit cards
- ▶ Charge cards
- ▶ Gas credit cards
- ▶ Home equity loans
- ▶ Store charge cards
- ▶ Any other loans or credit payments

You can use numbers for one month, but a full year's worth will be more accurate. If those aren't readily available, average as many months as you can get numbers for. This is especially important if your income fluctuates from month-to-month, because you know your expenses will also change.

◀ *SEE ALSO 2.2, "Tracking Expenses"* ▶

The results of your calculations should tell you what percent of your income is claimed by your expenses. Compare to this standard:

▶ 10 percent or less—this is an ideal level

▶ 15 percent or less—nothing to worry about

▶ 20 percent or more—your debt is beginning to become a problem

▶ 30 percent or more—it is unlikely you will qualify for any more loans

It is important to keep your debt-to-income ratio below 15 percent as a safety precaution in the event of a financial crisis. If you carry too much consumer debt (which is what the debt-to-income ratio measures) and you lose all or a substantial portion of your income, you will drain your emergency cash reserve much quicker paying off loans.

◀ *SEE ALSO 2.6, "Emergency Funds"* ▶

A high debt-to-income ratio also indicates there would be extra money available for an investment or savings program that is now paying off consumer loans.

4.2 CREDIT CARDS

Credit Card Abuse

The Math of Credit Cards

How to Find a Good Credit Card

Credit cards revolutionized the retail industry by granting consumers instant credit to make purchases. Credit cards are almost a necessity in today's consumer marketplace, but it's easy to abuse easy credit. In this section, you'll learn how that abuse happens, why the math of credit cards works against you, and where to find a good deal on a credit card.

4.2

Credit Card Abuse

Abuse of credit cards is a personal financial epidemic. Depending on the source, the average family carries between $8,000 and $10,000 of credit card debt. That translates into a tremendous national monthly expense that is, for the most part, wasted money. The largest source of bad debt—the financing of consumables— is credit cards, along with charge cards and "affinity" or in-store cards. These sources of almost instant credit make it too easy for some people to give in to impulse buying.

Credit cards are a form of **revolving credit,** which means the issuer sets a limit and you can charge up to that amount. As you make payments, your credit line is refreshed by that amount. As long as you make the minimum payments or more, you can keep using the card. It is possible and probable that most consumers have several credit cards, along with charge cards and in-store cards. If you are employed and make regular payments, you may have a significant combined line of credit across all cards. Tapping all that credit is too tempting for some people who find themselves in terrible financial trouble because of over spending.

WORDS TO GO . . . WORDS TO GO . . . WORDS TO GO

Revolving credit is a form of consumer credit that renews the amount of credit available (up to a limit) by the amount of payment you make. You don't have to reapply—the credit line renews automatically.

Credit cards often become a source of cash for nonemergency spending. Cash advances are available up to a certain percentage of the credit you have remaining on your card. You can get cash at a participating bank or, in many cases, at ATMs. Except in true emergencies, cash advances are bad personal financial decisions. Most cards will charge a fee upfront for the privilege of taking the advance, and then charge a higher interest rate on the advance than on other charges. Some cards also apply your payments to lower-interest charges first, before applying them to higher-interest cash advance charges. In an emergency, cash advances from a credit card are usually better than "**pay-day loans**" or other personal loans from nonbank lenders—but *only* in an emergency.

WORDS TO GO . . .WORDS TO GO . . .WORDS TO GO

Pay-day loans let you borrow against your next paycheck. There are fees for the service and, if you don't pay back the loan in a short period, it renews with additional fees and interest. Some of these loans can result in consumers paying well over 100 percent interest on an annual basis.

You can reduce the temptation to abuse credit cards by only having one card and committing to paying off the outstanding balance every month, or as quickly as possible. Avoid buying items that have no lasting value until you are able to pay the credit card bill in full every month. If you need to make a large purchase on your credit card, budget an amount to pay off the balance in three to six months. This will reduce the interest you pay.

The Math of Credit Cards

Credit cards charge interest on the unpaid balance of your account. However, there are two ways of calculating the interest charges—one is much better for you than the other. It is best if you pay the full balance every month, but if you don't you should use a card that calculates interest charges that are better for you. Here are the two methods:

▶ The two-billing-cycle method looks at your average daily balance over two months. This method works against consumers who only pay part of a large charge in the first month, because the credit card company looks at the first month and second month. The full amount of the charge is calculated in the first month, the partial amount is calculated in the second month, and this is averaged together, so you get no credit for the payment in the first month.

▶ The one-billing-cycle method is better for the consumer. If there is a large charge in the first month and a partial payment, the consumer only pays interest on the remaining balance in the second month, not the full balance.

Your credit card statement should tell you which method is used to calculate interest. If you can't find the information on your statement or in any of the information you have from the issuer, call the customer service number and ask how interest is calculated. If the company uses the two-billing-cycle method, consider switching to a card with the one-billing-cycle method.

4.2

Minimum Charges

Credit card companies are required to set a minimum payment on your statement that covers the interest payment and pays down some of the principal amount. Companies use several methods for computing the minimum payment, which should be explained on your statement. One of the most common methods is a percentage of the outstanding balance or a minimum dollar amount, whichever is greater. There is pressure from consumer groups to make credit card companies raise the minimum payments even higher. The reason is that at most minimum payment levels it will take many years to pay off the average $8,000 per family credit card balance.

Using the $8,000 balance, a 14 percent interest rate, and assuming the minimum payment is calculated as 2.5 percent of the balance, you will pay over $93 in interest the first month and by the time you pay the $8,000 balance off in 278 months, you will have paid over $6,792 in interest charges alone. If you only pay the minimum, you'll pay almost $14,800 for that $8,000 worth of goods and services. And this assumes, of course, that you never charge another penny on that card!

If you took the $14,800 that you paid over 278 months to pay off the credit card and invested it evenly (about $53 per month) over the same period in an account that earned 8 percent, your financial picture would be much different at the end of 278 months. Instead of having a paid-up credit card and nothing else, you would have $42,468 in your account! This is just an example of how the math of compounding either works against you (paying the minimum) or works for you (investing steadily).

Fees

Some credit cards and charge cards have an annual fee that you must pay for the privilege of carrying the card. Unless you have poor credit and have to settle for a secured credit card, there is no reason to pay an annual fee for a credit card unless it buys you a lower annual interest rate. Some premium cards offer a variety of products and services with their top-level card that requires a fee. If you want and will use these services, decide whether they're worth the price of the annual fee.

Many **charge cards** have fees that go with their services. Charge cards differ from credit cards in that they usually do not have a fixed spending limit. Your spending limit is more a function of past spending patterns and your overall financial worthiness. American Express is the most famous of all charge cards. It has different levels that allow you to buy increasing amounts each month. Charge cards don't allow you to carry a balance: you are expected to pay off the balance each month.

WORDS TO GO . . .WORDS TO GO . . .WORDS TO GO

Charge cards differ from credit cards in that they don't offer a true line of credit. You are expected to pay the balance each month. How much you can charge during the month depends on previous spending patterns and other financial factors.

Other Fees

Credit cards give you a window from the end of the billing cycle until the date the payment is due. They expect to receive your payment during this period. If your payment is even a day late, you will get hit with a hefty fee that may exceed $35, *and* your next month's interest will be calculated without subtracting your late payment from the principal. Credit card companies don't count the payment until it is in their possession, so a postmarked envelope the day payment was due doesn't count. To be safe, make sure the payment will arrive several days before the due date and avoid a hefty fee.

If you go over your credit limit, the company will likely hit you with a fee. How much of a fee may depend on how much over the limit you went. If you try to charge an item that will put you too far over the limit, the card company will deny approval. If you go just a little over your credit limit, the card company will let the charge go through, but may hit you with a fee.

How to Find a Good Credit Card

Finding a credit card is easy—and a lot of times they'll find you. Finding a *good* credit card, one that works for your financial situation, may take some work. The market is awash with offers of no-interest or very low interest cards for some introductory period. These companies are primarily looking for customers to transfer balances from old cards to their card. This may or may not be wise. Like most financial decisions, it is not hinged on one number or one factor.

A good place to begin looking for a credit card is www.bankrate.com. This website has comprehensive information on rates in every state and nationwide. You do not have to have an account at most banks or institutions to have a credit card. Look at the deals in your state or look nationwide for the best deal.

4.2

Low introduction periods pass, so base your decision on the rate that remains. Credit cards have either a fixed interest rate or a variable interest rate. When interest rates are falling, a variable interest rate card may be the best choice; however, if rates are going up, locking in a fixed rate makes sense. The best choice is a low fixed rate card over a low variable rate card, but credit card companies can raise or lower rates on both cards. The difference is that with a fixed-rate card, the company has to give you notice, usually 15 days. Variable rate cards can change rates with no notice to you.

If your history is that you pay off the balance almost every month, look for a card with no annual fee. If you frequently carry a balance, look for a card with the lowest fixed interest rate, even if it means paying a reasonable annual fee.

4.3 DEBIT CARDS

How They Differ from Credit Cards
Using Them Instead of Checks

In this section, you'll learn about bank debit cards and how they differ from credit cards. These versatile cards perform a variety of functions, but be careful that you stay on top of your record keeping.

How They Differ from Credit Cards

Debit cards are connected with bank checking and savings accounts, which makes them different from credit cards that are independent of such accounts. This is just the beginning of the differences. Debit cards do not extend credit; as the name implies, they draw funds directly from the associated account. When you use a debit card to buy $50 worth of goods, the $50 is withdrawn from your account—there is no bill at the end of the month and no interest to pay.

With a debit card, you can perform several functions with most bank accounts. You can:

▶ Access ATMs

▶ Use the card at terminals requiring a PIN (personal identification number)

▶ Use the card like a credit card, but the money is debited from your account within a few business days

Most debit cards now carry either the Visa or MasterCard brand, which means they are accepted into those respective verification systems. If you want to buy something at a store with a debit card, the system verifies your account is good for the charge. The merchant receives an authorization and you sign a slip just as you would sign a credit card slip. The difference is the funds are transferred out of your account, usually within a few business days, if not sooner.

Some merchants—grocery stores, for example—have terminals at the checkout where you can swipe your card and choose credit or debit. If you choose debit, you will enter your PIN and verify the amount. Some terminals will ask if you want cash back. This is not unlike writing a check for more than the amount, which some stores will let you do. However, be aware that some retailers and banks charge a fee for getting cash this way, because it is considered the same as accessing an ATM that doesn't belong to the bank. If there are fees (usually several dollars), you may want to look for an ATM from your bank for your cash needs and avoid the expensive withdrawal.

Using Them Instead of Checks

Debit cards provide much of the convenience of credit cards without the danger of running up a large bill that results in high-interest debt on impulse purchases. Debit cards are easier to carry than checks and may be more widely accepted, thanks to the affiliation with Visa and MasterCard.

Some vendors will allow (or encourage) you to set up an automatic payment of their bill on your credit card. Each month you get a notice that the company has billed your credit card to cover this month's charges. Use a debit card instead of a credit card and you avoid having that charge on your statement in case you don't or can't pay the credit card bill in full one month.

A potential problem with debit cards is failing to note each use in your check register. Because debits come out of your account quickly, you need to keep your register current so you know the correct balance. It is too easy to let a few debit card purchases or cash withdrawals from the ATM go by without recording and you may run the risk of overdrawing your account.

One record-keeping method that defeats this is to check your bank account online (some banks have a way to access the information over your telephone) several times a week and record all transactions in you register. That way you know what has actually happened and what has cleared.

4.3

4.4 PERSONAL LOANS

Consolidating High-Interest Loans

Lines of Credit

Trading debt for debt is normally not a good financial decision unless there are exceptional benefits in doing so. Getting rid of high-interest credit card debt with a lower-interest home equity note can make a bad situation better. This section explains why.

Consolidating High-Interest Loans

The burden of high-interest credit card debt can be oppressive, both financially and emotionally. Homeowners have a way to potentially rid themselves of high-interest credit card debt, but the maneuver carries some risks. Homeowners can tap into the equity of their home for a home equity loan to pay off a large credit card debt.

The benefits are twofold. First, the interest rate on home equity loans, while higher than primary mortgages, is lower than credit card interest. Second, in most cases the interest is tax deductible—always check with a competent tax advisor to verify tax deductions. Interest payments on credit card debt are not tax deductible.

This strategy can erase a big credit card bill in one maneuver. However, several other things must happen. You must halt your spending habits that ran up the debt. Once you have paid off the cards, destroy all but one. Don't close the accounts, though—that may actually hurt your credit rating, which is discussed in 4.5, "Credit Rating."

The risk of this strategy is that if you do not curb your spending, you will run up a large credit card debt again, then you will owe not only the credit card debt, but a loan on your home. If you default on the home equity loan, it could put your house in jeopardy.

A home equity loan requires an application and fees may run several hundred to several thousand dollars depending on the size of the loan and other factors. Your home will get an independent appraisal of its value, which will determine how much equity is available. This, along with your ability to repay the note, will determine how much the lender will let you borrow. You can use the money for any purpose, not just paying off credit-card debt. You can pay for an addition to your home, college tuition, a vacation, or whatever you choose. Getting rid of high-interest debt is a popular and wise use of the funds if you have the discipline to not let your credit card balances get out of hand again.

Lines of Credit

In addition to a home equity loan, you can get a line of home equity credit. This will be much like a loan except you only draw what you need, when you need it. People doing remodeling or other construction work find this convenient. Others may want to use some of the money now, but not tap the rest of the equity until a later date. They pay interest on that portion of the equity they have actually borrowed, which keeps interest expense low.

4.4

The application and approval process is the same as the home equity loan. You are given a special set of checks or a debit card as a way to access the credit line when you need it. The loan may have a time limit in which you must use the equity—five years, for example. At the end of the time limit, your credit line expires and you must pay off the outstanding balance under the terms of the loan agreement. You may be able to extend the credit line, but some banks will require you to go through the approval process again. Like the home equity loan, the interest may be tax deductible and your home is collateral for repayment of the outstanding balance.

4.5 CREDIT RATING

Credit Score

Credit Agencies

Your credit score may be one of the most important numbers in your life. It is checked not just by potential lenders, but also by potential employers, landlords, and others. In this section, we'll look at credit scores and where they orginate.

Credit Score

Your credit score or rating is so important to your financial well-being that an industry has sprung up that monitors people's numbers and credit reports and notifies them of changes. Your credit score not only determines if you will get a loan, it determines in part, what interest rate you'll pay.

The FICO number, which stands for Fair Isaac Company, the company that computes and sells the numbers, is the single most important number in the credit industry. With a high FICO, you can get a loan at a good rate and have a better chance renting an apartment or landing a job. A low FICO score may mean no loan or a loan at a much higher rate than advertised. Some property owners will not rent to you, and there's a chance you could be turned down for a job if it involved fiscal responsibility.

FICO scores are complicated mathematical calculations based on information from credit agencies and crunched to come up with a three digit number that is your score. According to the FICO website (www.myfico.com), your score is composed of these parts:

- ▶ Payment history: 35 percent
- ▶ Amount owed: 30 percent
- ▶ Length of credit history: 15 percent
- ▶ New credit: 10 percent
- ▶ Types of credit used: 10 percent

The FICO website provides detailed information on each of these categories. There are tips for improving your score or not harming it. For example, one item the score considers is length of credit history. You want your credit history to be as long as possible, so never cancel your oldest credit card, even if it is the one with the highest interest rate. Pull it out of a secure hiding place once or twice a year and charge something you can pay off when the bill comes. This extends your credit history back to this card and improves your score.

You can check your FICO score from the FICO website; however, it will cost you. You can also check your credit reports from the three credit reporting agencies listed later. FICO scores range from 300 to 850 and the higher the better. A score of 720 and above will get the lowest interest rates on loans. Scores between 720 and 675 can still qualify for loans at decent rates, but scores below 675 are considered risky.

Improving your FICO score is a lengthy process that usually involves improving your creditworthiness (35 percent). This includes making sure all your payments are on time. This is a big part of your score. If you have past due items, find a way to clear them up as soon as possible. Bad marks on your credit—bankruptcy, judgments, liens, wage garnishments, and such—will improve as time puts them farther in your history.

The other area that accounts for a big portion of your score is the amount owed (30 percent). Here an obvious help is to reduce your outstanding debt. Pay off credit cards, personal loans, and in-store financing of items like furniture.

It is a mistake to think that if you cancel all your credit cards, your score will improve—it could have the opposite effect. One of the measures is portion of credit available and amount used. If you have five credit cards with a total available credit line of $40,000 and you carry a balance of $5,000, that looks better than one card with an $8,000 credit line and a $5,000 balance. That is why it is better to put the unused cards in a safe place rather than canceling them.

Another misconception is that checking your credit reports will lower your score. Your inquiries don't count in the equation, however, if your credit bureau accounts show multiple inquiries for new credit, this repeated activity may indicated you are opening new accounts. One of the reasons you check your credit reports is to spot new inquiries that you did not originate. This could be a sign of identity theft.

◀ *SEE ALSO 3.8, "Identity Theft"* ▶

If your score is low because of errors on a credit agency report, you can and should get those corrected, but even that will take time. If you are planning on a major purchase, such as a house, it is best to check your FICO score and allow ample time to correct any mistakes and take whatever other steps are necessary to improve your score—reducing your overall debt for example. Don't wait until it is time to apply for the mortgage to discover there is a problem.

Credit Agencies

Three major credit-reporting agencies track your credit rating. Companies that extend credit to you report your payment history and lapses. Any negative credit events such as bankruptcy, judgments, or wage garnishments go on your report. This information is available to anyone you give permission to see it. If you apply for credit or a loan, somewhere on the application is your consent to view your credit history.

You should review your credit reports several times a year for accuracy and to make sure that there is no unusual activity such as strange accounts at stores you don't recognize. This could be a mistake or evidence of identity theft.

You can order a copy of your credit report directly from the reporting agencies. Their contact information is in Appendix B. They must provide you with a free copy once per year, which you can get by calling 1-877-322-8228 or ordering the reports at www.annualcreditreport.com.

If you find a mistake, there is a procedure for correcting the entry. Contact the company that filed the incorrect report—a common mistake will show a balance when you have paid off the account. Ask the company to file a corrected report. At the same time, alert the credit agency to the mistake and ask them to remove it from your record. Provide any written evidence you have of the mistake.

The credit bureau must respond to your request within 30 days. They may ask for more information or deny the request if you can't provide sufficient evidence. If it is a significant mistake that you believe is having a negative impact on your ability to obtain credit, consider turning the matter over to an attorney. Most mistakes can be corrected without going to that extreme. Remember to check all three credit agencies for the mistake. You must contact each one separately.

4.6   REPAIRING YOUR CREDIT

Debt Counseling

Restoring Your Good Credit Rating

If your credit is severely damaged, you may want and need some professional help to correct your spending habits and get a plan to repair your credit. Help is available, but so are organizations that prey on people in trouble. This section discusses the right way to repair your credit.

Debt Counseling

People in serious debt may turn to debt counselors for help. Several legitimate counseling services offer assistance to people in financial distress. Some of the larger ones are listed in Appendix B. These organizations don't make promises to wipe out your debt or any other quick fixes. They will help you understand what you need to do to control your spending and what you can do to work with creditors on a repayment plan.

This is a responsible approach to the problem. Unfortunately, an industry of legal, semi-legal, and illegal operations makes outrageous promises and charges equally outrageous fees to make your debt problem disappear. These credit-repair "clinics" and "doctors" sound like they have special information or "insider" secrets that will make your problems go away.

There are, however, no secrets or special deals or anything else that can legally make debts go away, unless you file bankruptcy. Some of these operations are, in fact, fronts for bankruptcy lawyers. Bankruptcy is a legal option to resolve your debt situation, but it is a drastic step that has long-term consequences and should be the solution when nothing else will work.

Restoring Your Good Credit Rating

It is possible to restore your good credit rating even after a bankruptcy. It will take time and a determination to not commit any financial indiscretions such as late or missed payments. You will need to reestablish your credit as soon as possible. One way you can begin this process is with a secured credit card. If you have a job, you may be able to get a credit card with a low credit limit that requires a substantial deposit, such as a $500 credit limit and a $125 deposit that stays with the account until you have demonstrated your creditworthiness, which may take several years.

If you show you can handle the responsibility of credit, over time you will be able to rebuild your credit. One of the first large extensions of credit will likely be for a car loan. Don't buy a car just to reestablish your credit, but responsibly repaying a loan is another step to rebuilding your credit.

The ironic thing is that many credit problems and up to one-half of personal bankruptcies are not caused by irresponsible handling of credit, but by large medical bills, loss of jobs, and other financial emergencies that overwhelm family finances. If families run up large credit card bills it is because of pressing financial circumstances, not irresponsible behavior. Yet, to rebuild a good credit rating you must prove again that you are responsible with money and credit.

4.7 BANKRUPTCY

New Rules May Limit Choices

Competent Legal Help Mandatory

When your debts are so overwhelming that there is no way you can repay them, bankruptcy may be your only option. Changes in the bankruptcy laws have made the decision more complicated and may result in a lengthy repayment process. In this section, we'll look at the alternatives.

New Rules May Limit Choices

When Congress rewrote the bankruptcy code in 2005, it dramatically changed the way debtors used the law. Most personal bankruptcy filings come under two types: Chapter 7 and Chapter 13.

A Chapter 7 filing wipes out all debts. Any personal assets that are not exempted by law are sold and the proceeds distributed to creditors.

A Chapter 13 filing is a reorganization of debts where a plan is developed to repay some or all of the creditors. Interest is often frozen on debts and collection proceedings stop.

Chapter 7

Prior to the reforms of 2005, most personal bankruptcies were Chapter 7 filings. Usually, by the time the debtor reached this point there was no money left in bank accounts or other liquid assets. Often there were few if any nonexempt assets. The federal law defined some assets as exempt, while individual states add other items. The Chapter 7 filing wiped out all debts, except those exempt from bankruptcy laws.

Bankruptcy—either filing—will not eliminate debts for back taxes to the IRS or state government, student loans, child support or alimony, and criminal fines.

The bankruptcy code allows you to keep certain "exempt assets" such as your house, home furnishings (to a certain extent), your pension, and any money in retirement savings accounts. Exempt assets are outside the proceedings and cannot be used to satisfy debts. Cash, stock, nonresidential real estate, and so on are "nonexempt assets." A trustee appointed by the court handles the sale and distribution of these assets.

Where an asset falls may depend on which state you live in, so seek legal advice from a bankruptcy attorney before assuming an asset is exempt or nonexempt.

Creditors have the right to challenge your list of assets or any claim of exempt assets. It is against federal law to hide assets in a bankruptcy filing. Once the asset question is settled, your list of debts is **discharged** when the bankruptcy is approved by the court. This means you are no longer responsible of these debts and the creditors can not attempt to collect from you—if they do, it is a violation of federal law.

WORDS TO GO . . . WORDS TO GO . . . WORDS TO GO

To **discharge** a bankruptcy is the final act by the bankruptcy court that completes process of eliminating the debts from your responsibility.

Chapter 13

Following the reforms of 2005, which were driven by credit card companies and other businesses that lose substantial sums in bankruptcy filings each year, the most common personal filing is now Chapter 13.

If you have an income, the odds are good that the bankruptcy court will insist on a Chapter 13 filing. The court may eliminate or reduce some debts and set a repayment plan for others. You are put on an allowance to cover your living expenses and everything else you earn goes to the repayment plan. Financial tests apply to determine much of the repayment plan.

One of the benefits of the Chapter 13 filing is that you generally can keep your property, which can be a real plus. The downside is living under a very tight budget for an extended period (up to five years, depending on various financial tests). If you miss a payment to the plan, there can be consequences or a change in the plan.

Counseling

Before you can file either chapter of the code, you must attend an authorized credit counseling session given by a court-recognized provider six months prior to filing. Before your bankruptcy can be discharged, you must attend an authorized financial planning class.

Competent Legal Help Mandatory

Bankruptcy is not a do-it-yourself process, nor is it something to trust to an attorney who is doing on-the-job training. It is a complicated process, and more so now that there is a new set of laws on the books that are still being tested as more cases go to the bankruptcy courts.

Although the new law has taken some of the decision-making out of the hands of filers, you should consider bankruptcy very carefully. The implications for your life are significant. A bankruptcy on your credit report is devastating. It will be difficult, if not impossible, to obtain credit for a period of several years. A bankruptcy stays on your credit report for 10 years, although it diminishes in importance each year that passes without more bad credit marks.

4.7

5

HOUSING

5.1 BUYING VS. RENTING

Which Is Best for You

Advantages of Buying

Disadvantages of Owning a Home

Advantages of Renting

Disadvantages of Renting

Owning a home is the American dream, at least it's some Americans' dream. Not everyone wants to be or should be a homeowner, but for many people it's the right and smart thing to do. In this section, we'll look at the pluses and minuses of buying and renting.

Which Is Best for You

The decision to buy or rent your home is complex and complicated. It is complex because where we live is an emotional topic and sometimes emotions confuse decision-making. It is complicated because both buying and renting have advantages and disadvantages. Deciding which is best for you may take some thought and research.

For some people, the decision is simple—they feel strongly one way or the other and wouldn't feel comfortable in any other arrangement. Most people, however, need to look at the advantages and disadvantages of buying and renting to decide what's right for them. What is right at this moment in your life may look different in a few years, when it will be time to reevaluate your position.

Advantages of Buying

The advantages of buying a home are both financial and emotional. For many people, it is something they dream of, a place to call their own. A home gives you and your family a sense of identification with the community. On the other hand, there's the maintenance, taxes, and other expenses that go with a house that apartment-dwellers don't have to bear.

Buying a home can be a great financial and emotional investment. Here are some of the benefits of home ownership:

> ▶ **Tax benefits:** Homeowners enjoy substantial tax benefits, such as being able to deduct the interest they pay on their mortgage and their property taxes. For many taxpayers this deduction makes itemizing practical, which

opens the door for deducting other items from your taxes that were not available if you took the standard deduction.

◁ *SEE ALSO 8.4, "Tax Savings Strategies"* ▷

▶ **Build equity:** In most markets, residential real estate appreciates— sometimes rapidly. Between your down payment, your mortgage payments, and the appreciation, you are building equity in your house. Equity is the difference (in your favor) between what you owe and what the house is worth on the open market. When you sell your house, you receive that equity, less any fees. You can also tap that equity in home equity loans.

◁ *SEE ALSO 4.4, "Personal Loans"* ▷

▶ **Remodel freely:** When you own your home, you can remodel, repaint, or redecorate however you choose without getting anyone's permission— although if you do remodel, building permits and zoning may be involved.

▶ **Put down roots:** If you plan to stay for a long time, owning your own home is a satisfying way to connect with your community.

Disadvantages of Owning a Home

Owning a home comes with much responsibility and considerable financial obligation. You should be sure you're ready for the commitment before you join the ranks of homeowners.

▶ **Money's tight:** Buying a home is a significant financial commitment— there's a down payment, closing costs, and other fees just to buy; followed by monthly payments on the mortgage, insurance, taxes, and so on. If you'll be stretched to make all of this work, this may not be the right time to buy.

▶ **Limited mobility:** If there's a chance you'll be leaving the area in three years or less, buying may not be a good idea. Here's why: at closing, you'll pay several thousand dollars in costs for a variety of fees. If you leave too soon after you buy the house, the market may not have gone up enough for you to recover these costs. In some markets, prices rise very fast, but these markets can cool just as quickly, so don't count on rapid appreciation.

▶ **Not feeling at home:** Maybe you're in a community because of a job transfer, but don't really like the area. If you're not emotionally connected to an area, it doesn't make sense to commit to it financially the way buying a home requires.

▶ **The market is up:** When interest rates and/or prices are high, it's usually better to rent. Rentals are a better deal, because you are not locking yourself into a long-term arrangement in an environment of high rates and/or prices.

▶ **Selling can take time:** It can take months or even years to sell your home, depending on what the residential real estate market is like in your community. This can be a real burden and may force you to sell at a price much lower than you wanted.

Advantages of Renting

Renting makes sense for people who have plans to move soon, or want to keep their options open. At the same time, every rent check you write invests nothing in your financial future.

Young people and older people, in particular, may be the best candidates for renting, although for different reasons.

▶ **No long-term commitment:** Your commitment is one-year at most for most rentals. Even then, if you are transferred out of the area, many property owners will let you out of your lease. For young people who may be changing jobs or moving around within a large company, renting makes more sense than being tied down to a house.

▶ **No bills:** Once you pay your rent and utilities, most of the other bills are the property owner's problem. There is no lawn maintenance, snow removal, exterior painting, and so on for you to worry about.

▶ **Cheaper:** Renting is usually cheaper than owning a home, especially for young couples with no children or singles. This advantage also works for retired folks, who may not want the headaches of a home to maintain. Their retirement income may be low enough that the tax advantages of home ownership would be negligible.

Disadvantages of Renting

Renters are at the mercy of the property owner, to some extent, in terms of raising rent or setting other conditions.

▶ **Rent payments go nowhere:** Your rent payments do you no future good. They are not deductible from your taxes and build no equity.

▶ **No control:** You have no control over the environment in the complex or building. If the owner lets maintenance slip, the property may begin to look shabby. Neighbors live all around you and you have no control over who they are or how loud they play their television.

▶ **No attachment:** Many people find it hard to become attached to an apartment that they can't paint the way they want or remodel.

5.2 PROPERTY TYPES

Single-Family Homes

Duplexes

Co-ops

Condominiums and Townhomes

Timeshares

Homes come in a variety of types and ownership configurations. A type will appeal to urban, suburban, or rural residents. In this section, we'll look at these types.

5.2

Single-Family Homes

A single-family home is just what it says it is—a home for one family. It is usually built on its own lot with some distance between neighbors on either side and the back. Developments in high-density areas may have zero-lot-line homes, where all the houses are built on one side of the property line. This gives more lawn space for each homeowner.

There is a distinction for single-family homes because zoning laws restrict developments in certain areas, so apartments or other multiunit housing can't be built there.

Duplexes

A duplex is a two-family home, where each family has its own living quarters. The duplex may be a ranch with the two units side-by-side, sometimes with garages separating the two living areas. Other duplexes are "stacked" one over the other.

You can also find a triplex and a four-plex, which move into the area of a small apartment unit. Duplexes are often approved for single-family developments, because they are not high-density developments.

Most duplexes are rental units, but it isn't unusual to find the owner in one unit, renting out the second.

Co-ops

Co-ops or cooperatives are a form of ownership where the residents own a corporation that owns the property. Residents or owners of the corporations get the right to live in an apartment called a proprietary lease. Because you become an owner in the cooperative corporation, the co-op board must approve you.

Co-ops are generally found in large cities, particularly on the East Coast; however, you may come across one almost anywhere. If you are interested in buying into one, you should make sure the corporation is financially sound and able to cover all of the building's outstanding bills and future maintenance needs. Look over any covenants or restrictions on the use of the property or common areas.

One big area of concern is the resale procedure. Will the co-op board be helpful in expediting applications for potential buyers?

Another area of concern is financing the co-op purchase. Conventional financing may not work, because you're not buying a house, you're buying shares in the co-op corporation. As such, your tax deductions look different from traditional homeowners. Consult a tax professional for advice on what options are available to you.

Condominiums and Townhouses

Condominiums or condos describe a form of ownership in which you own an individual living unit and other areas are held in common ownership by the residents. The common areas could include parking lots, lobby, recreational areas, and so on. The condo board makes rules governing the use of the common area and manages the money collected from residents to pay for the maintenance of those areas.

Residents own the interior walls of their unit and are responsible for all the maintenance and repairs. The exact ownership arrangements (where your responsibility begins) are defined in the condominium agreement.

Condominium owners get to deduct interest expense and property taxes. However, they also pay a portion of the fees necessary to maintain the common area. If there is a fire, other major damage, or a big repair required, condo owners will be hit with a special assessment to pay for the expense.

How these assessments are handled and other important details are found in the bylaws and deed restrictions. You should study these carefully before you buy a condo, because they are binding and could make life unpleasant if you suddenly find after you move that no pets are allowed, for example.

A townhouse is somewhat like a condominium in that it is attached to another townhouse, but there are no condominium fees or associations. The owner holds complete title to the property under (and over, usually) the home.

Timeshares

Timeshares are a way to own time at a vacation property. Judging the financial benefits of timeshares is difficult, but they are generally not sound investments. There are high fees associated with maintaining them, and it may be difficult to get an accurate read of what to expect. While some timeshares may work for your vacation needs, they are probably not good investments overall.

Some timeshares tout your ability to "trade" time with other timeshare owners so you can vacation in different places. Although this may or may not work out, it is best to approach with caution, because you may have an unpleasant surprise when it comes time for a visit.

It is easier to buy a timeshare than it is to sell one. The market is usually full of timeshares for sale, and it should be a caution if there are many for sale in an area you are interested in.

5.2

5.3 BUYING A HOME

Location

Affordability

Second Homes

Real Estate Agents

Buying a home, whether it's a primary residence or a second home, is a process of gathering information and then acting on your conclusions. This section will help you understand the information you need and who can help you with the research and decision-making.

Location

Where you want to live is a personal decision, but where you buy a house is also a financial decision. Not only will the neighborhood determine in part the price of the house, it will play a role when it comes time to sell.

Your lifestyle will push you towards certain neighborhoods: close to schools, near shopping, retirement communities, and so on. Is your family growing or shrinking? Here are factors to consider when picking a location to buy a house:

▶ How long do you plan to live in the house? The average is around seven years. What will the resale value be then? If you know you are going to stay longer, will the house accommodate your needs for that long? Is it big enough for more children? Will it be *too* big when they leave home?

▶ If you have children or plan to have a family, are the schools suitable?

▶ What is the property tax situation? In some communities, living across a tax boundary (school district, incorporated area, and so on) can mean a big difference in your taxes.

▶ Think resale. Whether you buy the house planning to live there forever or knowing you will be moving in a few years, think about a house's potential resale value when you look at locations. Is the area growing, declining, or stable? What might it look like in 5 or 10 years?

A house is your biggest financial investment, as well as a place to call home. It is worth the investment to gather some information about the area you are considering. The local chamber of commerce will have "newcomer" packets, which usually contain directories and other sources of information. If you are unfamiliar with the community, subscribe to the local newspaper or visit its website to get a feel for what's important in the area.

Affordability

The first question you need to answer before you go house hunting is, how much can you afford? When you have a good sense of what your budget will bear and what you will qualify for in a mortgage, you can narrow your house hunting to realistic possibilities.

This is one part of qualifying for a loan (the other parts are income verification and credit rating) that you can do yourself, because the process is mathematical and lenders follow the same guidelines to determine lender debt-to-income ratios. These ratios differ from the consumer debt-to-income ratios because they look at long-term debt and housing expense.

◀ *SEE ALSO 1.3, "Personal Finance Plan"* ▶

The two numbers used by conventional lenders for debt-to-income ratios are 28 and 36. FHA loans use 29 and 41 for their ratios. The first number, 28, is the front-end ratio and is the percentage of your income that you can spend on housing. This is figured by calculating 28 percent of your gross monthly income. That number is how much you can spend on housing for the mortgage, taxes, and insurance each month.

The second number, 36, is the back-end ratio, which lenders look at for your total debt ratio as a percentage of your gross monthly income. This calculation looks at all your debt plus the expense of your housing. Take 36 percent of this number and that is your maximum total debt expense.

Calculating the cost of the loan payment is easy. A number of online mortgage calculators will do that for you. Bankrate.com has one that will figure your monthly payment on different loan types. However, you also need to include taxes and homeowners insurance. Taxes vary widely by city and state. If you are working with a real estate agent, ask them for an estimate. If you are just exploring an area, call the county tax office and ask for their help in estimating taxes on the price home you are considering.

The lender will require you to carry adequate homeowners insurance. Policies differ in cost and coverage, but you can estimate $35 per month per $100,000 of value.

A final cost is private mortgage insurance (**PMI**). If you do not put down at least 20 percent of the purchase price, the lender will require you to pay for PMI, which compensates the lender in case you **default,** or stop making payment on the note. If you can't make up missed payments, the lender may start **foreclosure** proceedings, the legal steps to repossessing your house. PMI can cost between one-half and one percent of the mortgage amount and it is built into your monthly payment. On a $200,000 loan, PMI could add up to $167 per month.

WORDS TO GO . . .WORDS TO GO . . .WORDS TO GO

PMI, private mortgage insurance, is required by lenders when the buyer does not put down at least 20 percent down payment. The insurance protects the lender against default. When the homeowner's equity passes 20 percent, the policy can be canceled; however, the lender may need to be prompted.

Default, in the context of a loan, means the person owing the money fails to make payments. A mortgage loan in default may lead to foreclosure if the responsible person does not make back payments.

Foreclosure is the legal process of seizing your house for not paying your mortgage or your taxes. The property is sold and the proceeds go to paying off the note or taxes.

These ratios are just one part of the picture that lenders look at when deciding what you can afford to pay. If you have a large down payment, that will weigh heavily in your favor. However, if you know these ratios and costs, you will save yourself time wasted looking at homes that are clearly out of your range.

Second Homes

Second homes for most families mean vacation homes. All of the same financial considerations exist for buying a second home as for buying your primary residence. The lender will look at the same debt-to-income ratios and include the second home's mortgage payment. But you do need to consider other factors when buying a vacation home:

▶ **Maintenance:** How often will you use it and how will it be maintained during your absence?

▶ **Taxes:** What are the tax implications? Check with your tax professional for questions about what can and can't be deducted. This will be different if you rent the place out while you're not using it.

▶ **Income:** Are you counting on rental income to help pay the mortgage? What is the rental history in the area? Who will rent the property, clean it, and so on? You may need commercial insurance if renters are going to use the property.

Vacation homes can take many physical forms. Each presents its own set of considerations. Owning property that you do not live in can be challenging.

Real Estate Agents

Unless you are an attorney familiar with real estate law, you're probably better off using a real estate agent to help you buy a home. A real estate agent can expedite the process of finding homes in your price range by tapping into their database. The Internet has opened vast amounts of information to consumers, but when it comes to setting up appointments to see houses, getting questions answered, and following up on leads, real estate agents are invaluable.

When you're ready to make an offer, the agent can do the paperwork and make sure the legal steps are followed. As you go through the process, there will be more paperwork, inspections, counter-offers, and other matters. Your real estate agent deals with the seller's agent to make all of this happen in a timely manner and according to the real estate laws of your state. They will prepare you for closing, where all the paperwork is signed and checks are written.

You may think that the real estate agent who helps you find the house and guides you through the process is working for you. Be aware that is not exactly correct in some states. You may notice that your agent never says anything negative about houses you look at nor will comment on whether the price is high or low. In some states, the real estate agent technically is representing the seller when they show you a house.

In most cases, this is not a problem, but if you are concerned about the exact role of your real estate agent, ask them what they can and can't do. If you want the agent to absolutely represent you, ask if the agent will sign a "buyer's agent" agreement. This is a contract between you and the agent that says they are working for you exclusively. The agent will disclose this to other agents representing sellers. It also means any house you look at for the term of the contract must be through this agent. Most agreements don't require any changes in compensation, but ask before you sign.

5.4 FINANCING AND REFINANCING

Qualifying for a Loan

Fixed Rate

Adjustable Rate

FHA and VA

Hybrids

The Closing

When Refinancing Makes Sense

To Pay Off Debts

Buying a house is the largest financial commitment most people make. Qualifying for a mortgage and choosing the right type of loan require careful thought and preparation. In this section, we'll look at how that process works and when it makes sense to refinance.

Qualifying for a Loan

Lenders consider a number of factors in deciding who gets a mortgage loan. If you show real strength in one area, it may counter a slight weakness in another. Here are the areas they consider:

▶ **Debt-to-income ratios:** The front-end ratio is 28, while the back-end is 36.

◀ SEE ALSO 1.3 *"Personal Finance Plan"* ▶

▶ **Employment history:** Lenders like a stable employment history. Three years or more at your current employer is best. Self-employed people are not excluded from getting loans, but will need more documentation to prove income.

▶ **Stable address:** Have you lived at your current address for three years or more? What about your previous addresses? Lenders want to see people who are stable and not moving every six months.

▶ **Credit score:** Your credit score is very important—the higher the better—for the lender to approve your loan and interest rate. Scores that are not near the top may still be approved, but the loan will be at a higher interest rate. Mortgages are available for people with credit problems, but they are very expensive.

◀ SEE ALSO 4.5, *"Credit Rating"* ▶

▶ **Character:** Your record will be checked for criminal or civil convictions or outstanding warrants.

It's a good idea to get preapproved before you make an offer on a house. This may cost an application fee, but it tells you if you are going to qualify for the loan. The lender will check everything and issue a letter saying you are qualified for a loan up to a certain amount for a period of 30 to 60 days. This is a good bargaining tool with the seller but, more importantly, you know there's a 95 percent chance the loan will go through.

Fixed Rate

The 30-year, fixed-rate loan was the industry standard for many years; however, when interest rates began to fluctuate in the 1970s, lenders began developing alternatives such as the adjustable rate mortgage.

5.4

The fixed-rate mortgage is still the loan of choice when rates are relatively low for most homebuyers because it locks in a loan payment that they can count on for the life of the loan. This stability makes planning and budgeting easier. Taxes and insurance costs may change, but the principal and interest payment remains constant for the life of the loan.

The downside is that when interest rates are high, why lock in that expense? In addition, it is harder to qualify for fixed rate mortgages because of higher payments compared to adjustable rate mortgages.

Variations

Some variations of the 30-year fixed mortgage shorten the time it takes to pay off the note and reduces the total interest you pay. The most common variation is the 15-year fixed mortgage, which is paid off in 15 years. The savings on interest charges is dramatic, but monthly payments are quite high. If you want to build equity quickly and pay off your mortgage (a popular option for people who want to retire without a mortgage payment), the 15-year note may be your answer.

For example, a $200,000 mortgage at 6 percent compares this way:

	15-year	30-year
Interest rate	6%	6%
Payment	$1,687	$1,199
Interest paid	$103,788	$231,676
Total paid	$303,788	$431,676
Difference:	$127,888	

Another variation on the 30-year note is to set up your payments on a biweekly schedule. This means make a half payment every two weeks, which results in paying an extra month each year. With a biweekly mortgage, you will pay off the note in 24 years instead of 30. Some lenders charge a fee for this service, which may reduce its benefit.

Points

Most lenders require you to pay **points** and closing cost when you get a fixed-rate mortgage. You may be offered two notes, one with a higher rate and no points or another with a lower rate and points you pay at closing.

> **WORDS TO GO . . .WORDS TO GO . . .WORDS TO GO**
>
> **Points** are equal to one percent of the loan amount and are charged by the lender at closing to reduce the interest rate.

It may seem that buying down the interest rate is always the best choice—after all, that lowers your monthly expense for the life of the loan. However, that may not be the case if you don't plan to live in the house very long. You should calculate how much the points will save each month in your loan payment and divide that into what you would pay in points. That gives you how many months it will take to recoup the cost of paying the points in lower monthly expenses. If that number of months is longer than you plan to be in the house, or even close, you're better off not paying the points and saving the money.

Adjustable Rate

Adjustable rate mortgages (ARM) were the industry's answer to high interest rates that kept a large number of buyers out of the market because they could not qualify for a fixed rate mortgage or did not want to lock in a high interest rate. An adjustable rate mortgage begins at one interest rate that is usually lower than fixed rate loans and then adjusts the rate at a predetermined point in the future.

You can find ARMs that set the adjustment point at almost any interval from one to seven years. At the adjustment point, the loan's interest rate is adjusted up or down based on a formula that is stated in the loan document. The interest rate is tied to some recognized index such as the prime rate or the interest rate of U.S. Treasury securities. The lender uses the index to determine the change in rates, but the index itself is not the sole factor. The lender adds a margin to the rate to arrive at the mortgage's interest.

ARMs change on the anniversary of the note and at the interval of the loan—that is, a three-year ARM will adjust at the end of three years and may adjust every year after that if the loan is structured that way. It is important that you understand how often your loan will be adjusted past the initial adjustment.

Most lenders put a cap on the increases and decreases to which your ARM is subject during the life of the loan. There are two types of caps: the rate cap and the payment cap. The rate cap is the best, although it may not initially sound that way. The rate cap puts a limit on how high your loan's interest can eventually go. For most ARMs, this is usually quite high and somewhat disturbing.

Here's an example of how a rate cap works. The rate cap limits how much the interest rate can go up during an adjustment period and how much the interest rate can rise over the life of the loan. An ARM may limit the adjustment period increase to 2 percent and limit the lifetime increase to 6 percent. Both of those are large increases when you're talking about a mortgage.

5.4

The payment cap limits how much your payment can rise during an adjustment period. This may sound like a better arrangement, because actual payment amounts are capped; however, it can be a real problem when interest rates are rising. Here's why: if the loan adjustment calls for a higher payment than the cap, you may not pay enough each month to cover the entire interest portion or any of the equity. If this is the case, that interest is accumulating and you continue to pay more interest on it. Instead of building equity, you're going the other direction and losing money because your loan balance is increasing instead of decreasing. This is **negative amortization,** and all you can do is make extra payments—which defeats the purpose of a payment cap—or refinance.

WORDS TO GO . . . WORDS TO GO . . . WORDS TO GO

Negative amortization is a loan situation where your payment does not cover all of the interest or any of the equity. You make payments, but the balance of the loan keeps going up because you pay interest on the interest you did not cover in your payment.

ARMs may make sense if:

▶ You don't plan to own the house for very long and want to keep the cost of ownership low.

▶ You are confident your income will grow in the near future and you will be able to handle increases in monthly payments.

▶ If current rates are high and you can't qualify for a fixed rate loan.

ARMs may not make sense if:

▶ There is not much difference between the rates for fixed-rate loans.

▶ You plan to stay in the house for a long time and fixed-rate loan rates are reasonable.

▶ You are very risk-averse and want the comfort of a locked-in rate.

FHA and VA

The government has two main programs to help people afford a home. The Federal Housing Authority (FHA) and the Veterans' Administration (VA) insure loans, mainly to first-time buyers, but others qualify also.

FHA

The FHA targets first-time homebuyers who may have trouble coming up with a large down payment. FHA loans may require only 3 to 5 percent down and you can finance some of the closing costs. A lower down payment may mean a higher interest rate.

FHA loans are assumable, which means if someone wants to buy your house and they qualify, they can assume your loan. Even though the buyer still must qualify, this may be a nice selling point.

FHA loans require a mortgage insurance premium (MIP) up front and the fee can run as much as 2.25 percent of the loan, plus a monthly premium. This insurance protects the lender the same as PMI for conventional loans. You can finance this amount if you want, but it will raise your monthly payment.

Veterans' Administration

The VA offers a loan program to any veteran who has served 180 days of active duty since September 16, 1940, or 90 days in any war. If you enlisted after September 7, 1980, you must have two years of service.

VA loans are attractive because they can be obtained with no money down and are assumable. One of the other benefits of VA loans is they never require PMI. Check with a banker familiar with VA loans for their requirements. VA loans go up to $240,000.

Flex 97

The Flex 97 mortgage is a conventional fixed-rate loan for first-time homebuyers. It requires a minimum of only three percent down and is very liberal about where you get the money. Fannie Mae sponsors the program and generally requires a good credit score to qualify.

Hybrids

Fixed-rate loans and adjustable-rate loans are not the only choices. Hybrid loan products that combine features of both may suit some situations, depending on your plans for the house and your current situation.

5/25 and 7/23 Mortgages

The industry has created products that act like one type of mortgage for a while, then change. The products are usually called either a 5/25 or a 7/23 mortgage. They can be convertible or nonconvertible.

Here's how they work. The interest rate during the initial period of the loan is fixed for either five or seven years. At the end of the initial period, your rate adjusts. If you have a convertible loan, the rate is adjusted just once and the loan becomes a fixed rate loan for the balance of the years. If you have a nonconvertible loan, it becomes a traditional ARM at the end of the initial period.

If you do not plan to live in the home beyond the initial five- or seven-year period, these loans offer a better interest rate than a 30-year fixed product. They are not as inexpensive as ARMs, but they don't carry the interest rate risk, either.

Be mindful of what happens at the end of the initial period to see if, five or seven years from now, you can live with the possible change. If you have a nonconvertible loan, at the end of the initial period it will become a traditional ARM, so check out the terms and conditions of what that loan looks like, just as you would in the previous section.

Balloon Loan

A balloon loan starts with an initially low interest rate for a defined period—say five years—then the balance of the note is due in one payment. The idea is to enjoy a lower interest rate in the initial period and sell or refinance before the balloon is due.

Interest-Only

Interest-only loans require you to pay the interest on the monthly payment for the first three to five years of the note. After the initial period, the loan payment converts to a regular principal-and-interest payment. The advantage of this loan is that it lowers your monthly payments in the beginning, which may help you qualify for the loan.

During this period, you are not building any equity through your payment, although in the initial years of a mortgage most of the payment is going to interest expense anyway.

The Closing

The closing is when the actual transaction occurs—papers are signed, money changes hands, and loans are funded. Depending on the state you live in, the closing may take place at the real estate agent's office, the title company, the bank, the courthouse, an attorney's office, or some other customary location in your community.

Prior to closing, someone—your banker, real estate agent, or title company—will give you a final closing statement that details all the costs you have agreed to and the other administrative expenses involved.

In many cases, you will be asked to bring a certified check for that amount to the closing. Often the check will be made out to the title company or **escrow agent,** which will disperse the funds to the buyer and pay all the other legal and administrative fees. If the closing occurs somewhere other than the bank, the title company agent will notify the bank that all is in order and the bank will release the funds to pay off the note on the house (if there is one) and the balance less fees and commissions will go to the seller.

WORDS TO GO . . .WORDS TO GO . . .WORDS TO GO

An **escrow agent** serves as a disinterested third party to the real estate transaction and its role is to hold funds (often down payments) until all matters in the real estate transaction have been resolved. When the seller is satisfied, the buyer is satisfied and the lender is satisfied that everything is in order, the escrow agent will disperse funds to the appropriate parties (usually the seller).

Here are the major fees and charges you (the buyer) will normally pay:

▶ **Points:** You may have to pay points with your loan. A point is equal to one percent of the loan amount. Points are considered prepaid interest and usually deductible in the year they are paid.

▶ **Loan fee:** Your lender may charge you an origination fee, which may be one percent of the loan amount. This expense is not tax deductible.

▶ **Credit report:** You must pay to have your credit checked. Sometimes you pay this fee at the time you apply for the loan.

▶ **Appraisal fee:** The lender will require an independent appraisal of the property. This fee may be paid before closing or at closing.

▶ **Mortgage insurance:** If you don't put down 20 percent or more, you'll have to pay PMI.

▶ **Prepaid interest:** Depending on when you close, you may have to pay interest for the month you move in.

▶ **Homeowners insurance:** You will be required to prepay one year's worth of homeowners' insurance acceptable to the lender and have proof prior to closing.

▶ **Title insurance:** The lender will want a clean title (to prove the seller was the rightful owner) and title insurance. You will have to pay for this service.

▶ **Recording and transfer fees:** Various governmental districts require title filings and deed transfers that must be paid.

▶ **Survey:** The lender will require a survey, especially if there is acreage involved, to determine the property boundaries.

▶ **Condo, homeowner association fees, and so on:** If there are fees associated with the property, you may have to pay a prorated share for the remainder of the year.

▶ **Taxes:** The owner may have paid property taxes for the year or part of the year. You may have to pay a prorated share to cover the time you will occupy the property.

Depending on the property and circumstances, there may be other fees. The company that organizes the closing will probably have some administrative cost to split between the buyer and seller.

The actual closing itself is a process of going over all the paperwork and signing all the legal documents. You should have received copies of most of the major documents prior to closing so you would have time to review them. Ask questions if you don't understand something.

The seller may or may not be present. Sometimes they are in a different room and documents are shuffled back and forth. It is possible to do a closing by mail with the seller in another town if they've already moved.

The important concern is understanding in advance how much money will be required at closing. When you qualified for the loan, the banker should have given you an estimate of closing costs. If what you're being asked for now is much higher, go to your banker and ask why.

When Refinancing Makes Sense

When interest rates start dropping off prolonged high rates, it is common to see people rush to refinance their mortgages. As interest rates dropped in the first years of this decade, an unprecedented number of mortgages were refinanced. Continued low interest rates through 2005 drove a huge growth in the real estate market.

If you have a mortgage with a high interest rate or an ARM that is about to adjust, and interest rates seem very low to you, it may be time to consider refinancing. Lowering your loan's interest rate can reduce your monthly payment significantly, but refinancing is not free, so you have to weigh the cost with the benefits.

The old rule was interest rates must be two percent better for refinancing to make sense. However, competition drove down the cost of refinancing so that now even a one percent difference makes the deal worth considering. Although costs have come down, you still must weigh the benefits against the expense.

Part of that decision is how long you plan to stay in the house. If you think you might leave in a few years, refinancing may not pay for itself. Here's why: if you could lower your monthly payment by $45 dollars by refinancing and it cost $2,500 to complete the process, it will take four-and-a-half years to recoup the $2,500 cost. If you are going to stay in the house for another 15 years, then this is an easy decision. However, if you are only going to be in the house another seven years (the average stay), does it make sense to go to the expense when you could invest the $2,500 for seven years?

There are other considerations, of course. If the refinancing gets you out of a bad ARM or you use the money to pay for college costs, then you have to consider those factors also.

To Pay Off Debts

Some 26 percent of the people who refinance their homes do so to pay off debts. Taking equity out of your home to pay off debts is risky. Although you are potentially getting rid of high interest consumer debt and replacing it with lower interest mortgage debt, you are placing your house at risk if you can't keep up with the payments.

If you have money-handling problems, they may return and burden you with high consumer debt *and* a big house payment.

5.5 BUILDING A HOME

Construction Loans

Find a Builder

Building a home is a creative and complex process. There are a thousand details and decisions. In this section, we'll discuss two of the biggest decisions: your loan and your builder.

Construction Loans

Building a home involves financing in two stages: the construction stage and the permanent stage. In most cases, you'll need excellent credit and substantial equity to build a custom home. If you decide to build in a planned development, you may have more options.

Custom Homes

Financing the building of a custom home involves working with a banker with experience in this area. There will be a lot of interaction between you, your architect, the banker, and the builder. You probably want to have your attorney involved in reviewing documents as you go.

How the loan is structured will vary somewhat from bank to bank, but the basics are a two-part process. There will be an agreement of the ultimate value of the home, based on the architect's drawings and finish schedule. The builder's construction bid will detail supply needs by date.

The bank will fashion a construction loan that pays the builder on an agreed-upon schedule for work completed. As the house and lot are finished and inspected for completion according to plans and specifications, the builder is paid off. The building process could take eight months or more depending on a number of factors.

By an agreed-upon schedule, the house is refinanced under a conventional mortgage. While this is a complicated financial arrangement, if you have a banker who is used to working with custom homes, it will go much smoother.

Planned Development

Building in a planned development may be easier than building a custom home. You often have a small number of builders (or just one) to choose from and there are a limited number of floor plans. Your options include the interior finish and perhaps some exterior options as well (patios, and so on).

Financing in a planned development can be easier because the developer may have secured financing in advance for the construction. You may only need a large down payment to begin your house, which will go towards conventional financing once the house is complete. Depending on the market, you may find building in a planned development not much more expensive than buying an existing house.

Find a Builder

If you do want to build a house, finding the right builder is a process of checking references and looking at previous work. If you are moving into a subdivision, look at other subdivisions the builder has done (if any). How do they look after five or ten years? Ask around to see if a name keeps coming up that is highly recommended.

If you are new to an area and want to build, you might do yourself a favor by renting for six months or so and taking the time to do some research.

When comparing developers, always check what's included and what's extra to get a good comparison. If you are not interested in some of the features a builder includes in the price, maybe a different developer will let you pick the features you do want for close to the same price.

5.6 SELLING YOUR HOUSE

On Your Own

With an Agent

Preselling/Selling Things To Do

Sales Agreement and Other Forms

Closing

Selling your house is usually the other side of buying a new one; one doesn't happen without the other. This section looks at what needs to happen for the sale to go through.

On Your Own

Thanks to the Internet and access to tools that provide homeowners with more information, many are offering their homes for sale themselves. There are some advantages to selling your house, one is the savings on commissions and more control over the process. The disadvantage is that it is a lot of work.

Here are the steps you must perform if you want to sell the house yourself:

▶ **Set the price:** This may not be as easy as it seems. What you think your house is worth and what it will sell for may be two very different prices. One way to do this is to have an appraisal done. If you don't get the price right, you may give your house away or not sell it for a very long time.

▶ **Put it up for sale:** How will you market your house? A sign in the yard may work, but unless you are lucky and have a long time to wait, that's not the best way. You can advertise a variety of ways including listing the house on the Multiple Listing Service. You have to pay a substantial fee and a commission to any real estate agent (2–3 percent) who brings you a buyer.

▶ **Screen potential buyers:** How do you know which lookers are serious and which are just wasting your time?

▶ **Negotiating:** You must handle offers and counter-offers directly. You should have an attorney review any offers or other legal documents.

▶ **Do it legally:** Just because you are not a licensed real estate agent doesn't get you off the hook on real estate law. You are responsible for knowing the law when it comes to offers, discrimination, property condition statements, and so on. You should have an attorney knowledgeable in real estate law to back you up.

With an Agent

If you decide to use an agent to sell your house, you will sign a listing agreement, which gives them the right to market your house. With that right comes the obligation to represent you as the seller and to do their best to sell your home for the highest possible price given current market conditions.

For this work, you will pay a commission of 6 or 7 percent at closing. The commission may be split with another agent if that agent introduces the buyer.

You should expect the agent to:

- ▶ **Suggest a listing price:** The agent will use their information and judgment to set a sales price that is reflective of your desire. If you want to get out of the house in a hurry or get the most money possible, the agent will suggest a price accordingly.

- ▶ **Market the home:** The agent will list your home in the MLS and offer to show it to other agents so they will be familiar with the property. Your agent may also do an open house, produce flyers, run ads in the local newspaper, or take whatever steps necessary to get your home in front of buyers.

- ▶ **Suggest repairs or fix-ups:** The agent will also suggest repairs or items around the house that can be fixed, painted, or repaired that will improve the marketability of the property.

- ▶ **Screen buyers:** The agent can screen potential buyers and eliminate people who are not qualified or not good fits for your house. They can also show your house when you aren't home.

- ▶ **Do the leg work:** The agent can handle the paperwork of offers and counter-offers. They can follow up on leads and, if a closing is near, make sure all the details of inspections and other procedures are done on time.

Preselling/Selling Things to Do

Before you put your house on the market, there are items to clean, fix, repair, or remodel that will increase the value of your home and ease the task of selling it. Some items require just cleaning up and picking up, while others may need some professional help and an investment of money.

Improvements That Pay for Themselves

Your real estate agent is a good source of information on what will add more value to the price of your home than it will cost. Be careful that you don't add too many expensive improvements just before putting the house on the market, because it may be difficult to sell. If your kitchen is dated and shabby, ask your real estate agent if it is worth remodeling. Kitchen updates along with updating bathrooms are usually big improvements, and often return more in a sales price than they cost. When remodeling for resale, remember to leave your personal decorating style out of the process and stick to simple, clean, neutral colors and finishes.

Avoid adding things like patios, decks, sunrooms, and so on. They will probably not add enough value to recover the cost. Work with your real estate agent to make sure you don't raise the value of your house out of the neighborhood's price range. You don't want to have the most expensive house in the neighborhood— or the least expensive.

Repairs and Replacements

Fix any walls that need patching or ceilings that are cracked. Make sure all doors and windows work and the glass isn't broken or cracked. Fix any plumbing leaks and replace damaged tiles. Have the heating and cooling systems inspected and make any needed repairs (save the paperwork to show the buyer). Make sure all your appliances work. Ask your agent about replacing some or all dated appliances or making an allowance in any offer.

Replace any worn carpet and have the rest professionally cleaned. If you have a pet, see if you can house them elsewhere after the carpets are cleaned—some people are sensitive to pet dander or object to pet odors. Have wood floors refinished if necessary and replace any damaged vinyl tiles.

Where necessary, repaint the walls in a neutral color—white or an off white.

Clean Up and Pick Up

Once your repairs and replacements are complete, do a thorough cleaning of the house, including the woodwork and windows. Consider hiring a professional service if you don't want to do this yourself.

Pick up the house and store all of the personal "stuff" that we all accumulate. An uncluttered house looks bigger and is easier for potential buyers to envision as their own. Clear all surfaces of personal objects and put them in storage, not the closet (where buyers will look).

Your goal is to make the house as neutral as possible so potential buyers can see their stuff in the house. Your real estate agent can help you "undecorate" those areas that may be distracting to potential buyers.

Exterior or Curb Appeal

You can improve the curb appeal by trimming the shrubs and keeping the lawn cut. Plant flowers if it is the right time of year. Clean the gutters and paint the front door. Make sure the house makes a good first impression. Research shows that houses with a clean, well-kept appearance from the street sell faster by 15 days on average than houses where the outside either has been neglected or appears bland and uninviting.

Sales Agreement and Other Forms

The sale of a house requires many forms, but two in particular are important. The forms may differ slightly from state to state, but they accomplish the same thing. Your real estate agent will guide you through those particular to your state and local jurisdiction. Two of these forms are very important: the Property Condition Report, which is provided by the seller, and the Sales Agreement, which is the offer to buy the house from the buyer. They may have slightly different names where you live, but they will provide essentially the same information.

The Property Condition Report

Most states require the seller to provide a statement or report that lists any known major defects or problems with the property. This form discloses problems before the sale so the buyer knows what the condition of the property is before committing to the deal. For example, if there is water in the basement after a rain, the seller is required to disclose that information. The seller must disclose more than general information—you must be specific: "When it rains, there are two feet of water in the basement."

You should disclose anything that would or might change the value a reasonable buyer would place on the house. Include all major mechanical systems, electrical, plumbing, the roof, flooring, and walls. You are also required to disclose any problems with environmental hazards such as asbestos, lead, radon, and so on. You may also be required to disclose any known changes in zoning or local ordinances that will materially affect the property.

The purpose of this form is to protect the real estate agent who represents the seller and to protect the buyer from problems. If the buyer discovers that the roof leaks in five places and has been doing so for a long time, they may have the basis for a lawsuit against the seller if that information was known and not disclosed.

Save all the paperwork from recently done repairs and any major appliances that have been replaced. If there is a problem with these after the sale, the new buyer will have documentation to know what work was done and by who.

The Sales Agreement

The sales agreement, also called purchase agreement, is the buyer's offer to purchase the home and it always contains a number of contingencies that give the buyer a way out if something doesn't look right.

Your best bet is to structure your offer so that you are protected as the buyer, but don't put too may contingencies in or the seller will feel you aren't serious about completing the deal. The major contingencies are:

5.6

▶ **Loan details:** Lists how much time you have to secure financing, what type and rate of financing, the maximum interest rate, the amount of the loan, the type of loan, and the down payment.

▶ **Sale of your home**: If your house is for sale and it must sell in order for you to buy the new house, make that one of the contingencies.

▶ **Appraisal and inspections:** Most sales agreements require the house be inspected and appraised. The sales agreement makes these steps contingencies in the event either turns up negative.

▶ **Personal property:** What, if any, personal property is included in the sale (appliances, ceiling fans, and so on)?

The buyer should include anything else in the sales agreement that is normal for your market. Your real estate agent is your best guide in preparing your offer.

The sales agreement is accompanied by a check for a deposit to show your sincerity. In some markets, this is called **earnest money.** The money goes into an **escrow account** where it sits until the offer is accepted or rejected. If the offer moves forward, the earnest money becomes part of the down payment. If the offer is not accepted, the potential buyer gets their money back.

WORDS TO GO . . . WORDS TO GO . . . WORDS TO GO

Earnest money is a check that accompanies your offer to buy a house. It may be known by different names in different markets, but the purpose is to show the seller that you are serious about your offer and willing to tie up your personal funds to demonstrate your interest.

Earnest money is held in an **escrow account** while the seller considers your offer. In some states, the real estate company may have an escrow account for holding the funds, while other markets may use a title company, bank or other financial institution. If the offer to purchase is accepted, the earnest money becomes part of the cash down payment and is conveyed to the seller at closing.

Closing

At closing, the seller turns over the property title and money changes hands in a very structured process that is organized to protect all the parties involved.

The seller will need to complete some steps prior to closing and have other documentation prepared so the transaction goes smoothly. The seller is responsible for organizing the closing, which is usually done at a title company, escrow agent's office, bank, or other location. In many states, the title company serves the role as the escrow agent and coordinates with all interested parties when and where the closing takes place.

The seller will usually have to provide proof of a termite inspection and title search at closing, so these should be done in advance. You will also need to bring any proof of repairs that were required in the sales contract or any other action called for in the list of contingencies. It is likely the escrow agent or title company will want this information in advance of the actual closing so they can verify everything and make copies.

The important documents that will be needed before closing include your current mortgage information, property tax statements, utility bills, and so on. The agent organizing the closing will give you a list of documents needed to complete the closing process. These will be used to figure out prorated costs between the buyer and seller of various expenses. Any problems with the appraisal, inspection, or title search must be cleared up before closing. The seller is responsible for paying some of the fees associated with the transaction. These include:

- ▶ **The real estate agent's commission:** This is what you agreed to pay the agent when you signed the listing agreement.
- ▶ **Title search:** You are responsible for the title search.
- ▶ **Taxes:** You and the buyer split taxes based on how long each of you will own the property during the year.
- ▶ **Administrative fees:** You may be charged some administrative fees by the company organizing the closing.

Depending on the negotiated sales agreement, the seller sometimes picks up some of the costs normally paid by the buyer. This will vary from deal to deal, but you will know about this before closing.

After all the papers are signed by the buyer and seller, the company handling the closing verifies all is in order and notifies the bank which funds the loan.

Depending on the bank and how your loan is paid off, you may get your net proceeds—that is, what's left after paying off your loan and all the fees—that day or soon thereafter.

5.7 RENTING AND LEASING

Getting Approved

Common Terms

Financial/Legal Aspects

For some people, life circumstances are such that renting or leasing a place to live makes more sense than the commitment of ownership. This section looks at some of the important aspects of renting and leasing.

Getting Approved

Residential property for rent or lease varies from apartments to single-family homes. The terms rent and lease may have a different meaning in some markets although the distinction is usually one of length. To rent a property is considered more short-term than a lease. Either way, the property owner, often represented by a management company, must approve the person wishing to occupy the apartment or house.

The general rule is the more upscale the property, the harder the approval process. Add this to that rule: the fewer vacancies, the harder the approval process. Rental property is often abused and property owners want to screen out potential problems if possible. In addition to damage to property, some tenants skip without paying their rent, which means landlords may look at potential renters very carefully.

Most properties require an application and a fee to even consider you for a unit. The application will require several previous addresses to be checked as references. The property manager will also want to check your credit. If you have a problem credit report, you may be turned down.

◀ *SEE ALSO 4.5, "Credit Rating"* ▶

Common Terms

Lease agreements spell out the terms of your occupancy and what is expected of you. The document is written to protect the property owner and, other than what is legally required, will have almost nothing that protects the tenant.

Your lease defines when your occupancy begins and ends. It states the rental rate and if there is any provision to raise the rate during the term of the lease. It also spells out:

▶ If you are responsible for utilities

▶ What pets, if any, are allowed and what the deposit is

▶ How many people can occupy the unit

▶ What the rules are regarding decorating

▶ What the rules are regarding noise, odors, and so on

▶ Where and when to pay the rent and what the late fee is

▶ If the unit has a yard, who is responsible for its upkeep

▶ Rules regarding illegal activities

You get the picture. Leases can go on for pages of very small print. The more upscale the property, the more pages in the lease.

You can try to change some of the wording, but it is almost impossible except in the very upscale units.

Financial/Legal Aspects

Leasing has no tax benefits like those that homeowners enjoy. There are no deductions that make the cost of leasing more affordable. In some markets, leasing is less expensive when you look at lease payments versus mortgage payments for comparable property. However, when you factor in the tax benefit of deducting mortgage interest, it is difficult to make a financial case for leasing except as a short-term solution.

The legal obligations of the person renting or leasing to fulfill the terms are strong. Most of the leases in use have been in use for some time and tested in court. If you need to break a lease, it is best to go to the property manager and negotiate some arrangement. Some leases will let you sublet the unit or you may be able to pay a month penalty or so and get out of the lease without a fight. Note that in some states, if your job takes you more than 50 miles away, you can break your lease without penalty.

6

AUTOMOBILES

6.1 BUYING A CAR

New vs. Used

Where to Find the Actual Price

Negotiating

Buying a car is the second most expensive purchase most people make after a house. Your decision may be clouded by the emotionally driven advertising that obscures the underlying finances. This section examines the process of buying a car.

New vs. Used

Buying a car has two components: the financial part and the emotional part. Some people are able to keep those separate, and they will get the best value for their money. Unlike the other large purchase you will make (your house), autos begin depreciating the minute you drive them off the dealer's lot. Unfortunately, most people need a car for transportation, so they go into a considerable amount of debt for an asset that loses value every day.

There are several strategies to making the most of this awkward situation. The largest spilt is between those who believe it is best to buy a new car and those who opt for a late model used car.

Buying a New Car

The idea that buying a new car is a better financial move comes from two areas—financing and maintenance. New cars are usually easier to finance with dealer and manufacturer incentives; if you pay attention, you can save a significant amount of interest expense over the life of the loan.

The other area of concern is maintenance. New cars come with extended warranties that cover major items such as transmissions, drive trains, and other major components. These warranties may cover 10 years or 100,000 miles.

The average new car price is over $30,000, which means you are possibly financing $20,000 or more depending on your down payment and trade-in. To make financial sense of buying a new car, you should plan to drive it several years past the date you have paid off the loan. This period without a note payment is a good time to save money for a down payment on the replacement car you will have to eventually buy.

◀ *SEE ALSO 4.1, "Debt Management"* ▷

If you "need" a new car every two or three years, you will pay a steep price for the privilege. You might consider leasing, which is still expensive but lets you get into a new vehicle every few years with relative ease.

Buying a Used Car

The argument for buying a used car is that someone else has already paid for the most significant drop in value, which comes in the first year of ownership. You may have heard the cliché that a new car loses 20 percent of its value the minute it is driven off the car lot. That's not far from the truth. Even a one-year-old car is significantly less expensive than a new one. Following the first year's decline or **depreciation,** the perceived loss of value tends to be more gradual.

WORDS TO GO . . . *WORDS TO GO . . . WORDS TO GO*

Depreciation is the loss in value an asset experiences over time. In the case of cars, depreciation is a function of not only mechanical wear, but the fact that each year cars are different in design (some more so than others) rendering last year's model out of fashion and so worth less because it is no longer "new."

Late model used cars often carry some of the original manufacturer's warranty, and you can purchase extended warranties. Because of the way car dealers price used cars, you may not be getting the bargain you think, but using available information resources, which we'll discuss shortly, can improve your chances at getting a reasonable price.

The Best Value

The best value for your automobile dollar is a vehicle you buy at the best price, finance at the best rate, and drive for many years. Thanks to advance manufacturing techniques, you can drive a car, with proper maintenance, for 150,000—200,000 miles before repairs become prohibitively expensive.

Buying new cars is usually not a good financial decision, regardless of what interest rate you get on the loan. You can't make the case for leasing either as a sound financial decision.

If you need a car for business—that is, you are able to deduct some or all of your car expenses on your tax return—you may be financially justified in buying a newer car more frequently. Leasing may also be an option for business use. Driving to work doesn't count as business use. If you are unclear about the tax implications of using your car for business purposes, consult competent tax counsel for clarification. It can be a substantial deduction if justified.

Where to Find the Actual Price

You can improve your chances of getting a decent deal if you know the actual price or value of the car you want to buy. Thanks to the Internet, that information is readily available.

You want the **actual dealer invoice price,** not the sticker on the window, which is more sales material than financial disclosure.

WORDS TO GO . . . *WORDS TO GO . . . WORDS TO GO*

Don't be confused by the commercials you hear on television. Car dealers are not using their **actual dealer invoice price** when they have ads saying "1% over dealer invoice!" Do your homework and find out what their real cost is (or close to it) and you'll get a better price on your new car.

Three websites have this information:

▶ The National Automobile Dealers Association—www.nada.com; an industry trade group site

▶ Kelley Blue Book—www.kbb.com; this site also has used car prices

▶ Edmunds.com—www.edmunds.com; has detailed information on the manufacturers suggested retail price (MSRP) and what people are paying for the car you want in your area

This detailed information will help you set the price you are willing to pay. Without this information, you are stuck with the price the dealer is willing to sell the car to you.

Negotiating

If you do your homework on the price of the car you want to buy, you can negotiate with the dealer from a strong position. You should negotiate, because if you don't, you won't get the best deal.

Always negotiate the sticker price of the car and not what you can afford in monthly payments. Dealers can structure a way to get you into a car that is close to your monthly payment, but that deal will almost certainly not be in your best financial interest. The dealer can extend the term of the loan, put you in a heavily financed lease, or any number of other plans to get you committed to the car.

You want to stay with the sticker price, because you know the number there and can negotiate fairly and from a position of strength. You should note several areas on the sticker:

▶ **Destination and delivery charges:** The dealer may inflate these, but you will have the actual cost from your web investigation. The dealer shouldn't make a profit on these charges.

▶ **Add-ons:** These extra services such as rust proofing are not needed on modern cars and you shouldn't pay for it. Watch out for these types of services, many haven't been performed when you are looking at the car, but will be if you agree to the service as part of the sale.

▶ **ADM:** ADM stands for "additional dealer markup," which is simply more profit for the dealer. Never pay this charge.

Your goal is to pay no more than three to five percent over the dealer's actual invoice price (the price you got off one of the websites). This is what you are negotiating with the dealer for, not the sticker that is on the vehicle. If you want the latest "hot" car and the dealer has a waiting list of potential buyers, don't expect many concessions in negotiating. However, if the model year is ending and the dealer still has an inventory to move, you might get an even better deal.

If you aren't getting anywhere with a dealer who sticks to an inflated price, walk out and find another place to buy a car.

BUYING VS. LEASING

Benefits/Drawbacks of Buying

Benefits/Drawbacks of Leasing

In this section, we'll compare the benefits and drawbacks of buying a car and leasing a car.

Benefits/Drawbacks of Buying

The benefits of buying a vehicle are that, even if you own the car a number of years, it will still have some value when you want to sell it or trade it in for another vehicle. Although cars do not appreciate, they don't lose all of their value unless they don't run anymore or become so old that no one would want them. (If you hold it long enough, it could become a "classic" and begin appreciating—but it will need to be 30 plus years old.)

When you own the car, you can drive as many miles as you want and decorate or paint it to your personal tastes. Many people make a personal statement with their car. However, owning a car has its drawbacks. Unless you can pay cash for it, a car must be financed and that means you owe what could be the second largest debt on your personal financial statement. New cars cost around $30,000 on average, so loans can be pricey. Some extend 60 months or more, which means interest expenses can be steep unless you take advantage of low-interest dealer or manufacturer incentive financing.

Benefits/Drawbacks of Leasing

Leasing a car has few financial benefits unless you can legitimately deduct all or most of the lease cost off your personal or business taxes. For people who must have a new car every few years, leasing is a way to do that, often without a large cash down payment as may be required with purchasing a car.

◀ SEE ALSO 8.4, *"Tax Savings Strategies"* ▶

But leasing is an expensive way to have a car. Your monthly payment builds no equity and only gives you the right to drive the car for a predetermined period. At the end of that two or three years, you either turn in the car or you can buy the car at a residual price that is inflated over the true market value of a similar model. If you want another car, your choices are to lease one or buy a car without a trade-in.

6.3 WHAT TO DO WITH YOUR OLD CAR

Sell

Trade-In

Donate

When you are ready for another car (new or used), you need to dispose of your old one. This section looks at your options.

Sell

Depending on the condition of your car and your patience, you may get more money for it if you sell it yourself rather than trade it in on a newer model. There are several steps in the process:

6.3

- ▶ **Set a price:** Use the web resources mentioned above to determine the car's value. You can then add something to that for your profit.

- ▶ **Clean it up:** Clean and fix up the car so it looks nice. If the finish is in good shape, give it a wax job and thoroughly clean the interior. If you expect to sell the car for several thousand dollars, consider taking it to a detailing service.

- ▶ **Fix it up:** Make any minor repairs that are pending and make notes of anything major that may be coming up.

- ▶ **Market it:** Place an ad in the local newspaper and consider an ad in one of the many auto specialty publications that carry pictures of cars for sale.

- ▶ **Transfer title:** When you make a sale, you will need to transfer the title to the new owner. Someone at the state department of motor vehicles or your county courthouse can explain how this is done in your area.

If you have the time to deal with phone calls and people wanting to see the car and test-drive it, selling your own car probably makes good sense.

Trade-In

For many people, trading in their car when they buy another is the simplest route. Unfortunately, you may not get close to the same value as selling it. Here's why: dealers use the trade-in as part of the equation when figuring what to charge you for the car you want. They can make it sound like you are getting a good deal on the new car, but that may not be the case at all. By manipulating the price of the trade-in, dealers can make the new car seem less expensive, but it could cost you several thousand dollars compared to what your trade-in was actually worth.

If you know the value of your trade-in, you can prevent those types of maneuvers and get a better deal by insisting on a higher value for the trade-in.

Donate

Some people drive their cars to the point of collapse. The vehicles need more work than they are worth and may have stopped running altogether. A number of charities will take your car as a donation, whether it runs or not. This is often a better use of the vehicle than hauling it off to the junkyard.

You can claim the donation on your income taxes if you itemize, but if the value of the vehicle (or any noncash donation) is over $500, you must receive a letter from the charity acknowledging the gift before you can claim the deduction.

6.4

6.4 THE AUTO LOAN

Dealer Financing

Bank Financing

Internet Sources

Third Party Financing

With the rising price of vehicles has come longer and more incentive-driven financing. This section looks at auto loans, the lenders, and the terms.

Dealer Financing

As the price of autos climbed and sales flattened, dealers and manufacturers looked for ways to get people back into the showrooms. Their two-pronged strategy over the last few decades has been low interest financing and leasing.

Low interest financing was combined with cash-back rebates from the manufacturers to make owning a new car seem affordable to almost anyone. The low interest rates, which often went down to 0 percent, were designed to draw people into the dealerships. In many cases, only people with perfect credit qualified for the lowest interest rates, while everyone else was directed into another program at much higher rates.

Even if you got the great interest rate, it was usually for the inflated sticker price on the window, not the price you discovered on one of the websites. If you want a lower sales price, it will be at a higher interest rate.

You may still find a good financing deal at the dealer, but don't assume that the one that is advertised is the best for you. There are many other sources of auto financing—and the dealer knows it.

Bank Financing

Banks, credit unions, and savings and loans all want to give auto loans, making it a very competitive market. If you have decent credit and a stable job history, you can probably qualify for bank financing. This is handy to have when negotiating with the dealer. If you know the value of the car and what you are willing to pay, you can get a commitment from the bank and go to the dealer without needing any help on financing. This puts you in a strong bargaining position.

◀ *SEE ALSO 4.5, "Credit Rating"* ▶

Internet Sources

The Internet can turn up sources of financing for your auto purchase. Several websites have information on auto loans:

▶ **Bankrate.com:** This site can tell you what auto loans are going for in your community so you can get an idea of what the range is in interest rates.

▶ **eLoan.com:** You can apply for a loan and banks that participate offer you their deal.

▶ **Capitalone.com:** This finance and credit card company lets you apply for an auto loan online and you can have a check in a few days.

Third Party Financing

There are personal finance companies that will make auto loans to just about anyone regardless of credit, but the loans come with a high price. Interest rates are very high and payments must be made weekly in many cases. If you fall behind, the finance company will take the car and you will still owe the difference between what they could sell it for and the note, which will be large because of the high interest.

6.5 THE AUTO LEASE

Lease Terms

True Cost of Leasing

The auto lease has become a popular way for people to get into a new vehicle every few years. It is also an expensive way to acquire a car. This section looks at the terms of a typical lease and the true costs of leasing.

Lease Terms

A lease is a contract between you and the leasing company that permits you to drive the vehicle for a specified period. At the end of that period, the lease will detail what options and obligations you have to the leasing company. As with most leases, the contract is mainly about protecting the leasing company and their property. Here are the general terms found in most leases:

▶ **Term of lease:** The term may run from two to four years, although it can be longer.

▶ **Upfront money:** The lease will require you to pay some money up front. This could be the first and last month's rent along with the tax, title, and license fees.

▶ **Number of miles:** You are allowed a total number of miles during the term of the lease. If you go over the allowed total, there is a per-mile charge.

▶ **Insurance coverage:** The leasing company will require you to carry comprehensive insurance coverage on the vehicle, often with zero deductible.

◀ *SEE ALSO 7.2, "Auto Insurance"* ▶

▶ **Residual price:** At the end of the lease, you have the option of buying the auto at a predetermined price called the residual price or value. This is usually inflated over what the car is actually worth on the open market and is a profit center for the dealer.

▶ **Excessive wear:** If you have excessive wear, which would be more wear than would be expected for a car of this age and miles, you will be responsible for repairs.

The lease will also discuss who pays the sales tax charges on the lease payments if that is appropriate in your state and any other tax questions.

If you need to break the lease, the contract spells out your obligation to pay off the balance of the lease. Some companies will let you try to sell the car and pay off your obligations that way or find someone to take over your lease. However, these documents are tightly written and most have been refined after many court challenges.

True Cost of Leasing

The true cost of leasing is made up of three components. Leasing, like purchasing, should be a negotiated process. If you don't negotiate the lease, you'll pay too much. The price of the car, called the **capitalized cost,** is something you can discover using the Internet and insisting the cost not be an inflated retail price.

If you lower the capitalized cost, you narrow the gap between it and the **residual value,** which is what is financed in the lease. The smaller this number, the lower your lease payments will be.

The third component of a lease price is the interest rate. You do not have to use the dealer or leasing company's financing. You can use your own bank or other source. If you bring a lower interest rate source to the bargaining table, you may win concessions to match your rate.

WORDS TO GO . . .WORDS TO GO . . .WORDS TO GO

The **capitalized cost** is the price of the car. The **residual value** is what the car will be worth at the end of the lease (the depreciated value)

However, unless you can deduct some or all of the lease payment from your tax return, there is no real benefit in leasing. Lease payments buy the use of the vehicle for another month and that is all.

7

INSURANCE

7.1 LIFE INSURANCE

Term

Whole

Universal

Calculating Need

How to Buy

Life insurance protects your most valuable personal asset—your ability to support your family. No product can replace your life, but adequate insurance can replace your income so your family doesn't suffer financially. In this section, we'll look at the most common types of life insurance.

Term

Term life insurance provides protection or coverage for a specific period or term. There are several different term products, but they all have in common an end date when they lapse. On this date, you have the option to renew the policy for another term or do nothing and let your coverage end.

WORDS TO GO . . . WORDS TO GO . . . WORDS TO GO

Term life is a life insurance policy that offers a death benefit for a defined period (the term). The policy may be guaranteed renewable, but at a different premium. Terms can run from 1 to 30 years. When the term ends, so does your coverage. Most term life insurance products have no cash value nor do they build any residual value. Term policies are popular because they are cheaper than other forms of life insurance such as whole life insurance.

You can buy policies that renew annually or for a set number of years, such as 5 or 10, although you can find policies up to 30 years. Life insurance companies market a variety of policies with different terms and options.

Term insurance may work best for people who have different needs for coverage at different times in their lives. For example, while children are at home and through college, insurance needs may be higher than after they are adults and off on their own. In this scenario, a term policy that lapsed when less coverage was needed would fit a financial plan.

Term is generally less expensive than whole life or cash value life as it is called. That's because you pay for insurance protection and nothing else. However, all insurance is priced in part on age and, as you grow older, term becomes more expensive. There are two concerns with using term policies as people age: the first is renewability and the second is price of coverage.

Most term policies let you renew them without another medical exam, but make sure that feature is in place before you purchase the policy. If you develop a serious medical condition, you don't want to find out your life insurance won't let you renew.

Even if you can renew your policy, it will be at a new, age-driven rate. While term policies are much cheaper than whole life policies for young people, that gap narrows considerably and may reverse as people age. The overall cost advantage still goes to term in most cases; however, it can be pricey for people over age 60. In most cases, older people don't need as much life insurance as young people and couples with young families.

Term products are priced one of two main ways. **Increasing term** policies raise the premium on the anniversary date of the policy annually. The second way is level billing. **Level billing** takes the anticipated increases over the policy term and effectively bills you an average premium. Increasing premium products work best for younger people, whose costs will be low, and for people who may cancel the policy in the early years. Level premium products work best for people who want a constant price so they can budget accordingly. With a level premium policy, you will pay more for the insurance in the early years and less in the later years than you will with an increasing term policy.

7.1

WORDS TO GO . . . WORDS TO GO . . . WORDS TO GO

Increasing term policies raise the premium on the anniversary date annually. These policies tend to be less expensive than level billing in the early years when you are younger and more expensive if you hold the policy until your older years.

Level billing policies look at the term of the policy (10 years, for example) and determine a premium that is appropriate for the whole period. The premium will fall in the middle, but remain constant for the term of the policy. These policies are convenient for planning purposes, because you'll know what the premium will be.

Most term policies provide a level benefit, for example a death benefit of $200,000 whether you die in the first or last year of the policy period. You can buy a decreasing term policy that reduces the death benefit by a predetermined amount each year. These policies can be used while you are paying off a debt such as a mortgage and wouldn't need as much toward the end of the loan as at the first.

Whole

Whole or cash value insurance provides the same basic protection, but goes beyond term insurance by adding a savings component that accumulates on a tax-deferred basis until it is withdrawn, and then it is taxed at ordinary income tax rates.

The savings component and the high commissions paid to sell whole life products make them so much more expensive than term life policies. Whole life policies are designed to be held your whole life; they do not end as long as you keep paying premiums and only make financial sense if held a very long time.

Depending on how your premium is structured, you generally pay a level premium—there are no increases with age like term life products. It may take a number of years for your premium to build substantial cash value. Your premium is split: part of it pays for the insurance, part goes to cash value, and part pays the commission and sales expense. If you cancel the policy in the early years, most of your premium will have gone to the death benefit and paying sales commissions and little to cash value. The result is that you will lose a lot of money that you could have saved by buying a term policy and only paying for the death benefit.

If you keep a cash-value policy long enough to build significant cash value, you have a choice of what to do with the money:

▶ Surrender the policy and claim the cash.

▶ Borrow the cash (if you die while the loan is outstanding, it is deducted from the payout, plus interest).

▶ Use the cash to pay future premiums (this feature, often called "vanishing premiums," is often touted by salespeople as a real benefit).

The forced savings feature of whole life is often cited as a plus for people who may have trouble saving for retirement. A whole life policy bought at a young age might accumulate a significant amount of cash that could be used in retirement.

The downside is people need the most life insurance when their children are still at home, and that is usually when they can least afford high premiums.

Universal

Universal life insurance is a variation of whole life insurance. It has the same features—a death benefit and a savings component—but offers consumers a great deal of flexibility in how their premium is applied. Consumers can change the death benefit and apply more of the premium to the death benefit or lower the benefit and put more into savings.

The universal policy is very popular for its ability to change with a customer's insurance and savings needs. Unlike regular cash-value policies, universal life has more options on interest rates for savings, loans, and repayments than regular policies.

A variation of universal life is variable universal life, which lets the insured invest the savings portion of the premium in a set of mutual funds rather than a fixed-rate savings account. This shifts the risk of what return your policy may or may not earn to you and the market. Combining stock market risk and insurance is not considered a wise financial move.

Calculating Need

Calculating how much life insurance you need is part math and part lifestyle. The math part is determining how much income the insurance needs to replace for how long. The lifestyle part is more subjective.

Assume that both you and your partner work, and you travel a great deal in your job. If your partner dies, will you still be able to travel that much and maintain a household for the children? You could hire a housekeeper/nanny, but that is expensive and may not be in keeping with your desire to raise your children. If you have to find different work or take a different position, what will that do to your income? Maybe you would not want to work at all for a while to ease the children through their grief.

When you have an income figure that the insurance settlement needs to provide (figure a conservative return of no more than five percent) and how long it must last, you can arrive at the amount of insurance you need. If you need $40,000 a year, you need a policy that will pay $800,000 at death. If you want that income for the rest of your life, recognize that inflation will reduce its purchasing power if you never withdraw any of the principal or keep it in very conservative investments. Most people will need it the most to get the children grown and out on their own. If they have to draw down some of the principal in the last years (for college expenses), it should not be a financial burden.

A more comprehensive method of determining your life insurance needs looks not only at replacing an income but at those special funding needs that will arise, such as college, retirement for the surviving spouse, paying off the mortgage, and so on. This more comprehensive method often requires more than one policy and will be helped by the services of a financial planner. Detailing those special needs will depend on the age of the adults and the children and what other resources are already in place to meet those special needs.

How to Buy

You can buy life insurance three ways:

The Independent Agent

An independent agent is not employed by any one life insurance company. They are free to sell policies from several different companies. In theory, they find the best policies for you and represent you to the company. In reality, they are paid a commission when they sell a policy, so the odds that they are going to seek out the lowest priced policies seem slim. Still, they are not obligated to try to sell you the latest product the company is pushing, which may not be in your best interest.

Captive Agent

A captive agent works for the company that issues the policy. They sell only life insurance policies from that company. On one hand, you may not get to see a broad range of products, yet these agents tend to be the best trained and most knowledgeable about life insurance products. Most of these agents also sell other company products such as annuities, mutual funds, and savings products. Many have completed advanced financial training classes that are offered by industry groups, which help the agents provide better advice.

From the Company

Some insurance companies sell directly to consumers. These companies offer the lowest cost products and commissions, but don't usually have offices you can go to or agents that will come to your house to explain policies. Most, if not all, of their business is done by phone, mail, or over the Internet. If you know what you want, these companies offer savings. Some have outstanding customer service, even though it is delivered over the telephone.

7.2 AUTO INSURANCE

Collision

Comprehensive

Liability

Other Coverages

How to Buy

Automobile insurance goes beyond fixing a fender-bender. If a person is hurt or killed in an accident, you could be sued and face a severe civil judgment. This section discusses the different types of auto insurance coverage.

Collision

If you finance or lease a car, you will be required to carry collision insurance. This is wreck protection and it covers your car regardless of who is at fault or if you hit a tree or other stationary object. The policy has a deductible (except for some leases, which require a zero deductible). You pay the deductible first and then the policy pays the rest of the repair costs. You can select the deductible that fits your budget. A higher deductible will lower your monthly premiums, but don't set the deductible so high it empties your bank account and savings to meet it.

In addition to financed and leased cars, newer vehicles should have collision coverage. However, this is expensive. If your car isn't worth much, consider dropping collision coverage.

Comprehensive

Despite being named comprehensive, this coverage doesn't cover accidents at all. Comprehensive insurance protects you from theft, fire, vandalism, hail, wind, and other types of damage. It is also required for financed and leased vehicles. You can have some control over premiums with the deductible, but if you have an older car that is not mandated to have the coverage, consider dropping it because it's expensive.

Liability

Liability covers the other person in the accident and is required in most states. This is the most important insurance to have because it can protect you in an accident by compensating the other party. If you cause a wreck that injures or kills someone, there is an excellent chance you will be sued. This is the context in which you must view liability insurance: what assets do you have to protect and what is it worth to you to protect them? There is other insurance you can buy, an **umbrella policy,** to provide supplemental protection, but liability insurance is your first line of protection.

WORDS TO GO . . .WORDS TO GO . . .WORDS TO GO

An **umbrella policy** is liability protection that begins after your automobile or homeowners liability protection has been exhausted. It covers a variety of liability issues including libel and slander cases.

Liability is sold in number combinations like $50,000/$100,000, which is the minimum in many states. These numbers describe the limits the insurance company will pay on a single accident. They represent $50,000 per person and a maximum of $100,000 per accident. If your protection needs are higher (you have more assets at risk in a lawsuit), you can get the coverage bumped to $250,000/$500,000.

Other Coverages

You can buy some additional coverage with separate policies or riders to existing policies. This extra coverage is often worth the price for the peace of mind it buys:

Uninsured/Underinsured Motorists

This coverage protects you in the event the person who hits your car does not have adequate or any insurance. The law says everyone must have liability insurance, but don't count on it. If the person has no insurance, there's a good bet they have no assets to fix your car.

Medical Coverage

You can buy medical coverage for yourself, your passengers, and people in the other car in the event of an accident. Whether you need it will depend on the sufficiency of your health insurance, however having it for others is a good idea. There are two forms, personal injury protection, which may be mandated by your state, and medical coverage for you and anyone hurt in the accident. If you aren't required to get personal injury protection, the expanded medical coverage is usually a better deal.

Roadside Assistance

Two riders cover you if your car breaks down. One provides coverage for the cost of towing your car to a repair facility and the other provides some reimbursement for the cost of a rental while your car is being repaired.

Gap Insurance

If you buy a new car with little or no money down, there will be a period where you will owe more than the car is worth thanks to instant depreciation. If you total the car during this period, the insurance company will pay you what the car is worth in the market or its **actual cash value,** not what you owe on the note, which will be more.

> **WORDS TO GO . . .WORDS TO GO . . .WORDS TO GO**
>
> **Actual cash value** is what the insurance company determines your car was worth just before the accident. This value is not what you paid for the car, but factors in depreciation, resale value, and other factors.

7.2

Gap insurance will pay the difference between what the car is worth and what you still owe on the note.

How to Buy

You can buy auto insurance three ways:

The Independent Agent

Independent agents are not employed by any one insurance company. They are free to sell policies from several different companies. In theory, they find the best policies for you and represent you to the company. In reality, they are paid a commission when they sell a policy so the odds that they are going to seek out the lowest priced policies seem slim. Still, they are not obligated to try to sell you the latest product the company is pushing, which may not be in your best interest.

Captive Agent

A captive agent works for the company that issues the policy. They sell only insurance policies from that company. On one hand, you may not get to see a broad range of products, yet these agents tend to be the best-trained and most knowledgeable about insurance products. Most of these agents also sell other company products such as life insurance, annuities, mutual funds and savings products. Many have completed advanced financial training classes that are offered by industry groups, which help the agent's provide better advice. You can often get discounts on insurance if you have multiple policies with the same company.

From the Company

Some insurance companies sell directly to consumers. These companies offer the lowest cost products and commissions, but don't usually have offices you can go to or agents that will come to your house to explain policies. Most, if not all, of their business is done by phone, mail, or over the Internet. If you know what you want, these companies offer savings. Some have outstanding customer service, even though it is delivered over the telephone.

HOMEOWNERS INSURANCE

What's Covered

Actual Value

Replacement Value

Flood and Earthquake Insurance

Umbrella Policy

Riders and Provisions

Homeowners insurance has some key provisions that are easily misunderstood, which can lead to an unpleasant surprise if you file a claim. This section reviews these key provisions of homeowners insurance.

What's Covered

Homeowners insurance covers the main structure, including any attached buildings or structures such as garages or sunrooms. Sheds and fixtures like fencing, driveways, and so on are also covered. The policy assigns a percentage of the house's value—often 20 percent—to unattached structures and fixtures. If you have a significant investment in an outbuilding—a pool house, for example— you may want to buy extra protection. If you own a second home, most policies will let you add it to an existing policy.

Homeowners policies do not cover business equipment or supplies. If you operate a business out of your home, you will need separate coverage for that.

Homeowners policies cover personal possessions up to a percentage of the structure's insured value. Most policies assign personal property 50 to 60 percent of the value of the insured structure. Using the 50 percent value, a home insured for $200,000 would have personal property insured up to $100,000. Homeowners should keep as much documentation as possible along with photographs or a video inventory of their personal property. Insurance companies provide kits to help with this process. If you have jewelry, computers, collections, or other high-value items, you should get specific riders to cover these items.

Actual Value

Insurance companies place a value on property that is damaged by several methods. One common method is called **actual cash value**. This method of valuing items for claim purposes places a value on the item just before it was destroyed or stolen. For example, a living room setting that cost $5,000 new three years ago might have an actual cash value of $2,600 now. That is what the insurance company will compensate the homeowner for their loss. This can be a shock if you were expecting to buy another $5,000 setting with the insurance check. If you don't know if your policy uses actual cash value, ask your agent or call the customer service number on the policy.

WORDS TO GO . . . *WORDS TO GO . . . WORDS TO GO*

Insurance companies use **actual cash value** to compensate you for items damaged or stolen from your home. This value is what the insurance company says the item was worth just before the incident and not the replacement value. It is the least expensive form of coverage because it provides the least coverage. The actual cash value considers depreciation, market value, condition, and so on.

Actual value policies are the least expensive, but provide the lowest level of coverage in terms of refurnishing your house. This becomes especially important if your house is severely damaged or destroyed. An actual value policy may not provide enough money to replace your house.

Replacement Value

Replacement value policies cost more, but are generally considered a better investment. These policies provide a settlement that is adequate to replace the damaged property exactly or with items of comparable quality. When your house is damaged or destroyed, replacement value policies will pay to rebuild it the way it was and to the same quality standards.

There is an expanded version of this coverage called guaranteed replacement value policies or extended replacement policies. These policies provide the best protection, but are the most expensive. The guaranteed replacement value policies are open-ended and will pay whatever it takes to restore your house and possessions. Extended replacement policies add 20 to 25 percent extra on to the policy limits to cover any additional costs in restoring your house and possessions. If you live in an area prone to storms, this is important coverage, because after widespread disasters, construction costs often rise and stay high for lengthy periods.

Flood and Earthquake Insurance

Flood and earthquake insurance are typically special-issue policies. You have to buy a separate flood insurance policy from the Federal Flood Insurance Program (1-800-427-4661, www.fema.gov/nfip). Your agent can arrange the coverage, but the actual policy comes from this government program.

If you live in a flood prone area, your lender will require you to have flood insurance. Flood insurance goes into effect 30 days after you apply, so don't wait until a storm is coming!

Earthquake insurance is more important in certain areas of the country than others. However, note that most homeowners policies do not cover ground movement, whether it is an earthquake or something else. If you are new to an area, find out what the incidence of earthquakes is and whether lenders require the coverage.

Umbrella Policy

"Slip and fall" is a common term among lawyers who work personal injury cases. As a homeowner, you are potentially liable for the injury someone suffers if they fall on your property. However, your potential liability doesn't end there. If you are in a car wreck, you could be sued for much more than the limits of your auto policy or someone could accuse you of slander and sue you for damages. Unfortunately, the list goes on.

To provide an extra measure of liability protection, you can buy an **umbrella policy** that kicks in after other policies reach their limits. The umbrella policy can offer help in personal injury cases and other civil matters. Most policies start at $1 million in protection. You can buy more coverage if you need it. Because the policy comes in after other coverage is exhausted, the premiums are reasonable and the extra protection is well worth the money.

7.3

WORDS TO GO . . .WORDS TO GO . . .WORDS TO GO

Umbrella policies, as the name implies, provide a coverage that protects you from liabilities resulting from accidents in your car or at your home. They can also protect you in a number of civil matters beyond accidents, such as libel and slander cases. Umbrella policies take over after your other (homeowner, for example) insurance is exhausted.

Riders and Provisions

Riders and provisions are attachments of extra coverage to homeowners policies that address specific insurance needs. Some riders are beneficial and address important issues, but be aware that others can simply duplicate other coverage or add little of real benefit. Here are some examples of riders and provisions:

- ▶ **Jewelry:** If you have expensive jewelry, you'll want special protection, which will include a schedule listing and describing each piece and a value based on an appraisal.

- ▶ **Collections or other valuables:** Art, stamp, coin, and other valuable collections should be covered by specific provisions. Your agent can tell you the best way to provide protection for valuables that are not normal household possessions.

- ▶ **Computer, business equipment:** If you have personal computers or run a business, even part-time out of your home, these items will not be covered under most homeowners policies without a special provision or separate policy.

- ▶ **Inflation protection:** This is becoming common in most policies, but if it is not included, add it as a rider or provision to protect your coverage by increasing it at the rate of inflation.

- ▶ **Extended theft protection:** This extends coverage to boats and recreational vehicles as well as other vehicles. It also protects against credit card fraud.

- ▶ **Additional living expenses:** This provision allows you up to 20 percent of the house's value in living expenses while your house is being rebuilt. It also covers government order evacuations.

7.4 **RENTER'S INSURANCE**

Coverage

Riders

If you rent, you need an insurance policy that covers your possessions. The property owner's policy covers the structure, but you are responsible for your own insurance. This section covers renter's insurance.

Coverage

Renter's insurance, which is available whether you are renting an apartment or house, covers smoke, fire, theft, wind damage, water damage (but not flooding), and other general perils. The insurance is sold on your possessions, not the building, so calculating the amount of coverage is limited to what you own. It will speed processing and help resolve conflicts if you have documentation of the items, especially high-value appliances, furniture, or entertainment equipment. Keep sales slips, photographs, and/or a video inventory off site for safekeeping.

7.4

Insurance companies pay off claims on renter's policies using one of these two valuation methods:

▶ **Actual cash value:** This option pays you the value of your possessions minus any depreciation.

▶ **Replacement value:** Pick this option if you want the insurance company to pay for replacing your possessions with the same or comparable quality items up to the limits of your policy.

Riders

If you have expensive jewelry, computers, or business equipment in your rental unit, you should have a specific rider protecting those items. Most policies will only pay a fixed amount for jewelry and may not pay anything for business-related equipment without a specific rider.

You may also want to consider extra liability protection, as either a rider or an umbrella policy. This is an important consideration if you run a business, even part-time, out of your rental unit. Extra liability protection is not expensive in most cases.

7.5 HEALTH INSURANCE

Group Policies

Individual/High Deductible Policies

Health Savings Accounts

Prescription Drug Policies

Dental and Vision Policies

Healthcare costs have been rising faster than the rate of inflation and faster than the growth of personal income for a number of years. Health insurance is very important to your personal finances, but it can come at a high price. This section examines health insurance coverage and costs.

Group Policies

Group health policies through employers or the government offer the best buy and often the best coverage of all health insurance policies. The reason is that insurance costs go down when the **risk pool,** or the number of people insured, goes up. Group policies are cheaper than individual policies and larger groups are less expensive to insure than smaller groups.

> **WORDS TO GO . . .WORDS TO GO . . .WORDS TO GO**
>
> **Risk pool** is the number of people who share the risk for a particular group insurance policy. A basic principle of insurance is the larger the risk pool, the less risk to the insurer and the lower the premium.

Employers may offer one or more policies to employees for their selection as a benefit. Usually, the employer will try to offer a mix of lower cost insurance that requires using certain providers with more expensive policies that allow a wider selection of healthcare providers.

Almost all group policies are **managed-care** plans, which means the insurance companies negotiate with providers to manage the cost of service. The policies offer two levels of coverage: in-network and out-of-network. Use network-approved providers and the policy will pay more than if you use non-network providers. You still have a choice, but choosing a non-network provider may be expensive. Another way insurance companies manage the cost of medical services is requiring patients to get referrals to see certain specialists before paying maximum benefits. In general, the greater freedom to choose providers you have, the higher the premium.

Managed-care insurance plans attempt to control costs by managing the care patients receive and the providers that dispense the services. By negotiating discounts with providers and driving patients to them, insurance companies can lower overall healthcare costs.

Group managed care insurance policies fall into three basic varieties:

▶ **Health Maintenance Organizations (HMO):** The HMO plan is usually the least expensive choice, but has the most restrictions in terms of who you can see for your healthcare needs. From the list of approved physicians, you will choose a primary healthcare provider. This physician coordinates all your healthcare needs. If you need to see a specialist, you must receive a referral from your primary care physician. If you see a specialist without a referral, the insurance may not pay any of the bill or only a small portion.

▶ **Preferred Provider Organizations (PPOs):** A PPO encourages users to stay within the approved network of healthcare providers by requiring a small or no co-payment. If a non-network provider is used, the co-payment may be much higher and the coverage more restrictive than for the same service provided by a network provider. You may see a specialist without a referral. Some PPO plans do not cover preventive care. PPO rules vary by provider and state.

▶ **Point-of-Sale (POS):** These policies are an expanded form of HMOs that use a primary provider, but are not quite as restrictive when it comes to using out-of-network specialists. POS plans usually cover preventive care.

Insurance policies share common features and terms. These terms are often sources of confusion for insurance consumers.

Deductible

Insurance policies that require a deductible want the consumer to pay for the first dollars of healthcare. This is seen as a way to slow down unnecessary healthcare spending. There is a deductible for the primary insured and another deductible for the family, if they are included in the policy (for example, $300 for the employee and $600 for the family). Insurance benefits do not begin until the insured has paid these deductibles within policy year. As you pay medical bills, you should get statements from the company showing how much of the deductible has been met. Not all expenses count toward the deductible.

Co-Payment

When you visit a healthcare provider, many policies require you make a co-payment of some amount at the time of your appointment. Depending on the policy and who you are seeing, the co-payment could range from $10–$40. HMOs typically don't require a co-payment or only a very small one.

Coinsurance

Coinsurance is the amount you pay along with the insurance company after the deductible is met. A typical coinsurance split is 80/20, which means the insurance company pays 80 percent of the cost and you pay 20 percent.

Out-of-Pocket Limits

An out-of-pocket limit caps the amount of coinsurance you have to pay in any one year. Once you hit it, the insurance company pays for 100 percent of all future costs of "usual and customary" charges for covered expenses. If your healthcare provider charges more than the **usual and customary charges,** you are still responsible. The out-of-pocket maximum resets each year.

WORDS TO GO . . .WORDS TO GO . . .WORDS TO GO

Usual and customary charges are a list of fees that the insurance company says it will pay for healthcare services. Doctors in the company's network have agreed to these charges; however, if you go outside the network, a provider may charge more and not agree to the insurance company's fee schedule.

Lifetime Limits on Benefits

Lifetime benefits to an individual available under their policies are capped to protect insurance companies from paying for a healthcare situation that could cost them millions of dollars. A policy that has lifetime benefits of at least $1 million is desirable.

Preexisting Conditions

A preexisting condition is a medical problem that you had before joining a new health plan. The Health Insurance Portability and Accountability Act (HIPAA) protects you if you have a preexisting condition and have been insured during the past 12 months. Your condition cannot be excluded under the new policy. If you have a preexisting condition and have not been covered by insurance during the past 12 months, the longest the policy can exclude the condition under the new group policy is 12 months.

The HIPAA law does not apply to individual coverage, so if you have or are looking for individual coverage and have a preexisting condition, it may be excluded permanently or for an extended period.

COBRA

COBRA is the Consolidated Omnibus Budget Reconciliation Act and it allows you to maintain your group health insurance coverage for up to 18 months if you lose your job. If your spouse does not have coverage, this can be an important, although expensive, benefit, especially if you have a preexisting condition (see the previous section). You can maintain health insurance for your protection and remain insured, so when you find a new job, your preexisting condition won't be excluded under the new group policy. COBRA only applies to companies with 20 or more employees.

You must pay the full premium where before, as an employee, the company was undoubtedly paying a substantial portion. However, it still may be cheaper than finding an individual policy, and if you have a preexisting condition, you may not be able to qualify for an individual policy anyway.

Here are the conditions where COBRA applies:

- ▶ You leave your job and are self-employed or unemployed.
- ▶ You are the dependent, widow, or widower of a worker who dies while employed at least three years.
- ▶ You are the divorced spouse or child of a worker employed three years or more.
- ▶ You are the child under the age of 23 of a worker who left the company.

You have a 60-day window to file for COBRA benefits after you leave the company.

Preauthorization of Benefits

The insurance company will require you get preauthorization before some types of treatment. For example, most surgery will require preauthorization from the insurance company. In an emergency, the company will want you or someone to notify them within 24 hours or so.

You should check your policy or call the insurance company to see if you need preauthorization for a procedure out of the ordinary. Failure to get preauthorization or notify the company promptly after an emergency may reduce your benefit by as much as 50 percent.

Individual/High Deductible Policies

Individual health insurance policies are very expensive and usually limited in coverage when compared to group policies.

Basic individual policies cover major medical or catastrophic coverage. This protection will pay for hospital stays and surgery in the event of serious illness or emergencies. Routine doctor visits, tests, and so on will come out of your pocket. Even covered expenses will have a high deductible. Your premium will depend, in part, on how high a deductible you choose. It is not uncommon for these policies to start at $5,000 for an individual and $7,500 or $10,000 for the family. Because these policies don't cover routine healthcare visits, the deductible only is met with a serious illness or hospital stay. You should consider whether you and your family's health is such that you can afford to chance this coverage. Another consideration is affording the deductible. Although $5,000 sounds like a lot, even a short stay in the hospital will run up that much in a hurry.

A managed-care plan that offers many of the same benefits of a group plan is available in many states, but for a high premium. These plans differ from group plans in two major ways. First, the premium is much higher; second, the deductible is very high. You may have many of the benefits of a group plan, including choice of provider and having routine medical services covered. However, the premium for an individual may be in the hundreds of dollars each month. To help lower premiums, most of these policies have very high deductibles—$5,000 to $10,000. As a practical matter, they become much like the basic policy because the consumer is paying for many routine healthcare services out of pocket before the deductible is met.

Consumers with a high deductible healthcare policy often use a health savings account to help pay for the out-of-pocket expenses.

Health Savings Accounts

Health Savings Accounts (HSAs) are a tax-preferred way to put aside money to pay out-of-pocket expenses for people who have high deductible healthcare insurance policies. The money is taken out of your pay before payroll taxes are calculated, so your current taxes are reduced. The money is put in a special account set up at almost any financial institution and can be used to pay a variety of healthcare costs. If you don't use all the money in your account in one year, it rolls over to the next year.

HSAs have some specific restrictions that make many consumers ineligible to use them. Here are some of the features that make HSAs work for some consumers and prevent other consumers from using them at all:

▶ You must be on a high deductible healthcare insurance policy to be eligible for an HSA. If you have insurance through your employer or are covered by your partner's insurance, you are ineligible for an HSA.

▶ You must stop contributing when you reach age 65 and you can't use HSAs if you are on Medicare or are receiving benefits from the Veterans Administration.

▶ Contributions are limited to the amount of the deductible on your high deductible health insurance policy. You cannot contribute more than the deductible and the maximum contribution under any circumstances is $2,700 and $5,420 for individual and family respectively (2006). Persons over the age of 55 can take advantage of a catch up provision that allows extra contributions. These are:

2007: $800

2008: $900

2009: $1,000 from then on

These catch-up contributions, like regular contributions, must stop when you reach age 65. HSAs are complicated by many details. For more information, you can read about them on the U.S. Treasury's website: www.ustreas.gov/offices/public-affairs/hsa/.

Prescription Drug Policies

Prescription drug policies are sold with healthcare policies either as riders or as separate policies, but part of the total healthcare benefit. They are not sold as stand-alone policies.

Most prescription policies involve a co-pay for each prescription filled. Name-brand drugs have a higher co-pay than generic drugs. An important detail to note is whether the plan pays from the first dollar or whether prescriptions are included in your deductible that must be met before the drug plan begins to pay.

Many plans now offer a refill-by-mail program where you receive a 90-day supply of maintenance medications at a time. This process saves some money over buying three 30-day supplies and some policies require you to buy medicine you take on a maintenance basis this way.

Dental and Vision Policies

Dental policies pay for routine dental work, but most policies have an annual cap on expenses, which means serious dental work will not be covered in a meaningful way. Before signing up for dental insurance, look at your family's dental situation and previous dental expenses and see if the premium and limited benefit make sense for you. A high premium plus a high deductible will buy a lot of dental work.

Vision policies usually cover an annual routine eye examination at a fixed price and discounts on frames and lenses. If the premium is not too high and you have an annual exam, it is worth the money. Some healthcare policies include vision as part of the policy so there is no extra cost.

| 7.6 |

DISABILITY INSURANCE

Occupation and Income

Waiting Period

Length of Benefit

Key Considerations

The chances of a person becoming disabled for a significant period due to an accident or illness are higher than dying, yet more people have life insurance than have disability insurance, which protects the same thing: your ability to produce a paycheck. This section examines disability insurance features.

Occupation and Income

Disability insurance replaces a portion of the income you were making when you became disabled. You decide the level of benefit when you purchase the policy. There are two sources of disability policies: group policies through your employer and individual policies.

7.6

Group Policies

Disability policies that come with your benefit's package at work may not offer the same levels of benefit as an individual policy, but you don't have to pay the premium or the premium will be low because it is a group policy. Because you don't pay the entire premium, benefits received under a group policy may be taxed like ordinary income. Of course, when your leave the company, your coverage ends. Some group policies can be converted to individual policies.

Individual Policies

Individual disability policies generally offer the best protection and are more expensive than group policies. You can choose several different levels of coverage along with some other options to influence you premium. There are two main types of disability policies sold and they are identified by how they define disability:

▶ **Income replacement or modified occupation:** This definition of disability says the policy will not pay benefits if you are able to perform an occupation that is suitable for your age, experience, and education, even if it isn't your previous career. This policy is the lower cost of the two because it is more restrictive about when it will pay benefits.

▶ **Own occupation:** This definition of disability says if you cannot perform your occupation, you will receive benefits even if you could hold another job. This is the most expensive definition, but the one you should carefully consider. For many people, the definition of disability includes not being able to perform the job they are educated, trained, and experienced to do.

Another definition is sold in some policies, but you have to be unemployable in any job to earn benefits. This is usually not a recommended policy. The restrictions of this policy are close to those of the Social Security administration, which also makes disability payments.

◖ *SEE ALSO 14.5, "Pension Plans"* ▶

Waiting Period

Disability insurance doesn't begin right away in most cases. There is a waiting period before benefits begin. The waiting period is comparable to a deductible in other insurance policies—it is the period where you are responsible for covering your expenses out of pocket. This underscores the importance of an emergency cash fund.

◀ *SEE ALSO 2.6, "Emergency Funds"* ◗

Many policies pay at the end of the month, not the beginning, so a 60-day waiting period means you would receive the first check in 90 days. This is a financial decision that weighs the benefit of a lower premium against going without the benefit for 60, 90, or 120 days.

Length of Benefit

Disability by definition is not something that will end in a few weeks or, in many cases, months. The purpose of the insurance is to consider a worst-case scenario, which would be a permanent disability. Policies have terms of almost any length you want to buy, but most people look at one of two options. At age 65, you are eligible for Social Security benefits and Medicare, which may replace much of your disability insurance income. Many people use age 65 as the end date for their disability policy. The other school of thought is that a disability is going to cause problems long after age 65, so the income will be needed for the rest of your life. The longer benefit period will result in a higher premium.

Key Considerations

Disability policies feature some key provisions that should address important considerations, including the following:

Renewable

Three types of clauses deal with how you can renew the policy. It is important to know the difference because the choice affects your premium:

▶ **Noncancelable:** The company cannot cancel the policy or raise the premium. The only basis for canceling the policy is nonpayment of premium. This offers the best protection.

▶ **Guaranteed renewable:** You can renew the policy each year without an increase in premiums unless the insurance company raises premiums for everyone in the same group.

▶ **Conditionally renewable:** This is not as common as the other two clauses, and it's one you should usually avoid. It gives the insurance company the option to renew or not a group or class of policies.

7.6

Adjusting for Inflation

Disability policies should have a provision for adjusting the payment based on the cost of living increases. Payments may last for years, but if inflation keeps eating away at the purchasing power, your benefit will not be worth as much.

Purchase Options

Purchase options allow you to buy additional coverage at specified times in the future. This is important, especially for younger people who may see dramatic increases in their incomes and want to expand the coverage.

Partial Disability

A disability that limits the number of hours you are able to work might reduce your income if you are in a commissioned sales job or even on an hourly or salaried pay scale. Disability insurance would make up the difference (up to policy limits).

This often becomes important if you are coming off a totally disabling situation, such as recovering from an accident or serious illness. You may not be able to work full time in your own occupation, but can still perform some of the tasks. These payments could last to the policy limits or until you fully recover and can return to work full time.

Disability Presumed

This policy considers some conditions, usually associated with an accident, fully disabling whether you can perform some or all of your own occupation's tasks or not. These would include blindness, loss of speech, hearing, or loss of limbs. The policy will define these presumptions of disability.

Waiver of Premiums

Most policies contain this provision, which states you do not have to continue paying premiums on the policy once you have been receiving benefits for 90 days.

7.7 LONG-TERM CARE INSURANCE

Overview

When to Apply

Amount of Benefit

Length of Benefit

Waiting Period

Long-term care insurance, ungraciously called nursing home insurance, is a major concern to an aging population of baby boomers. With annual nursing home expenses running in excess of $45,000 per year in many locations, long-term care insurance makes good financial sense. This section looks at the fundamentals of this important insurance coverage.

Overview

Long-term care insurance covers care in a nursing home, in-home care, an assisted living facility, or a combination of these for people who can't care for themselves but don't need skilled nursing care for medical reasons.

The need for long-term care is the inability to perform two or more activities of daily living or cognitive impairment. The activities of daily living (ADL) are:

► Eating

► Bathing

► Dressing

► Toileting

► Continence

► Transferring (getting out of a chair or bed)

Cognitive impairment is a mental confusion so that the person poses a danger to themselves or others. This is not to suggest the person is violent, but they may get lost or wander off and forget simple steps to keep themselves safe (going out at night in the winter without a coat, for example). Persons meeting either the ADL or cognitive impairment definition need long-term care.

Health insurance and Medicare will generally pay for skilled care (performed by nurses under the supervision of a physician), but do not pay for custodial care, which is what most people need. Long-term care insurance pays for custodial care.

When to Apply

Premiums for long-term care insurance are fixed when you apply, so the younger you are, the lower your premium. Buying too young may be wasting money because most long-term care needs occur after age 65. The best age to apply is around age 59. However, long-term care is medically underwritten, which means you must be in relatively good health to qualify. If there is a history of chronic illness in your family, it may be wise to apply for the coverage at an earlier age. Once symptoms of a chronic illness or condition appear, it is unlikely you will find any company that will sell you a policy.

Amount of Benefit

Most policies pay a daily benefit that is offered one of two ways. You can receive a fixed amount every day you are receiving long-term care services or you can be reimbursed for your actual expenses up to a daily limit. If expenses go over this limit, you are responsible for the difference.

There are several variations on these payout plans and it will pay you to shop for a policy that fits your particular needs. If you have assets, you may not need the policy to cover every dollar of expense, but look for coverage that pays most of the daily expense. This will lower your premium, because you are not buying as large a benefit.

Your policy should include inflation protection that increases the benefit at the rate of inflation. If not, what seemed like a reasonable daily benefit may not come close to meeting your needs in the future.

Length of Benefit

Most stays in long-term care situations last around two years; however, that average may be skewed by including terminally ill patients or people who have just come out of the hospital after a serious illness. If you are under age 65, most financial experts suggest a four- to six-year benefit period. There's no way of telling, thanks to modern medicine, how long a stay in long-term care will last. The longer the benefit period, the more expensive the premium will be, but there is no point in buying protection that will end when you may need it the most.

Waiting Period

The waiting period is that time before benefits begin—much like a deductible in a regular insurance policy. The longer you can extend this period, the lower your premium will be. However, you must have the ready cash on hand to pay what could be $4,000 or more per month in expenses before the waiting is over. This is a personal financial decision based on your family's cash situation and how big of a strain it will be on them to wait for the insurance benefits to begin.

7.7

8

TAXES

8.1 INCOME TAX

Basic Structure

Itemize vs. Standard Deduction

Credit vs. Deduction

Record Keeping

We all pay federal income tax on a variety of earned and unearned income. The Internal Revenue Service is backed by a code so complex it takes over a million lines of regulatory language to explain. Little wonder it is routinely attacked by everyone from politicians to standup comedians. In this section, we'll look at the structure and major components of the personal income tax.

Basic Structure

The personal income tax is built on the premise that a person or family's income is adjusted by deductions and credits to arrive at an adjusted total. This adjusted total is used to compute the taxes due based on income tax tables.

For most taxpayers, the process starts every paycheck when their employer deducts payroll taxes. Here are the taxes collected:

▶ Federal income taxes

▶ State income taxes*

▶ Local income taxes*

▶ Social Security taxes

▶ Medicare taxes

(*If applicable)

Self-employed people are required to pay their own **Social Security** and **Medicare taxes** and make their own tax deposits. In most cases, quarterly deposits will cover the requirements. The IRS provides worksheets to help estimate deposit amounts and frequency.

◀ *SEE ALSO 14.5, "Pension Plans"* ▶

WORDS TO GO . . . *WORDS TO GO* . . . *WORDS TO GO*

Social Security taxes are collected on all wages up to a limit. Employees pay 6.2 percent and employers pay 6.2 percent for 12.4 percent on wages up to $94,200 (2006). Self-employed people pay the full amount.

Medicare taxes are collected on all wages. Employees pay 1.45 percent and employers pay 1.45 percent for 2.90 percent on all wages—there is no upper limit. Self-employed people pay the full amount.

When it's time to file the annual tax return, taxpayers gather records of income and possible deductions and credits. Some people find it helpful to use tax-preparation software to work through the filing process.

Itemize vs. Standard Deduction

The first decision facing taxpayers is whether to **itemize deductions** or take the **standard deduction** offered by the IRS. The standard deduction is for people who do not have enough qualifying deductions to itemize. The IRS reports that almost 65 percent of filers use the standard deduction.

WORDS TO GO . . . *WORDS TO GO* . . . *WORDS TO GO*

8.1

Itemizing deductions is the process of calculating individual allowable deductions that exceed the amount available under the standard deduction. Not every taxpayer can itemize.

The **standard deduction** is an amount allotted by the IRS for taxpayers who do not itemize deductions. It is a lump-sump deduction that comes off the taxpayer's income to lower the amount that will eventually be taxed.

Credit vs. Deduction

Your reported income for the year is reduced by two methods: **tax credits** and **tax deductions.** They are not equal in effect on your taxes. Credits are much better because they reduce your taxes dollar for dollar, while deductions only reduce your taxes by the percent of your tax bracket.

Deductions reduce the amount of income you report. If you are in the 25 percent marginal tax bracket and take a $100 tax deduction, you reduce your income $100, but only reduce your taxes by $25. (You have $100 less income to pay taxes on at 25 percent or $25 in taxes).

Tax credits, however, come off your tax bill. After you calculate the taxes you owe based on your income and deductions, tax credits are taken off this total. A $100 tax credit reduces your taxes $100, because it comes directly off taxes owed.

> **WORDS TO GO . . .WORDS TO GO . . .WORDS TO GO**
>
> **Tax credits** are dollar-for-dollar reductions in your tax bill and are more desirable than tax deductions.
>
> **Tax deductions** reduce the income that is ultimately taxed. Deductions reduce your tax bill, but only by your tax rate.

Record Keeping

Record keeping is important and the IRS insists on it. Most taxpayers will receive documentation of income from their employer. Other income, such as interest income from savings or investments, is supposed to be reported on various Form 1099s, which you're responsible for including with your return. If you don't receive those forms by the end of January, call your company to find out why.

If you're claiming deductions, you may need to prove those to the IRS, especially if you are audited. Charitable donations, unreimbursed business expenses and other deductions need supporting documents to prove they were legitimate deductions.

If you had income of any type during the year, the IRS expects it to be reported. The IRS may disallow a deduction if it believes it wasn't legitimate, but unless you engage in an obvious pattern of fraud you are unlikely to face more than paying the additional tax with interest and maybe a penalty. However, if the IRS believes you tried to conceal income to avoid paying taxes, it is possible you could go to jail.

8.2 | TAXABLE INCOME

Adjusted Gross Income
Standard Deduction
Itemizing Deductions
Exemptions
Determining Marginal Rate

There are two general steps in calculating your taxes. The first step is to figure out your adjusted gross income and the second is to decide whether to take the standard deduction or to itemize your deductions. When those tasks are complete, you apply the appropriate tax rate. This section discusses that process.

Adjusted Gross Income

Calculate your **adjusted gross income** (AGI) by taking your total income from all sources and adjusting it downward by all the appropriated adjustments. These adjustments include contributions to your retirement fund, health savings account, moving expenses, interest on student loans, alimony you pay, and other adjustments you are allowed to take. These deductions or adjustments are made before the standard or itemized deductions. Because the adjustments lower your AGI, your ultimate tax responsibility is lowered too.

8.2

WORDS TO GO . . . *WORDS TO GO . . .WORDS TO GO*

Adjusted gross income (AGI) is the first cut at adjusting your gross reported income. It includes those adjustments that are allowed whether you itemized deductions or not.

Standard Deduction

Once you have an AGI, you must then decide between the standard deduction and itemizing deductions. Most people go with the standard deduction because they don't have enough individual deductions to justify itemizing. The IRS sets the standard deduction schedule for each tax year.

According to the IRS, the standard deductions for tax year 2006 were:

If your filing status is:	Your standard deduction is:
Single or married filing separately	$5,150
Married filing jointly or qualifying widow(er) with dependent child	$10,300
Head of household	$7,550

If you or your partner were born before January 2, 1941, or are blind, special rules apply and there is a worksheet with the 1040 form to help you comply.

These numbers are adjusted each year and are for illustration only. The instructions for forms 1040 and 1040EZ have the current deductions. The standard deduction reduces your reported income by whichever amount you qualify for and this gives you (along with any other deductions or income) your adjusted gross income.

For many taxpayers, who have only a salary for income and take the standard deduction, the IRS provides several quick and simple Form 1040 variations, such as the 1040EZ, to file their taxes. You can complete these simplified forms (if you have all your records) in under an hour.

Itemizing Deductions

Itemizing works for taxpayers who have more deductions than the standard deduction allows. In most cases, this requires owning a home to take the deduction on interest paid on the mortgage. That is the largest deduction most taxpayers can take. Other deductions include medical expenses, unreimbursed business expenses, charitable donations, and others. Itemizing deductions can be tedious work, but well worth the effort. It will be easier if you've kept good records during the year.

◄ SEE ALSO 5.4, *"Financing and Refinancing"* ▷

Itemized deductions are reported on Schedule A and there are specific rules for how certain items can be counted as a deduction. Once your income reaches a certain level, depending on your filing status, the dollar value of your itemized deductions begins to phase out.

Exemptions

The last big reduction in your taxable income is the personal exemptions you are allowed. The rules allow you to claim an exemption for you and your partner, plus any children. You can claim step-children if you provide most of their support and no one else claims them on their tax return. For tax year 2006, the personal exemption for everyone in your house was $3,300. Once your income reaches a certain level, depending on your filing status, the dollar value of your personal exemptions begins to phase out.

Determining Marginal Rate

Your **marginal tax rate** is the rate you would pay on the next additional dollar of taxable income. In other words, it is the highest rate you pay on part of your taxable income. If someone says they are in the 25 percent tax bracket, they are usually referring to the marginal tax bracket and any additional income will be taxed at that rate.

WORDS TO GO . . .WORDS TO GO . . .WORDS TO GO

Marginal tax rate is the tax rate you pay on the last dollar of income. It is useful in determining what additional income will mean from a tax perspective.

However, your marginal tax rate is not the rate you pay on all your taxable income. That is often called the effective tax rate. The average tax rate is applied to all of your taxable income. For example a married couple filing jointly with taxable income of $100,000 would pay (using rates from 2006):

8.2

10% on $0 – $15,100 =	$1,510
15% on $15,100 – $61,300 =	$9,195
25% on $61,300 – $123,700 =	$9,675*
Total taxes =	$20,380
Effective tax rate =	20.38%
Marginal tax rate =	25%

*($100,000 – $61,300 = $38,700 × 25% = $9,675)

The effective tax rate tells you that a little over 20 percent of your taxable income was paid out in taxes. The marginal tax rate tells you that any additional income will be taxed at the 25 percent rate.

8.3 TAX PROFESSIONALS

Working with Tax Preparers

Using a Tax Accountant

Some taxpayers have very difficult returns that require the services of a Certified Public Accountant specially trained in tax preparation. Other people use tax preparation services that range in training from college degrees to several weeks. This section looks at the various types of tax preparers and how they can help you.

Working with Tax Preparers

Some taxpayers find it helpful or necessary to use a tax-preparation service to help them file their income tax return. The IRS has tried to make the code much more "user friendly," but it is still intimidating to many people. If you own a small business, are self-employed, or have a high income, you may need the services of someone with specialized knowledge of the tax code to help you file your return and plan tax strategies for the next tax year. Professional tax preparation services and consultants provide this type of assistance ranging from simply helping you fill out your return to preparing complex filings.

Simple Help

Many taxpayers have been using firms like H&R Block or Jackson Hewitt Associates for years to prepare their returns. For many, the modest fees are worth the investment to avoid the anxiety of deciphering the instructions. These national organizations and many local and regional tax preparation services rely on software to help their staff, which is often seasonal, correctly file returns. Many offer tax refund advances, which is a loan against the tax refund. The providers will file your return electronically for you. Although most taxpayers should be able to complete the easier 1040 forms without any assistance, the IRS is so intimidating, many feel more secure with someone else doing it.

Enrolled Agent

If you have a small business or are self-employed, you may find your taxes are more complicated than you have time or expertise to figure out. An enrolled agent is a former IRS employee with at least five years experience as an auditor and has passed a difficult two-day test on federal tax law. Enrolled agents can help with tax preparation as well as tax planning. They are experts in tax preparation and may specialize in some parts of tax law.

Certified Public Accountant

Certified Public Accountants (CPAs) who have specific training in tax preparation are the best resource for difficult tax situations. They have more education and experience than other tax preparers, and thus are the most expensive. CPAs can help you solve difficult tax preparation problems and work with you to develop tax strategies. In most cases, CPAs work on business taxes or for individuals with high incomes and high net worth.

Tax Attorney

Tax attorneys specialize in tax law, but do not prepare taxes. If you are in legal trouble with the IRS, you call a tax attorney. A tax attorney can also help you set up wills, estates, and trusts in a tax efficient manner.

◀ *SEE ALSO Chapter 16, "Estate Planning"* ▶

Using a Tax Accountant

Using a CPA to do your taxes can be a smart financial move if you have a complicated situation. However, CPAs are expensive and you should take some steps to ensure that you are getting the best value for your investment in their time.

8.3

Get all your records together and organized before you engage the CPA—this will save you time and money. The less sorting and looking the CPA does, the more efficiently your problem can be researched and a solution found.

Find out if the CPA charges a flat fee or by the hour. If they charge by the hour, get an estimate of how many hours this problem looks like it will take. Find out exactly what the flat fee includes—is there planning or other services included? If there is an audit based on the return, will the CPA represent you as part of this fee, or is that extra?

8.4 DOING YOUR OWN TAXES

Which Form?
Using Tax Preparation Software
Guides and Information Sources

Many taxpayers can and do prepare their own taxes, especially if they use the short form version of the Form 1040. Regardless of which form you use, there is tax-preparation software and a variety of guides that can help make the job easier and more accurate. This section looks at that process.

Which Form?

How easily you can complete your own taxes depends on how complicated your personal finances are and which IRS form you have to use for filing purposes. The two are related. Taxpayers use three main forms for filing tax returns, and you can file all three electronically.

1040EZ

The simplest and shortest form is the 1040EZ. If you have all the necessary information, you may be able to complete this form in less than 30 minutes. The main guidelines for using the 1040EZ are:

▶ You must file as single or married filing jointly.

▶ You can't claim any dependents.

▶ Your taxable income must be less than $100,000.

Other qualifications are listed on the tax instructions that come with the tax packet, but these are the main ones. The 1040EZ works for many young people and older people with grown children. Taxpayers using this form take the standard deduction and **personal exemptions.**

WORDS TO GO . . .WORDS TO GO . . .WORDS TO GO

Personal exemption is a dollar amount the IRS allows for you, your spouse, and every dependent in your household. The amount changes each year. There is a specific definition of dependent, which is in the instructions for completing the forms. You can claim personal exemptions on all three tax forms.

1040A

If you don't qualify for the 1040EZ, the next level up is the 1040A. This form is for returns that are more complicated and allows a broader inclusion of income sources, tax credits, and adjustments. Here are the main guidelines:

▶ In addition to wages, income can be from retirement plans, Social Security, interest, dividends, and other sources.

▶ Your taxable income must be less than $100,000.

▶ You are allowed certain adjustments and credits.

▶ You do not itemize deductions.

The 1040A has other requirements printed in the instructions on the form. One of the big differences between it and the 1040EZ is you can claim dependents. If you do not meet the requirements for 1040A, then you must file the form 1040.

1040

Form 1040, also known as the long form, is the most comprehensive of all tax filing forms. The form and accompanying schedules and supplementary forms cover all the tax situations under the IRS code. You must use form 1040 if:

▶ You have taxable income over $100,000.

▶ You itemize your deductions.

▶ You cannot use 1040EZ or 1040A.

8.4

Form 1040 is called the long form for good reason. Depending on the complexity of your return, it may take from 10 to 20 hours to complete.

Using Tax Preparation Software

Personal tax-preparation software has become widely popular because it streamlines the tax preparation process and checks for errors. You still must gather all of your information, but the leading software packages come with copies of all the forms most taxpayers will need. As your situation calls for a form, the program produces it and guides you through its completion.

The major vendors of tax preparation software have made the process as user friendly as possible. You complete your return by answering an "interview" conducted by the software. As you answer questions, the software will ask additional questions based on your answers. Along the way, the software may ask questions that could point to tax savings if you can supply the right answer and supporting documentation. If you have bought the state income tax add-on, it is completed as you complete the federal return. The software also checks to see if you are subject to the Alternative Minimum Tax and calculates that, if you are.

When the process is complete, the software checks for errors and asks you to resolve those. In many cases, these are data-entry errors or answering a question incorrectly. You can print out your return, sign it, and mail it along with a check if you owe taxes. You can also file the return electronically. The printout includes all the forms you needed to complete your return.

Personal tax-preparation programs all have to complete federal and state income tax returns. There should be no difference in your return whether you use one vendor or another. Three vendors hold most of the market. They are:

> ▶ **TurboTax:** This package from Intuit is the clear market leader. From the same company that makes the personal financial software, Quicken, this package, like the other vendors, comes in three levels of complexity, ranging from a basic product for simple returns to their top product designed to handle complex returns.

> ▶ **TaxACT:** The TaxACT basic package is free, so if you are doing a very simple return, this may be all you need. The more complex versions have a distinctive feature that looks at the tax ramifications of specific life events such as divorce, death of a spouse, and so on.

> ▶ **TaxCut:** This package has the credibility of H&R Block behind it and, with the top-level versions of the software, you can have one of their preparers look over your return.

All three packages have undergone numerous user tests and have passed by completing returns accurately, for the most part.

Guides and Information Sources

Because preparing your taxes is so complicated, there is a whole industry of books and websites that offer help. Several books are published every year with timely tax filing help. These include:

> ▶ Ernst & Young Tax Guide

> ▶ JK Lasser's *Your Income Tax*

> ▶ PricewaterhouseCoopers' *Guide to Tax and Financial Planning 2006*

There are other books, and those associated with known accounting firms are trustworthy, but avoid books, websites, and other sources of information that claim to know "secrets" that will help you avoid paying any taxes or make promises that seem too good to be true.

However, the Internet can be a ready resource, if you stick with reputable sites. The IRS's website has a tremendous amount of information including several online calculators, such as:

▶ An Alternative Minimum Tax calculator: This system, called the AMT Assistant, automates the worksheet in form 1040, and tells you in five to ten minutes whether you will have to pay this tax, according to the IRS.

▶ Earned Income Credit Assistant: This tool helps people determine if they are eligible for the earned income credit

Other sites that provide helpful information include:

▶ **Yahoo! Tax Center:** Part of the Yahoo! finance section, this site has many useful tools and articles to help you plan and prepare your taxes.

▶ **About.com Tax Planning:** This site is full of tax planning and preparation articles, including changes in tax law, so you'll know what to expect when filing time comes.

▶ **Moneycentral.msn.com Tax Center:** Another reputable site with tips, planning, and advice for taxpayers.

Contact information for these resources is found in Appendix B.

8.4

8.5 TAX SAVINGS STRATEGIES

Reduce Adjusted Gross Income

Itemizing Deductions

Credits

The way to pay lower taxes is to reduce the amount of your income that's subject to taxation. You do *that* by reducing the amount of your adjusted gross income and then applying more deductions. This section discusses those strategies.

Reduce Adjusted Gross Income

As a rule, you will gain the most tax savings through form 1040, because that method of filing affords the most opportunities for adjusting your income and taking the most deductions. Itemizing deductions is an important step in reducing taxes, but if you don't have enough qualifying deductions, itemizing won't help.

You may still be able to reduce your adjusted gross income (AGI) by deductions and adjustments. These items reduce the amount of tax you ultimately pay because they lower your ultimate taxable income. Here are some of the deductions and adjustments:

▶ IRA deduction

▶ Educator expense

▶ Student interest loan deduction

▶ Tuition and fee deduction

▶ Health savings account deposits

▶ Moving expenses

▶ Self-employment tax and heath insurance deductions

▶ Alimony paid

These common deductions and adjustments lower your AGI. These adjustments are available even if you don't itemize, but you will need to file form 1040A.

Itemizing Deductions

The purpose of itemizing deductions is to catalog more deductible expenses than the standard deduction figure. Here are the major expenses that make a difference between itemizing and taking the standard deduction:

▶ Mortgage interest expense

▶ State and local property taxes, including sales taxes

▶ Personal property taxes

▶ Cash and noncash contributions to charities

▶ Medical expenses

▶ Many unreimbursed job related expenses

▶ Home office expenses

▶ Losses due to casualty or theft

There are some limitations on certain expenses. Form 1040 instructions explain how much you can claim in certain deductions. Personal tax-preparation software makes these calculations for you so you don't exceed the maximum allowable deduction.

8.5

Credits

Tax credits are dollar-for-dollar reductions in your tax liability. Rather than reducing your amount of taxable income, tax credits reduce your taxes. Here are the major tax credits available to most taxpayers:

▶ Credit for child or dependent care

▶ Credit of the elderly or disabled

▶ Child tax credit

▶ Retirement savings contributions credit

▶ Education credit

▶ Adoption credit

▶ Earned income credit

▶ Foreign tax credit

These reductions in your tax liability, combined with itemized deductions and adjustments to your AGI, are the best way to lower your tax bill.

8.6 ALTERNATIVE MINIMUM TAX

The Other Tax Schedule

What Triggers the AMT

The Alternative Minimum Tax (AMT) was designed to catch wealthy people who were using loopholes in the system to avoid paying any taxes. Unfortunately, the AMT now catches many taxpayers who do not fall into that category. This section looks at the AMT and how you may fall victim to it.

The Other Tax Schedule

The **Alternative Minimum Tax** is, for practical purposes, a separate tax system that operates within the same code as the regular system but has very different rules. Conceived in 1969 to plug loopholes for wealthy taxpayers with huge deductions who paid little or no taxes, it now snares many middle-class taxpayers and unless it is changed will continue to trap even more. The reason is the AMT guidelines were not indexed for inflation, where the main tax code recognizes that much of the growth in income has come from inflation and not in real dollars. The tax brackets have been adjusted so that taxpayers don't pay more taxes just because inflation is pushing up their income, but the AMT guidelines were not adjusted, so many middle-income taxpayers now appear as "wealthy" to that system.

> **WORDS TO GO . . .WORDS TO GO . . .WORDS TO GO**
>
> The **Alternative Minimum Tax** is a parallel tax system that eliminates many common deductions to recalculate your taxes. The AMT was supposed to only catch the very wealthy who claim so many deductions they never paid any taxes. Instead, thanks to inflation, many upper middle class taxpayers are caught by AMT and forced to figure their taxes the traditional way and by the more stringent AMT method. Taxpayers must pay whichever tax bill is the highest.

AMT disallows many deductions and credits that are available under the regular system. For example, under AMT these items are affected:

- You can't use the standard deduction when figuring AMT.

- Interest deduction on home equity loans is not deductible unless you use the proceeds to improve your home.

▶ All personal exemptions are lost.

▶ The deduction for state and local taxes is lost.

▶ Incentive stock options can cause problems.

▶ Deductions for IRA contributions and other income-base calculations can be compromised.

The effect of these changes is to push deductions back into your income number.

What Triggers the AMT

AMT is triggered by income and deductions. As income naturally increases due to inflation, more taxpayers with children and itemized deductions will be required to pay AMT. The IRS predicts by 2010 that 39 percent of all married couples with children will have to pay the AMT.

Form 6251 is where you calculate your AMT. If that number is higher than your regular tax, you pay the difference. You will know you are getting close to being caught by AMT if you look at your return from last year and compare the AMT number to your regular tax number. If the two were close, you may be headed for AMT the next tax year thanks to increased earning due to inflation if nothing else.

You can employ some strategies to head off AMT, such as avoiding using your home equity for a credit line, because you can't deduct the interest under AMT. Prepaying taxes may not be a good idea either, as these are not deductible under AMT. The instructions for form 6251 spell out what is and isn't allowed for deductions. Tax software also does a good job of making these computations for you and warning if AMT is a problem.

8.6

8.7 AUDITS

Audit Triggers

Professional Help

Liability

An audit letter from the IRS ranks near the top of stress-inducing events in most people's lives. Specific indicators on your return may trigger the audit. This section looks at those triggers, professional help in your time of need, and what liabilities you may face.

Audit Triggers

Most taxpayers fear a **tax audit** by the IRS—and some with good reason if they have played loose with the rules. There are certain "red flags" that will make your return a more likely target for an audit. Avoid these and you reduce the odds of an audit:

▶ **Excessive itemized deductions:** If you have huge charitable deductions, for example, you had better have plenty of evidence to back up what you claim. Inflating deductions is one of the most common audit triggers. Don't let that stop you from taking a rightful deduction, but make sure you have the evidence to support it.

▶ **Offshore bank schemes:** Don't fall for the offshore tax dodges that claim to shelter money from the IRS in some foreign bank where it earns some fabulous interest rate tax-free. Check with your accountant before investing in one of these deals to make sure they are legal. Many are not.

▶ **Hiding income:** The IRS does not accept excuses for failing to report income. You may get by with a disagreement about a deduction, but don't try to hide income. People go to jail and/or pay heavy fines for that. One way the IRS finds out is if you are an investor in a partnership or Subchapter S corporation that reports a distribution to shareholders, but you don't report any corresponding income.

▶ **Abusive trusts:** Don't believe people who tell you they can put all your income-producing assets in a trust you control and avoid all taxes.

▶ **At random (almost):** Some returns are picked by a computer scoring method that rates all returns. Returns that score in a certain range may be selected for an audit because other returns scoring in a similar range exhibited problems in the past.

Tax audit is an examination by agents of the IRS of your current and, possibly past, tax returns to ensure they are in compliance with tax law.

Professional Help

If you are audited, you can get help from a tax professional, either a CPA or an enrolled agent. If one of those professionals helped you prepare your taxes, they should be available for the audit. After all, they'll get paid. If you do go with a professional, expect to pay $75 per hour and up.

If you are having a routine audit where no wrongdoing or illegal tax schemes are suspected, you may want to handle it yourself. Some audits are even conducted by mail, which eliminates some of the intimidation factor.

If the IRS is alleging you were involved in a tax shelter or arrangement that could be construed as fraudulent, consider hiring a tax attorney. The IRS is a formidable force that will pursue what it considers tax cheats with vigor.

Liability

Surprisingly, the IRS reports that some audits result in refunds to taxpayers rather than penalties. The rules on deductions are not very clear, so it may be easy for you to read the rule one way and the IRS to interpret it another. If the IRS sees no pattern of obvious deception when it comes to inflating deductions, your deduction may be disallowed and your taxes recomputed. You will likely pay the difference plus interest.

However, if the IRS sees a pattern of over-inflated deductions or, worse, hidden income, you could face severe civil and/or criminal penalties, including heavy fines and time in prison. In addition, if violations are found on returns from one year, the IRS may go back and audit previous years for other violations.

9
COLLEGE FINANCING

9.1 COSTS

Tuition

Books and Supplies

Living Expenses

Saving Expenses

Inexpensive Colleges

It costs a lot of money to send a child to college, but how much depends on many factors. This section looks at the major items you will have to cover and how you can figure out their costs.

Tuition

College tuition costs depend on the school your child chooses and can range from $9,000 to $30,000 a year for four-year institutions. Community colleges that offer two-year programs are still very reasonable in many states—$3,000 a year in many cases. Not everyone pays the same tuition, which is important to remember when it comes time to enroll. If your child is an academic star, top schools can put together "packages" that may include reduced tuition.

You should also be aware it is usually cheaper to attend public college in the state where you are a legal resident. Most schools charge an "out-of-state" tuition that is significantly higher than residents pay. Neighboring states may have reciprocity agreements that allow students to cross state lines and still pay in-state tuitions.

Published college tuition costs do not reflect a wide assortment of assistance that is available to almost every student. Some of this assistance is **needs based,** meaning the family's financial situation may increase the amount of aid the student is eligible to receive.

WORDS TO GO . . .WORDS TO GO . . .WORDS TO GO

Needs based financial assistance is driven by the financial circumstances of the family. This assistance specifically targets lower income households.

Don't consider tuition separate from other costs. If a community college has told you the aid package you qualify for is $x, don't assume that is all you will get at a four-year school, especially a private college. Tuition is very much a negotiated number when viewed in terms of accompanying aid packages.

Books and Supplies

The cost of books and supplies will fluctuate with majors. Science majors must buy expensive books and pay lab fees. Art and music majors have supplies and instruments to buy and maintain, along with lessons. Many colleges require students to have computers, but even if your child's doesn't, most students need one. Cell phones have replaced landline telephones for many college students, so they don't even provide landlines at college. All of these expenses begin adding up. In today's dollars, $3,000 per year is not unusual for these expenses.

Living Expenses

Living expenses can range from almost nothing if the student stays at home to $1,000 a month or more for a shared apartment. Fraternity and sorority houses are options, but they can be more expensive than apartments. Dorm rooms may be in short supply, but more affordable than an off-campus apartment. Many colleges let students buy **meal tickets** to on-campus cafeterias even if they live off campus.

WORDS TO GO . . .WORDS TO GO . . .WORDS TO GO

Meal tickets allow college students to eat at campus dining facilities even if they live off campus. They are often a bargain compared to fast food and may be more convenient than eating all the meals at a distant apartment.

9.1

An option that has attracted considerable attention is buying a place for your student to live while in college. This strategy involves buying a condominium, co-op, or a small house with the idea that in four years or so, you can sell the property for a profit and recover some of your college investment. If you have several children attending the same school, this can work even better assuming the living arrangements work out.

While sound in theory, you should go into this strategy cautiously. First, you should buy with resale in mind, not your student's neighborhood preference. You should also consider the possibility that half way through the first year, your student may decide to leave college. Can you afford the mortgage payments and college expenses simultaneously? College students are not the easiest on living facilities, so plan on some major repairs or renovations before you'll be able to sell the property.

◄ *SEE ALSO 5.3, "Buying a Home"* ▷

Saving Expenses

You can save expenses in a number of areas. One of the main ways is to assign your student some financial responsibility for the education they are receiving. This means summer jobs and possibly working some during the school year to help make ends meet.

Many students begin at a two-year school or community college. A number of states have a system of two-year schools that feed graduates into the four-year campuses to finish their degree. Community colleges in every state are more affordable than the four-year institutions. Getting the first two years out of the way on a less-expensive community college campus makes good financial sense.

Begin your search for a college early. Around 70 percent of all high school students are accepted by their first-choice school. For many families, getting into college is not the struggle—financing the education is the challenge. The system is complicated and time consuming. You should spend as much if not more time learning the financial aid system as you do considering which college your child may attend. The more time you have to work on the forms and with the college's **financial aid officer** (FAO), the more time you will have to tweak and negotiate the best deal for you and your student.

> **WORDS TO GO . . .WORDS TO GO . . .WORDS TO GO**
>
> **Financial aid officer** (FAO) is the key officer at each school who decides who is eligible for how much financial aid and what kind of aid they are to receive.

The expenses you must be particularly concerned about are those not completely covered by financial aid or scholarships. These include living expenses (housing, food, clothes, and so on).

Inexpensive Colleges

In terms of gross dollars, the truly inexpensive colleges are community or two-year schools. These are affordable in most states and offer **Associates Degrees** in different subject areas. However, their primary purpose is to cover the first two years of college so a student can move on to a four-year campus to finish the final two years needed for a degree. Besides community colleges, students can also choose to attend inexpensive state-supported schools.

Inexpensive or expensive is a relative term when talking about college tuition, because financial aid packages must be factored in to the equation. Some of the most generous packages are available at the more expensive private schools, making the net cost to the student relatively low. For example, a small, private college in New York State listed tuition at $17,300 per year, but reported that 92 percent of incoming freshmen received aid worth about $13,100, according to Hobsons Student Union ezine.

9.1

9.2 COLLEGE FINANCIAL AID

How the Process Works
Scholarships
Grants
State Aid
Federal Aid
Application Strategies

Financial assistance for college students comes from a variety of sources. This section looks at the different sources and how you can determine what works for your situation.

How the Process Works

The process of qualifying for financial aid begins with paperwork, specifically the **Free Application for Federal Student Aid (FAFSA)**, which parents can complete after January 1 of their student's senior year in high school. High school guidance offices will have this form, or go to www.fafsa.ed.gov for an online version.

> **WORDS TO GO** . . . *WORDS TO GO* . . . *WORDS TO GO*
>
> **Free Application for Federal Student Aid (FAFSA)** is the main federal form used to qualify for financial aid. It is a detailed questionnaire about your family's income and assets.

Some schools or states may require other forms, but the FAFSA is the main form used by all colleges to determine your family's **need.** The form asks for comprehensive financial information about income and assets of both the parents and the student. Once a college decides to accept your child, the file is turned over to the financial aid officer (FAO) to put together a package of aid that covers the gap between what the school believes you can afford to pay and what it costs. That difference is your need.

Your part is called the **expected family contribution (EFC)** and it should remain constant regardless of how much the school expenses are. For example, if your EFC is $12,000 per year and the state school cost $15,000 per year, your need is $3,000. However, if your child is accepted at a private school where tuition is $25,000 per year, your need is now $13,000. It doesn't always work that simply, because some schools apply their own adjustments to the need formula.

WORDS TO GO . . . WORDS TO GO . . . WORDS TO GO

Need in college financial aid is the difference between what you can afford and what the college costs. The FAO is responsible for presenting you with an aid package that addresses some or all of your need.

Expected family contribution (EFC) is the amount of money the college expects you to pay toward the total cost. The difference between that number and the actual cost of all college expenses for the year is your "need" and that is what the financial aid tries to cover.

The Aid Package

The FAO will present you with an aid package that may contain one or more of these types of aid:

▶ **Scholarships and grants:** These are outright gifts that you don't have to pay back, although some scholarships may require you to maintain a certain grade point average.

▶ **Student loans:** These loans to the student are usually backed by the state or federal government. There is no interest charged while the student is still in school.

▶ **Work-study:** This federally subsidized program provides part-time jobs to students around the campus to pay tuition or living expenses.

9.2

The Financial Deal

The package you are offered by the FAO will indicate how much the school wants your student. FAOs have latitude in making offers and can adjust the mix of aid to make the offer more or less generous. If the school is interested in your student, the aid will cover your need and then some. It will also have a greater portion of grants and scholarships and lesser amounts of loans. On the other hand, if the school is lukewarm about your student, the aid package may not even cover your whole need. There is room to negotiate, especially if the school really wants your student.

When you get the aid offer, look at the grants and scholarships to see if they are for the full four years or just one year. If they are just one year, what happens next year? Will the financial aid officer replace them with others?

Scholarships

Many people think scholarships are only for the athletically or academically gifted. While these students may attract the bigger scholarships, there are many other opportunities for students to cover part of their college cost with smaller scholarships.

Many scholarships are available from sources not connected with a college, but the reality is most scholarship dollars are awarded by colleges. You can use these scholarships (many are one-shot offerings) to pay part of the out-of-pocket portion of college costs.

However, if you are receiving financial aid, you are obligated to tell the college financial office about any outside scholarships you win. There's a good chance the FAO will reduce the amount of aid the college is providing by the amount of the scholarship, so you don't really gain anything. If you call the FAO and make your case that it was your hard work that won the award, you may keep your aid intact.

Some of the scholarships are multi-year and require your student to maintain a minimum grade point average, often in a specific discipline, while others are yours for the asking. All require an application of some kind and many want a short essay on some topic. Your student can often use the same essay or a version of it for multiple submissions. The most difficult part is staying motivated through the paperwork. Because most off-campus scholarships are one-shot awards, your student will need to go through this process every year to keep this type of scholarship money coming in to pay for out-of-pocket expenses.

Where to Find Scholarships

The first place to start is the high school counselor's office—larger schools may have a separate college admissions counselor. This office should have ample literature on available scholarships, especially those with ties to the local community, which are easier to win than ones awarded nationally.

Here are some of the possibilities:

▶ **Service clubs:** Service and civic clubs such as Rotary and Lion's Clubs often award local scholarships.

▶ **Unions:** If one of the parents belongs to a union, check to see if it offers a scholarship.

▶ **Sports groups:** Hunting, fishing, and outdoors groups often award local scholarships.

▶ **Churches:** Many churches provide scholarships.

▶ **Fraternities and sororities:** Local chapters of fraternity and sorority alumna may provide scholarships to children of members.

▶ **Professional organizations:** Chapters of organizations representing professionals may award scholarships.

▶ **Employers:** Your employer may provide a scholarship to students of employees.

This is not a complete list, but an example of the sources of local, noncollege scholarships.

Nationally awarded scholarships are usually worth more in dollars, but attract much more competition. These scholarships are often tied to specific academic endeavors such as music, a branch of science, engineering, and so on. Some require extensive applications, recommendations, and an essay. If your student is gifted in a particular area or field of study, there is undoubtedly a national scholarship offered.

How to Apply

The application process is simple for most noncollege, local scholarships. However, it does take some time and discipline on the part of your student to do the paperwork and write an essay if that's what is required. Because students are often reluctant to take on more "homework," there is often little competition for these scholarships. Extra work on the initial essay can pay off, because it can often be reused on multiple submissions with some tweaking.

9.2

If your student can win even one or two scholarships for $500 or a $1,000, that's less money out of your pocket (or the student's pocket). There are a multitude of websites on scholarships, some about specific offerings with instructions on how to apply, others with information on what individual colleges have to offer, and a third category of sites (some free and some paid) that offer help in finding scholarships.

It is the third category—sites offering help finding scholarships—which you should approach with caution. Some of the websites claiming to have access to a vast database of scholarships for a fee merely repackage what is readily available on the Internet. Before you pay any money for a web service or hire a "scholarship consultant," talk to your high school counselor about whether the services are legitimate or even necessary.

Grants

Grants are free money to pay for your student's college education. Most grant money comes through the college as part of the aid package the FAO will offer. You don't have to pay grant money back.

However, most grants are need-based, as determined by the FAO and federal or state guidelines. Grants are designed to help qualified students go to college without having to repay with interest all of their expenses.

Where to Find Grants

Most grants are from either the federal or state government or the college. You can find grants from other sources, but the bulk of the dollars flow through the colleges themselves. The college will often help you process the application as part of the aid process. The FAO will know, based on the financial information you have provided, what grants your student may get and for how much.

The largest and most well-known grant program is the Pell Grant. The Pell Grant program is federally funded and for under graduates. It is need based and uses the FAFSA to determine eligibility and amount. This is another reason to complete this form and get it to the college as soon after January 1 of your student's senior year as possible.

How to Apply

The application process for grants offered through the college will be coordinated by the FAO. Colleges are not the only sources of grants. The same types of organizations that offer scholarships may also award grants. These groups have a variety of application processes to follow. Your high school counselor's office will have details on many different grant programs available to your student. Some states offer grant programs based on extreme need.

Students may also receive grants based on achievement and/or recognition in a field of study in much the same manner as scholarships.

State Aid

All 50 states have need-based programs of state aid for their residents, and at least half of all states offer some form of merit-based assistance. In most cases, your student must attend a public college in the state where you are a legal resident to receive the assistance. In some cases, students attending private schools are also eligible.

States may use a different formula than federal guidelines for determining if your family qualifies for aid. This is good news for middle and upper-middle class families, because they may qualify for state aid in some states. Don't assume that, because you didn't qualify for federal aid, you won't qualify for state aid—that may not be the case.

How to Find Out What's Available

Your high school counselor's office should be able to tell you the status of aid in your state and what is available. Unfortunately, the function may be housed or named just about anywhere and under any name, so contacting the state directly without guidance from the counselor's office may be confusing.

How to Apply

A number of states use the federal FAFSA form to base their decision, although there may be supplemental forms to complete. Any state financial aid for which you are eligible will be a part of the aid package the colleges send you before April 15. If you apply at two schools, but one has a substantially higher tuition, you may receive a higher grant.

If you are fortunate, your state may also have low-interest guaranteed loans available. These will also be a part of the financial package the FAO offers your student.

Federal Aid

9.2

The bulk of dollars available for student assistance come through federal programs—either grants, loans, or work-study programs. Although some of the loan programs may be administered by private banks, the loans are guaranteed by the federal government, which keeps the interest rates low. Given the high cost of a college education, it is reasonable that a student will leave with some level of debt. These loans are all made to the students with repayment schedules that don't begin until after graduation.

How to Find Out What's Available

Your high school counselor's office will have the appropriate forms for the three main forms of federal assistance:

▶ Pell Grants and others

▶ Federal Supplemental Education Opportunity Grants

▶ Stafford Federal Student Loans

▶ Perkins loans

▶ Plus loans

▶ Work-study program

These programs make up the bulk of federal assistance for college students and appear in the aid package the FAO will offer your student.

Pell Grants

Pell Grants are the largest and best-known program of college aid. The grants are offered on a need basis to undergraduate students who have not earned a Bachelor's degree. The student must be a U.S. citizen and can only receive one grant per year. The amount is based on need and can be over $4,000. Pell Grants are awarded based on information found on the FAFSA.

Many other federal grants can enter the financial aid picture—some are tied to your student's field of study, especially math or science.

Federal Supplemental Education Opportunity Grants

Federal Supplemental Education Opportunity Grants are another source of assistance and are targeted at students in extreme need. Students who have received Pell Grants are given priority. Like Pell Grants, these supplemental grants use information off the FAFSA form.

Stafford Loans

The Stafford Federal Student Loan is the federal student loan program and it offers two types of loans.

▶ **Subsidized:** The government pays the interest while your student is in school and for the first six months after graduating. The loan is need based and is determined by the FAFSA form.

▶ **Unsubsidized:** This is a straight loan regardless of need. Interest payments can be accrued and rolled into the principal if the student wants.

The Stafford Loan program is for students. They are responsible for repayment. The amount a student can borrow depends on a number of factors. You can find out by visiting the federal student aid website www.studentaid.ed.gov.

Perkins Loans

Perkins loans are a federal loan program that offer the best interest rate (5 percent as of 2006) of all the federal loan programs. Colleges receive a sum of money from the government for the program and the FAOs get to parcel it out to their best prospects. Don't turn down a Perkins loan without carefully considering the consequences of losing this low-cost financing.

Plus Loans

A federal loan program for parents will let them borrow up to the total cost of college minus the aid the student receives. The Parents Loan for Undergraduate Students (PLUS) requires no asset or income limits, but you do need to pass a credit check. These are not need-based loans. You can find more information at the same website for Stafford loans.

Work-Study Program

This is a needs-based program that provides students a part-time job with the college. The salary goes to offset college expenses.

All of these aid resources will be noted on the aid package the FAO puts together for your student.

Application Strategies

The process of applying for financial aid is one that must be managed and organized. There are deadlines (different ones for different colleges) for you to submit material and applications. Your best source of those dates is the bulletins from the colleges themselves. General books on the topic may have the dates wrong, as may websites that provide general information. It is helpful if your student has narrowed the field of possible schools down to a half-dozen or less. Not only will this save paperwork, but also expense because it costs money to file multiple applications.

When to Apply

You only need to file one FAFSA form per student per year, regardless of how many schools the student is interested in. The form has a space to designate where it will be sent. You may be required to complete the College Board's CSS/Financial Aid PROFILE Application, especially if your student is thinking about a private school. In addition, many schools have supplemental forms for you to complete.

Based on the schools your student chooses, identify and gather all the forms you will need along with the deadlines for each form. If you miss a financial aid deadline, you may miss most of the funding you could have received. This is an absolute must. Schools award aid in bulk. If your student's application misses that bulk award, there may not be much left for the school to work with if you need substantial or even moderate assistance.

Your FAFSA and other material are sent to a third-party company that does a "needs assessment" and forwards that information on to the schools you name in your application. You can't submit a FAFSA before January 1 of your student's senior year. The aid application may go directly to the school or to a processor for analyzing.

Treat each college like a separate project, noting the dates when material is due. Be sure you mail it far enough in advance to arrive on time or consider using overnight mail with a return receipt so you'll know it got there on time. Make sure you have the correct address.

Filling Out the Forms

The FAFSA and other financial aid forms require detailed financial information. Don't wait until the last minute to begin work on the forms. You will need tax returns, bank records, W-2 forms, brokerage records, mortgage statements, and any other financial document relating to income or assets you own.

Many of the questions are directed at the student and others at the parents; be sure you are clear on who is answering the question. When answering questions on income and assets, it is very important that you understand exactly what the question is asking and answer it specifically—otherwise you might cost your student aid dollars or the processor might return the form to you for corrections, which will just slow the process down.

9.3 PREPAID TUITION PLANS

State Plans

Private Plans

Advantages and Disadvantages

Prepaid tuition plans help you aim to beat the escalating cost of college tuition by buying credits now. The plans let you invest in a fund that guarantees your student tuition credits at a price you know today. This section looks at the two main types of prepaid tuition plans.

State Plans

The rapidly rising costs of college have given birth to an investment vehicle named after Section 529 of the tax code that allows you to put aside money for qualified college expenses in an account that grows tax-deferred. There are two basic types of these "529 plans." One type is a pure savings program where earnings grow tax-deferred and the other is a way to purchase tuition credits now for use in the future. The prepaid tuition plans let you purchase tuition at state and, in some cases, private schools within the state at a current price for your student who may still be in elementary school.

Prepaid tuition plans are popular because, regardless of how high tuition climbs, you have locked in a price. The money grows, tax-deferred, until it is time to withdraw it for college expenses, when it comes out of the account tax free. Unfortunately, because tuition has risen so much faster than inflation in recent years, some prepaid plans have stopped accepting contributions, while others are now charging a premium on **tuition credits.**

9.3

WORDS TO GO . . . *WORDS TO GO . . . WORDS TO GO*

Tuition credits are a way to prepay college costs by paying a set price for tuition credits today that can be used in the future by your children. However, with college costs rising at a rate faster than many state university systems anticipated, many have stopped selling the credits or capped their future value.

The tuition credits the prepaid plan purchases can be used at any public college in the state and often their value can be assigned to private school tuition. You do not have to be a resident of the state to contribute to the plan, but you may give up some tax benefits if you are not.

Many of the plans have very high limits on annual contributions and allow you to switch the beneficiary if your student decides not to go to college.

Private Plans

One of the disadvantages is that the real benefits of prepaid tuition plans are limited to the state where the fund is located, but what if your student wants to go somewhere else? Some private (as opposed to state sponsored) plans offer more flexibility. One plan has arrangements with over 200 colleges and universities so students can attend any participating school with no penalty. It's hard to predict what your student will want when the time comes; this may ease some of those concerns.

Just because you have a tuition arrangement through a private plan does not guarantee admission to any of the participating schools.

Advantages and Disadvantages

Prepaid tuition plans are not easy to understand and can only be used for specific types of expenses. Although they were initially very popular, they have become less so in recent years. 529 savings plans offer more flexibility and have caught the imagination of many consumers. Here are some of the advantages of 529 prepaid college tuition plans:

- ▶ Lock in tuition rates years before they are needed
- ▶ Change beneficiaries if student changes mind
- ▶ May earn a state income tax deduction for contributions
- ▶ No worries about fluctuations in the stock market
- ▶ May work well if student is starting school within five years
- ▶ Out-of-state relatives can invest in fund

Here are some of the disadvantages:

- ▶ Some plans have stopped accepting contributions or are charging a premium due to rapidly rising costs
- ▶ If a student decides to not go to school and you don't have another child, you may have to pay 10 percent penalty to the IRS and taxes on the earnings
- ▶ You could pay penalties for early withdrawal if funds are not used for college

▶ Watch out for excessive management fees that will reduce the amount invested for education expenses

▶ There may be complications if you have to move out of state

▶ If you transfer fund assets out of state, you may have to repay any deduction from previous state income taxes

Prepaid college tuition plans make sense for some people, but not for everyone. You should consider talking to your accountant or tax advisor before committing to one of these plans.

9.3

9.4 TAX-FREE COLLEGE SAVINGS PLANS

What They Are

Investing in One

Tax-Free Investment Plans

Advantages and Disadvantages

Tax-free college savings plans refer to a group of programs and products that let you save money on a tax-deferred basis and use it tax-free to pay for college expenses. This section looks at the main tax-free college savings plans.

What They Are

College tax-free savings plans come in several forms, but the largest and most popular one is the 529 college savings plan. This is the other half to the 529 prepaid tuition plan offered by many states. The 529 savings plan is much more popular, probably because it is easier to understand and covers more expenses than the prepaid tuition plan.

Every state offers a 529 savings plan, while less than a third offer the prepaid tuition plan. The savings plan is a set of mutual funds that you invest in, much like a 401(k). The investment company managing the 529 savings plan for the state offers a family of funds ranging from aggressive growth to conservative for you to choose from. Some of the funds offer a version of lifecycle funds that adjust the asset allocation based on the age of your future student. If you enroll when your child is very young, the fund will be more aggressive, but as the child grows older and closer to needing the money for college, the fund reduces the risk by shifting assets into holdings that are more conservative and stable.

◁ *SEE ALSO 10.4, "Asset Allocation"* ▷

◁ *SEE ALSO 11.2, "Types of Mutual Funds"* ▷

Investing In One

In most states, there is one fund that is either sold direct to consumers or through brokers. There is usually a low minimum investment ($1,000–$2,000) and smaller minimum subsequent investments. However, you can put large sums of money in these accounts, as can anyone (grandparents, other relatives, and so on).

Investing in these accounts is a long-term commitment to let the fund build in value and let compounding work over time. Because the earnings grow tax-deferred, time will work in your favor. If your state offers a tax deduction on state income taxes for contributions to its 529 plan, it would be in your best interest to take full advantage of that benefit.

Tax-Free Investment Plans

In addition to the state 529 programs, the Taxpayer Relief Act of 1997 created Education IRAs, although they were never about retirement. Since then the accounts have been revised and renamed and are now called Coverdell Educational Savings Accounts. These accounts allow up to $2,000 a year to be contributed per child. The contributions aren't tax deductible, but if you use the money for qualified college expenses, the withdrawals are tax-free.

There are some limits on who can contribute based on income. You must have less than $190,000 in modified adjusted gross income ($95,000 for single filers) in order to qualify for a full $2,000 contribution. The $2,000 maximum is gradually phased out if your modified adjusted gross income falls between $190,000 and $220,000 ($95,000 and $110,000 for single filers).

You can establish a Coverdell ESA at almost any bank, mutual fund, or financial institution. Just make sure the parent remains the owner and the account won't interfere with financial aid.

You can contribute to a 529 plan at the same time you are funding a Coverdell ESA.

9.4

Advantages and Disadvantages

Tax-free investing plans like 529 savings plans and Coverdell ESAs have many advantages when planning how you are going to pay for college, but they also have some pitfalls. Here are some of the advantages:

- ▶ 529 savings plans and Coverdell ESAs let you pay for college with tax-free dollars.
- ▶ Both offer the chance for market growth given enough time.
- ▶ Coverdell ESA accounts are not tied to a school or a state.
- ▶ You can use 529 savings plans to cover many college expenses, not just tuition.
- ▶ Transferring assets from one 529 savings plan to another is cleaner because the assets convert to dollars, not tuition credits.

▶ Your state may offer a tax deduction for up to a limit for your contribution to its 529 saving plan.

However, there are disadvantages:

▶ 529 savings plans and Coverdell ESAs need years to allow the assets to grow.

▶ If the student chooses not to go to school and there is no other beneficiary, you will pay a penalty to get your money out.

▶ You are locking up your money for a long time.

▶ Management fees may be high.

▶ Coverdells are limited to $2,000 per student per year.

If you are confident your child will be a college student someday (or at least one of your children will be), these savings and investment plans may make sense.

9.5 COMMERCIAL LOANS

Personal Loans

Home Equity Loans

Other Loans

Advantages and Disadvantages

After student loans, borrowing by parents is often required to cover what financial aid does not pay for in college expenses. This section looks at loan options for parents.

Personal Loans

If the financial aid package, which includes student loans, does not cover the full cost of college, parents may need to borrow some or all of the difference. They have several alternatives, including one that was discussed earlier, the PLUS loan through the federal government. The remaining options are commercial loans that require a good credit rating. Some banks specialize in this lending and the college financial officer may have some recommendations.

These are not inexpensive loans, but if you have covered most of the expenses through savings and financial aid, you may not need to borrow much, either. A bank that is familiar with college-expense lending will be easier to work with in terms of getting the loan approved with terms that match your need.

9.5

Home Equity Loans

If you have substantial equity in your home or other real estate, a home-equity line of credit may be a smart way to finance those extra expenses. With home-equity lines of credit, you use only as much of your equity as you need. In most cases, you receive a special set of checks to tap the line of credit.

This works better than a straight home-equity loan or second mortgage, where you receive a lump sum, because you may not need the whole amount at once, but only part to pay bills at semester breaks, for example.

Interest on home-equity lines of credit loans is tax deductible in most cases, which is a nice benefit. As you repay the credit you use, it renews the amount available, so if you have more than one child in college you can continue to use the credit line.

Other Loans

There are other ways to borrow money for college funds. Some may make sense, while you should avoid others.

You can borrow from your 401(k) or pension plan. Many retirement plans will let you borrow money for college; however, unless this is your only option, it's a bad idea. First, your retirement is more important than funding college. Children can find ways to pay for their own college if they really want to go—they can take off a year and work to save money or go part-time or take more student loans. You can't finance your retirement. In addition, if something happens and you lose your job, the loan comes due immediately.

You can borrow on **margin** from your stock investments. That is a dangerous and highly risky strategy over a short period because it depends upon prices going up.

> **WORDS TO GO . . .WORDS TO GO . . .WORDS TO GO**
>
> **Margin** is an investment strategy that uses borrowed money to increase buying power. Investors with good credit can borrow up to 50 percent of the value of their assets from their broker. Usually the money is used to buy more stock. The investor must maintain the value of the account at a certain level. If the price of the stock begins to fall, the investor will be asked to put more money into the account or sell the stock and pay off the margin loan. This is known as a margin call.

Advantages and Disadvantages

Ideally, parents would not have to borrow money to put their student through school; however that's not the reality for many families today. Before plunging into debt, it would be smart to meet with a financial planner who could look at your whole picture and recommend a course of action.

Depending on your total financial picture, loans to the parents may or may not make sense. Here are some advantages to certain loans:

▶ PLUS loans are offered through the federal government and carry a low interest rate

▶ Home equity lines of credit let you draw down just what you need and not pay interest on a larger sum—in addition, the interest is tax deductible

Not all loans are the best of circumstances. Here are the disadvantages of some types of personal loans:

▶ Loans from retirement programs take money that should be earning interest out of the account and may be difficult to repay if you have financial trouble.

▶ Margin loans on stocks are risky because prices can drop, forcing your broker to issue a margin call for more money in the account.

9.5

9.6 EMPLOYER-SPONSORED PLANS

What Is Offered

Advantages and Disadvantages

Many employers, especially larger ones, provide a range of resources to employees to help with college expenses. In this section, we look at those options.

What Is Offered

If you work for a large company, you may have another resource to tap for scholarships and loans. A number of companies offer scholarships to children of employees. Sometimes these are needs-based, but often they are achievement-oriented, especially if the company is involved in technology.

Companies may also make low-interest loans available to employees, either directly or through contracting with a lender and negotiating a lower rate for employees.

Your company's human relations department should have complete information on what resources are available and how to apply for assistance.

Advantages and Disadvantages

There are some distinct advantages in working for a company that provides assistance to the children of employees:

▶ You are competing in a smaller universe for scholarships and grants, which increases the chances of winning.

▶ Loans are likely to be on very reasonable terms with repayment schedules that fit your compensation level.

There can also be disadvantages:

▶ If you have a special loan with your company and want to change jobs, the loan may come due as soon as you give notice.

▶ How many ties do you want to your company? If you love your job and your work and don't plan to leave, then this is not a problem; however, what if you have some financial problems not related to work and find you can't make the payment? Is that going to jeopardize your job?

9.7 ALTERNATIVES TO TRADITIONAL COLLEGE

Vocational Schools

Internet Schools

Not every young person is right for college and college is not right for every young person. There are alternatives to a four-year academic degree that may provide a satisfying career. In this section, we'll talk about other choices besides college.

Vocational Schools

Vocational schools prepare students for technical or skilled jobs in the workforce. These skills can range from electronics assembly to welding to heating/air conditioning repair. Some of the classes are one semester long, while others may last several years. To become a journeyman electrician or plumber requires a certain number of classroom hours along with in-field training.

Vocational schools may be standalone separate facilities or part of the curriculum offered at community colleges. The standalone facilities vary in quality and should be researched to ensure they provide a real education and aren't a front for generating financial aid dollars from the government.

Internet Schools

9.7

As the Internet gains wider penetration in households, schools have begun to offer online classes as a way to draw more students, particularly adult learners, into their system. At first, these efforts were looked at with disdain by traditional schools and as nothing more than updated diploma mills of earlier days when a person could get a degree from a phony college.

That still exists, unfortunately. However, many colleges have changed their ideas about online learning and added it to their offerings. Some offer degree programs that students can complete with most of the work done online and by telephone and mail. The students are required to spend a limited amount of time on the campus. Some programs do everything online and the degree the student receives is no different from one another student who spends four years on campus would receive.

Online classes are not cheap and may cost considerably more than regular classes. However, you can attend college from the comfort of your home and you don't even have to be in the same state to attend. Overall costs will be lower. Critics argue that a significant portion of the value of a college education is being physically on campus and participating in class and interacting with students and professors.

10

INVESTMENT PLANNING AND MANAGEMENT

DEFINING INVESTMENT OPTIONS

Mutual Funds and ETFs

Equities (Stocks)

Bonds

Cash

Annuities

Real Estate

Comparison of Options

Investors have a wide choice of investment options to reach their financial goals. However, not all investment options are equal—each has a place in your portfolio, but none should be the sole resident. This section examines investment options and how they compare.

Mutual Funds and ETFs

More people own mutual funds than any other single investment product. Mutual funds offer investors a tremendous range of investment opportunities, with over 8,500 different funds on the market. Funds can be sorted by investment objectives—some invest in rapidly growing young companies, while others take a more conservative approach.

Investors are drawn to mutual funds because of their professional management and **diversification,** which gives you a quality portfolio that would be difficult for an individual to replicate. Most mutual funds sell shares directly to investors and buy them back when the investor wants to sell, which makes it easy to get in and out of funds.

You can get into most mutual funds with a relatively low initial investment and still lower subsequent investments, which makes mutual funds ideal for automatic investment programs.

The success of an **actively managed** mutual fund (its return) depends, in part, on the expertise of the fund manager in buying and selling securities for the fund. A large measure of success is also helped or hindered by the fund's expenses.

Mutual funds with high **expense ratios** have a difficult time achieving good returns for investors over long periods. High expense ratios make it difficult for mutual funds to achieve better than average returns because of the drag the fund must overcome before showing a positive return to investors.

Low-cost, **passively managed** mutual funds are considered better choices for long-term investors. These funds hold expense ratios to one percent or less. Most of these low-cost funds are index funds, which track major stock and bond indexes.

WORDS TO GO . . .WORDS TO GO . . .WORDS TO GO

Diversification is the reduction of risk by spreading investment dollars over numerous stocks and or bonds to minimize the impact should one of the investments turn bad.

Actively managed mutual funds are open-end funds that employ a portfolio manger who buys and sells stocks and bonds in an attempt to post a better return than the market, usually represented by some stock index, such as the S&P 500.

Expense ratio is the percentage of assets used to cover the expenses of the mutual fund. These expenses are deducted from the fund's assets, which lowers the shareholders' return. The expenses include the management fee, operating expenses, investing fees, and other fees.

Passively managed mutual funds track specific stock or market indexes such as the S&P 500 or the Dow. The funds are passive because there are no investment decisions. The fund mirrors the index by investing in the stocks that comprise the index. This keeps expenses extremely low.

Exchange Traded Funds (ETFs) are a new type of security that looks very much like an index mutual fund, but is traded like a stock on the open market. ETFs track the major and numerous minor stock, bond, and commodity indexes. New ETFs are introduced on a weekly basis. Investing in an ETF is very similar to investing in an index mutual fund, except you buy it as you would a stock through a broker. Buying an ETF accomplishes the same diversification as an index fund, but with more trading opportunities.

10.1

Mutual funds and ETFs fill a variety of niches in a portfolio and can be the main investment vehicles for investors who want to take advantage of their many benefits. Most mutual funds are best suited for long-term investment strategies because of their ownership of common stock.

◁ *SEE ALSO Chapter 11, "Investing in Mutual Funds and Exchange Traded Funds"* ▷

Equities (Stocks)

Equities, popularly known as stocks, have been the bedrock investment for many people for years. A share of stock represents ownership in the company. As an owner, you have certain rights and benefits. You vote on important issues such as who serves on the board of directors and other matters.

If the company does well, you may share in the profits through stock **dividends,** which are cash payments to shareholders. Not all companies distribute profits back to shareholders. Some companies reinvest them back in the company to finance rapid growth. This is a fine strategy if the company is growing.

Stocks can be classified by the expectations placed on them by the market. **Growth stocks** are expected to grow at a pace faster than the rest of the market. **Value stocks** are said to be under priced by the market. Stocks are also classified by the size of the company and by the industrial sector they serve.

WORDS TO GO . . .WORDS TO GO . . .WORDS TO GO

Dividends are cash payments (usually, but not always) to shareholders by companies. Dividends are a distribution of profits to the owners. Companies that pay regular dividends are valued for that extra return they provide shareholders.

Growth stocks represent companies that are growing at a faster pace than the market in general. These companies often plow profits back into the company to finance more growth, which investors count on to keep the value of their stock increasing. If the company stops growing, even for a quarter, the stock market may lose confidence in the company and the stock's price can plummet.

Value stocks represent companies that investors believe the market has underpriced. The stock price may be depressed because the company's business is out of favor or for some other reason. Investors believe the stock will eventually return to a higher price that more accurately reflects the value of the company.

Stocks are more risky than mutual funds because investing in one stock is more risky than investing in 50 stocks like a mutual fund does. If one stock does poorly out of the 50 owned by the mutual fund, it will not have that much impact on the performance of the 50 as a whole. If you only own a few stocks and one does poorly, you are in trouble.

Your risk may be high with some stocks, but your potential return is also great. Stocks can grow and keep growing with no real limits. Microsoft is one of the largest companies in the world, yet there was a time when most people could have bought the whole company with their credit card limit (if it had been for sale). Many other investments have artificial or practical limits on how much you can make, but common stock has no ceiling.

Stocks, however, do have a floor. You can lose your entire investment if the stock becomes worthless because the company goes out of business or goes bankrupt. A company's stock price can also simply go nowhere. You may buy it at $25 per share—and five years later, it's $26 per share. Not a good return on your investment.

The key is to pick companies that exhibit growth qualities that are sustainable over the long term. That's more difficult than it sounds, but not impossible. Some investors enjoy the nitty-gritty of doing the research themselves, while others rely on stockbrokers or advisors to help them make selections.

Investing in stocks is a long-term commitment. No less than three years and preferably five is required as a minimum holding period. Over time, a broadly diversified basket of stocks has consistently returned in the 10 to 12 percent range in almost any 20-year period. That doesn't mean if you buy two stocks and hold them for two years, you should expect that return. It does mean that over long periods, stocks have been good investments.

◁ *SEE ALSO Chapter 12, "Investing in Stocks"* ▷

Bonds

Bonds are a debt that must be repaid. The U.S. Treasury, government agencies, municipalities, and corporations issue bonds of various lengths to **maturity.** A popular maturity for long-term bonds is 10 years, but you can find bonds with maturities ranging from 1 to 100 years. Although not technically bonds, the U.S. Treasury issues "bills" with maturities from 30 days to one year that have most of the same features bonds do.

10.1

Most bonds represent an income stream for the life of the bond, plus a repayment of the bond's principal or **face value** when the bond matures. For example, a 10-year, $1,000 bond with a $60 coupon pays $60 annually for 10 years and then pays the bond's face value of $1,000 back to the buyer. You can make money two ways with bonds: buy a bond and hold it to maturity, pocketing the annual income; or trade bonds for profit if they rise in value.

Most investors own bonds because they provide stability to their portfolio and a reliable source of income. This stability counters the unpredictable nature of stocks, which may change price dramatically in a short period. Bonds are appealing to conservative investors who are more concerned about the preservation of capital than growth—persons at or in retirement for example.

High quality bonds will make an annual interest payment that investors can count on and return the face value of the bond at maturity. Investors give up the opportunity to earn anymore than what the bond pays for the knowledge that they can count on this payment.

The other way to make (or lose) money with bonds is trading them on the **secondary market.** Bonds are very sensitive to interest rates because once a bond is issued, its rate is locked in. If market rates rise, the bond is no longer as valuable because newer bonds will pay a higher rate. If market interest rates fall, the bond increases in value because it is paying more than newer bonds. Traders attempt to capitalize on these differences. As with any trading situation, there can be winners and losers.

WORDS TO GO . . .WORDS TO GO . . .WORDS TO GO

Maturity is when a bond reaches the end of its financial life and the face value or principal is returned to the owner. Bonds may have maturities of just a few years or may stretch out for many years.

Face value is the amount the bond pays at maturity. It is usually the amount the investor pays for a newly issued bond, but may not be the price an invest pays on the open market.

Secondary market is any market for a security after the initial issue. In the secondary market, securities are bought and sold among investors rather than from the company or agency that issued the stock or bond initially. Stock exchanges are secondary markets. For bonds, most trades are done through brokers matching buyers and sellers.

For most investors, bonds fill two needs: first, as a mid-term investment (five to seven years) that generates current income; and second, as a relatively safe way to meet a financial goal in the future (tuition payment for college, for example).

◁ *SEE ALSO Chapter 13, "Investing in Bonds"* ▷

Cash

Cash management is an important part of any personal finance and investment strategy. Cash plays three roles in our financial life. First, it keeps the lights on and the pantry full. We need a certain amount of cash to cover our household operating expenses each month, plus some extra for those unplanned for bills we all expect. Secondly, we need a good **emergency cash reserve** to pay all those bills if we lose some or all of our income due to a job loss or medical problem or whatever. This cash has to be readily available without delay or penalty, yet earning as much as it safely can. Thirdly, we need cash as part of our investment program. This cash is money waiting to be invested or from a cashed-out investment. It needs to work as hard as it can for us, yet be available for reinvestment in something that has a higher chance of a better return.

WORDS TO GO . . .WORDS TO GO . . .WORDS TO GO

Emergency cash reserve is a ready supply of cash in bank products or a money market mutual fund that you can tap in a hurry in the event of an emergency such as the loss of a job, a big uninsured medical expense, or some other financial crisis. You should have enough to keep your household running for six months.

Most household money is in and out of checking accounts so quickly it has little time to earn much for us. If you can find an interest-bearing checking account that does not have high fees or high average daily balance requirements, you might earn enough to pay for your checks each year. Be careful, however, of fees that can negate any advantage of interest the account might pay.

Your emergency cash reserve can go into accounts that are more restrictive in account activity (because until you need the reserve, you shouldn't be touching the money) but pay a higher interest rate. In the event you need to access the money in an emergency, you can transfer it to your regular checking account.

Cash for your investing accounts must be placed with consideration of what other uses are available. If you're not comfortable with market conditions for investing at the moment, cash investments in certificates of deposit and money market mutual funds may be a good place to temporarily park your cash. Conservative investors, including people at or near retirement, may be more interested in preserving their cash than risk growing it.

◀ SEE ALSO *Chapter 3, "Banking"* ▶

Annuities

Annuities are sold by life insurance companies and are a regular series of payments that continue for a set period or until you die. Investors buy an annuity with a single payment or a series of payments that are more like deposits.

Annuity payments to the investor can begin immediately or be deferred to some time in the future. Typically, immediate annuities are bought with a lump-sum deposit and the investor begins receiving payments right away. Annuities are often used to fund retirement programs—earnings grow tax-free until they are withdrawn. Investors may make periodic deposits into a deferred annuity until retirement age and then begin receiving payments.

Annuities may pay either fixed or variable payments. A **fixed annuity** pays a constant income stream over the life of the contract, while a **variable annuity's** payments may change based on how the underlying portfolio does in the market.

WORDS TO GO . . .WORDS TO GO . . .WORDS TO GO

A **fixed annuity** is a contract with an insurance company that pays a fixed amount, usually monthly, for a stated period. The insurance company guarantees the principal and interest.

A **variable annuity** is a contract with an insurance company that pays a minimum interest rate, usually very low, and the rest of the payments vary depending on the market performance of the investments, which are mutual funds.

Payout options for annuities are numerous. You can receive the benefits of the annuity paid out over 5, 10, or virtually any number of years. You can also have the annuity pay you a monthly income for the rest of your life regardless of how long (or short) your life is. This solves the problem of out-living your money.

Annuities can best be used as a supplement to your retirement plan—there are no limits on how much you can invest in them. They're not as tax efficient as they might sound, because you face personal income taxes on the earnings (and deposits, if bought with pre-tax dollars).

Annuities come with fees that can eat into the returns offered by the various products. Variable annuities, in particular, may have high fees associated with managing the investment accounts.

By choosing low-fee products, investors can use annuities to supplement their retirement fund when they have maxed out other funding sources like 401(k) plans and individual retirement accounts.

Real Estate

Real estate is an investment most people should consider, but it requires some thought and personal assessment. You can add real estate to your portfolio by directly owning income-producing properties, or indirectly by owning investment products (mutual funds, mortgages, mortgage-backed securities, and so on).

Admittedly, the two methods aren't that similar, but they both allow you to get into the real estate market.

Commercial or industrial real estate ventures are beyond the financial limits of most investors. The opportunities for average investors are in residential properties—single family and small, multifamily dwellings.

Investing in income-producing real estate has many advantages, but it isn't for everybody. It's not the same as sending off a check to a mutual fund and letting a professional manager do all the work. To make it work—and take all the tax advantages available—you must play an active role in the management of the property.

One advantage of investing in residential real estate is that it is a local market you can get to know with some legwork. It responds to local economic conditions more sharply than to national factors. Real estate demand and prices in your community may be booming, while other markets are depressed. To succeed in this type of investing, there's no substitute for market knowledge: are prices rising or falling, where are rents going, how long does it take to sell a house, and so on.

Investing in residential real estate requires using leverage to make the most of your investing dollars, but that raises the risk factor too high for some people. **Leverage** is using borrowed money to increase your purchasing power. It works wonders when prices are rising and you can sell your property for a profit. However, if the real estate market slumps, as it does everywhere from time to time, leverage can work against you. In a deep real estate slump, it is possible, with a low money down loan, to owe more than the property is worth. Some markets take years to recover the real estate value lost in a major slump.

WORDS TO GO . . .WORDS TO GO . . .WORDS TO GO

Leverage is the use of borrowed money to increase your purchasing power. Because the money must be paid back, a slump will send the inherent values of real estate into a deep depression. Many investors will find it difficult to put their trust in stocks again.

Investing in income-producing real estate ties up your money, sometimes for much longer than you anticipated. Real estate is a long-term investment that's difficult to liquidate in a hurry.

You can also participate in the real estate market by investing indirectly through mutual funds or other securities. There are mutual funds that invest in real estate, including a hybrid called **real estate investment trusts** that have special rules for distributing income.

There are other opportunities to invest indirectly in real estate, such as buying mortgage-back securities and other types of notes tied to the market. However, none of these options is a substitute for actual ownership of income-producing property.

Comparison of Options

Investors have many choices when it comes to finding investment products to help them reach their financial goals. Some people may feel like there are too many choices. Here are the main jobs your investment program must accomplish and the products that will get you there:

Core Holdings

It is not necessary to invest in all the options presented here. Many investors can do without annuities or real estate. However, it is important to achieve the right balance for your situation and to adjust that balance as your life changes. Some mix of stocks (individual and/or mutual funds), bonds (individual and/or mutual funds), and cash is considered the core holding or portfolio for investors. That doesn't mean you can't own other options, but the bulk (80 percent plus) of your assets should be in this core portfolio.

Stay Ahead of Inflation

All of the investment options offer growth opportunities. However, you need to stay ahead of inflation or your assets won't really be growing. Stock mutual funds, if their expense ratios are very low, offer a chance for growth beyond inflation, as do common stocks. Real estate has been a traditional inflation hedge, but you shouldn't have more than 10 percent of your assets tied up in actual income-producing property. Bonds (with a few exceptions), annuities, and cash are not good places to protect large portions of your assets from inflation.

Growth with Acceptable Risk

This is a very personal assessment all investors must make based on their tolerance for risk. Some investment products are inherently more risky than others, but all investment products carry some risk. Here they are from least risky to most risky:

- ▶ Cash
- ▶ Annuities
- ▶ Bonds
- ▶ Real estate
- ▶ Mutual funds
- ▶ Stocks

You could reorder that list several different ways depending on how you view risk.

Liquidity

If you need to, how quickly can you get out of an investment with the least amount of penalty or possible loss? No one wants to consider the worst possible circumstances, but things do happen. If you need to liquidate fast, these go from easiest to hardest: cash, mutual funds, stocks, bonds, annuities, real estate.

10.1

10.2 INVESTMENT OBJECTIVES

Long-Term Objectives
Short-Term Objectives
Appropriate Product Selection

Investment objectives give you a target to aim for, and the right investment product is the tool that will help you reach your goal. This section discusses setting objectives and selecting investment products.

Long-Term Objectives

Long-term objectives are at least five years in the future and for most investors fall into two major categories: funding a college education for their children and building a comfortable retirement fund. We are not a society that easily works toward long-term goals. We are much more comfortable and familiar with goals and objectives that are immediate or in the near future, which may account for why so many retirement accounts are under-funded.

You can finance a college education if you don't have enough saved, but you can't borrow your way through retirement. Accomplishing this goal takes commitment and a willingness to sacrifice something now for a benefit in the future. Rather than picturing a bank account, picture yourself in retirement doing what you want to do. If your dream is to sail to the Caribbean, go price the boat you want, start planning your trip, find out what it will cost to live on the islands, and so on. Come up with a number to make your dream a reality—and assume it will cost more by the time your retire. The point is to put some emotional energy behind your objectives rather than sterile numbers.

Short-Term Objectives

Short-term objectives are less than five years away, and may be in three years or less. These might include saving for a down payment on a house or a second home, buying a new car, or some other major expense. Short-term objectives have immediacy that may draw your attention away from far-away objectives such as retirement. You must find a balance between those short-term needs (or wants) and your long-term goals. It's too easy to put retirement funding, in particular, on hold while other, more immediate (and fun) objectives are met. This is a mistake you will pay for in later years.

Appropriate Product Selection

Your best chance at reaching your long-term objectives is through stocks and bonds (either individual and/or mutual fund ownership). Historically, these vehicles working together have produced the best results over long periods. However, stocks are not appropriate for investment objectives that are less than five years away. The volatility in the markets makes them too unpredictable for short-term objectives. Long-term bonds (ten years or more) offer higher yields, but have higher risks. Intermediate bonds in the five to seven year range may be the best approach.

In the short-term, bonds and timed bank products such as CDs offer the best and safest way to meet investment objectives. Bonds of less than two years may not be competitive with bank products, but this is easy to check before investing.

If you have some small portion of your assets in real estate, you can target them at long-term objectives. This gives you a big window so you can choose when conditions are best to sell. That window may come in five years, or seven, or ten, or never. The point is, you can't count on selling at a specific time, because the real estate market operates on its own schedule.

10.2

10.3 RISK AND REWARD RELATIONSHIP

Risk Tolerance

Risk Premium

Expected Returns and Risk

Managing Returns

Calculating Return on Investment

Investing involves some degree of risk. How much you are willing to accept depends on your tolerance and what you expect as a potential return. This section discusses risk tolerance and the price and expected return for taking a risk.

Risk Tolerance

All investing involves some risk. The market is unforgiving on this point: the higher the potential reward, the higher the risk you will not achieve that reward and may lose some or all of your investment. There are no "insider secrets" or "millionaire tricks" like the ones that show up in your e-mail inbox. Every experienced investor knows their tolerance for risk and adjusts their investment strategy accordingly. Risk-adverse investors choose conservative products and strategies that have a lower chance of failure but offer a limited chance for growth. They can do quite well, but may need to invest more to achieve their goals.

Investors with a higher risk tolerance may be more aggressive in their product selection and investing strategies. Does this mean they will do better than conservative investors? Not at all, nor does it mean they will fail. It means they have increased the odds that their investments will grow faster than with a more conservative strategy and accepted the risk that this strategy could fail and they could lose money.

Which is the correct strategy? The one that is right for you.

Risk Premium

Investors must be rewarded for taking risks—if not, what is the point of taking a risk? If a very safe investment and a very risky investment could both pay you 5 percent, which would you choose? There would be no reason or incentive to pick the risky investment. However, if the risky investment might pay you 11 percent, you may want to think about it—is the extra 6 percent worth the risk?

In this case, the extra 6 percent is called the risk premium. It is what investors expect for the risk over a safe investment.

Here's how you can calculate it: Many investors use an absolute safe return as the base, such as the return on U.S. Treasury Bills. This is considered the safest investment there is, because it is backed by the full faith and credit of the U.S. government. If Treasury Bills are yielding 4 percent, that's the safe number. Any investment that has any risk at all will have to pay more than that. How *much* it will have to pay depends on the type of investment and how risky it is.

This is somewhat subjective, because each individual investor's risk tolerance will influence how they rank products for risk premium. If you believe a large, established company's stock should return twice the safe number, then those investments would need to return at least 10 percent or they would not meet the risk premium test.

Small, high-tech companies (many don't survive long) should yield quite a bit more to be worth the risk. If that number is 16 percent, then you should expect that level of return.

The risk premium measurement gives you a way to gauge the potential return relative to the risk you are taking. You know that high-risk investments have a higher potential for failure, so they must have a higher potential reward; if not, then pass on the investment.

Expected Returns and Risk

Expectations of returns and risk are often way out of alignment for inexperienced investors, often because of misleading advertising by various hucksters promising huge gains with minimal risk. While it is true that some investors do make huge sums investing in what turns out to be the "next big thing," most successful investors make money by consistently moving forward and cutting their losses quickly. They don't look for stocks that are going to double in price overnight. They look for stocks that are on an upward growth pattern and have been for some time. They look for companies that are leaders in their market and unlikely to be dethroned.

You can expect the stocks of large, established companies to grow in the 10 to 12 percent range over time. That's roughly their historical average. That doesn't mean that in any one year they may be up 25 percent or down 25 percent, which is why stocks are not suitable for short-term objectives. Smaller company stocks should grow at a faster rate, but are more risky. Sector stocks, such as high tech, can shoot up one year and collapse the next.

Bonds will track the safe number very closely, with corporate bonds and longer-term bonds yielding more and short-term bonds yielding less. Annuities will also track the safe number closely, paying a premium, but not much in most cases. Variable annuities are based on stock market results and may not track the safe number at all.

Cash (bank products) will usually be close to the safe product, not because they are safer, but because their investment periods are short.

Here is a chart that looks at relative returns. Actual market returns change almost daily, but the relationships give you an example of how products match up:

Investment	Expected return	Risk-free return	Risk premium
Large company stock	12%	4%	8%
Small company stock	16%	4%	12%
Corporate bonds	7.1%	4%	3.1%
U.S. Treasury Bills	4%	—	—
Inflation	3.2%		

Managing Returns

Investors can manage returns by choosing investment products that match investment objectives. Stocks work best over long periods and should be matched with long-term objectives. Allowing stocks, with continuous monitoring, the time to grow over long periods is the best way to manage those returns. Very few investors succeed in improving their returns by actively trading in and out of the market in an attempt to capture profits when they happen.

Interest-sensitive products such as bank CDs and bonds can benefit from a strategy called laddering which uses various maturities to capture the best of short and long-term interest rates.

◀ SEE ALSO 3.3, *"Savings Accounts"* ▷

◁ SEE ALSO 13.1, *"Basics of Bond Investing"* ▶

Calculating Return on Investment

You need to know how much, if anything, you made on an investment. Some simple math will give you this answer—and you can also do this as a "what if" exercise before selling to see where you are. The first formula is known as the Simple Return and it gives you a quick number, but it has some limitations.

The formula is:

Simple Return =
net proceeds + any dividends / what you paid – 1

For example: If you bought 200 shares at $30 per share and paid an $18 commission, the total cost would be

$6,018 (200 × $30 = $6,000 + $18 = $6,018).

You sold the stock for $36 per share and paid an $18 commission. If you received dividends of $1 per share, that equals $200.

Plugging those numbers in:

$36 × 200 = $7,20 – $18 = $7,182 for net proceeds.

Simple Return = $7,182 + $200 / $6,018 – 1

Simple Return = $7,382 / $6,018 – 1

Simple Return = 1.23 – 1

Simple Return = .23 or 23%

This number has limited use; it's really only valid for investments held for very short periods, because it does not consider the time value of money. To get a valid picture of how a stock or other investment has done over time, you need to calculate the compound annual growth rate.

The compound annual growth rate takes into account the time value of money and evens out the ups and downs so you can see the growth as a single number. To get the compound annual growth rate, you use the Simple Return with the adjustment of eliminating the subtraction of 1 at the end of the calculation.

From our example above, the Adjusted Simple Return would be 1.23.

The next step is to factor in the length of time you have held an investment. Let's assume you held the stock for four years.

Divide 1 by the number of years the investment has been held (4) and this will give you the factor to adjust the return:

$1/4$ = .25 power or exponent

Compound annual growth rate = adjusted simple return $^{\text{(raised to the power)}}$ – 1

Compound annual growth rate = $1.23^{(.25)}$ – 1

Compound annual growth rate = 1.05311 – 1

Compound annual growth rate = .05311 or 5.31 percent

You will need a calculator that allows you to enter the exponent or power. You can also make the calculations using Microsoft Excel. In the "Insert Function" under the "Insert" menu, pick "Math & Trig" from the drop down box and scroll down to "POWER." This function allows you to enter the number and the power you want to raise it to.

As you can see, our 23 percent Simple Return looked pretty good until we factored in the time you held the stock. The Annual Compound Growth Rate of 5.31 percent is nothing to get excited about. After you pay taxes and factor in inflation, this investment may have lost money. If you want an after-tax calculation, substitute after tax proceeds and after-tax dividend numbers.

10.4   ASSET ALLOCATION

The Proper Mix of Assets

Matching Risk and Return

Asset allocation is the process of allotting your portfolio among the three major asset classes: stocks, bonds, and cash. Experts agree that this allocation is more important to investing success than any other decision. In this section, we'll discuss asset mixes and risk and return.

The Proper Mix of Assets

The proper mix of assets depends on the individual investor. The best mix for a 30-year-old is not the same as for a 60-year-old. That is the function of **asset allocation**—to decide the proper mix of major asset classes for your particular situation. Finding and keeping your asset allocation in correct relationship with your life circumstances is the most important factor in long-term investing success.

Investors must also consider their level of risk tolerance. When you factor that into your asset allocation process, it tailors your portfolio to your individual style. Here's what an asset allocation range might look like:

WORDS TO GO . . .WORDS TO GO . . .WORDS TO GO

Asset allocation is the allocating of major asset classes (stocks, bonds, cash) based on your life circumstances. Typically, younger investors can afford to be more aggressive in their allocation because time is on their side, while older investors need to be more conservative.

10.4

Ages 20-30

Investors in this age range can afford to be aggressive. They have time to correct mistakes or wait out setbacks in the market. Here are some suggested ranges:

- ▶ Stocks: 80–90%
- ▶ Bonds: 0–5%
- ▶ Cash: 10–15%

Ages 30-45

Investors in this age range can still be somewhat aggressive, but less so, especially in the upper limits of the range. There is still time to correct mistakes, but you will lose valuable growth time recouping loses if you have too many. Here are some suggested ranges:

▶ Stocks: 60–75%

▶ Bonds: 10–30%

▶ Cash: 10–15%

Ages 45-60

Investors in this stage are entering or in their peak earnings period and should be putting away as much as possible. Although they can be more conservative as they approach age 60, they still need a presence in stocks to protect against inflation and to continue to build their asset base. Here are some suggested ranges:

▶ Stocks: 45–60%

▶ Bonds: 30–55%

▶ Cash: 10–15%

Ages 60 plus

As investors enter their retirement years, preservation of capital and protection against inflation become most important. Preservation of capital is accomplished with careful selection of bonds, however a continued presence in the stock market is required to provide some protection against inflation. Here are some suggested ranges:

▶ Stocks: 25–40%

▶ Bonds: 50–65%

▶ Cash: 10–15%

You can use individual stocks and bonds or mutual funds to achieve your mix. We didn't include real estate for the sake of simplicity, but it should not be more than 10 percent, especially in later years. These ranges are simple starting points, not absolutes. Your asset allocation may look different, but if it differs radically from these ranges, you should ask yourself if you are taking full advantage of the asset classes.

Matching Risk and Return

Asset allocation allows you to adjust your portfolio to match your risk tolerance with expected return. For example, adding more stocks to the mix and lowering the percentage of bonds can have the effect of raising the risk. This increases your potential for a higher return. Ideally, you would find the asset allocation that would give you the highest possible return for the level of risk you were willing to accept. This is not a plug-in formula, but a process that investors come to over time of working with their portfolio and understanding their tolerance for risk.

10.4

10.5 TRADING THROUGH A BROKER

Different Types of Brokers

Finding a Good Brokerage Firm

You need a stockbroker to buy and sell stocks. There are two broad types of brokers: full service and discount. Within those categories are some brokers that blur the lines. This section looks at your options in choosing a stockbroker and how to find a good brokerage firm.

Different Types of Brokers

Investors have two types of brokerage firms to consider when selecting a company to handle their trading business. The traditional **full service** companies such as Merrill Lynch offer research, investment advice, and a host of investor services. **Discount** brokers such as Charles Schwab focus on executing trades and providing low-cost services to investors.

WORDS TO GO . . .WORDS TO GO . . .WORDS TO GO

Full service brokerage firms provide account representatives to handle your business, along with research and other services. Many are converting from charging commissions to charging a fee based on assets under management.

Discount brokers focus on quick trades and straight-forward execution. They offer their services for much less than full service brokers, but don't provide personal advice or research.

The days when the gulf between the full-service brokerage firms and discount brokers was wide are gone. There are still differences—not the least of which is pricing of services, but many of the distinctive features of both sides have melded into hybrid brokerage firms that offer à la carte services. You can buy research services at formerly pure discount firms, and full service firms are offering discounted trading fees for active traders.

Many full service brokerage firms are moving away from a commission-based structure to a fee-based pricing system that charges customers a percentage of assets under management (one to two percent annually is common) for services including some research and advice. Full service firms offer recommendations and an account executive to discuss your goals and plans. You will pay more in investing costs, but many investors feel the advice and recommendations they get are worth the price.

If you want to do your own research and make your own decisions, a discount broker is probably the best choice for you. The Internet has opened up a tremendous amount of information to investors, most of it free, so many feel they can make their own decisions. Some discount brokerage firms offer research for a fee and other services once just offered by full service brokers. If you are an active trader, you can get an even deeper discount on commissions.

Finding a Good Brokerage Firm

Whether you are looking for a full service or discount broker, you should consider how your personal trading and investing style would work with the company. Ask yourself these questions about potential brokerage firms to see if you can find one that fits better than the rest:

- ▶ All brokerage firms have a website, even if you don't trade through it. Is it useful and full of information or does it waste your time looking for research that isn't there and links that go nowhere?

- ▶ How hard or easy is it to get an actual person on the telephone to ask a question?

- ▶ Does the site offer live quotes to customers? (Most stock quotes you see on the Internet are delayed up to 20 minutes from actual live action.)

- ▶ Does the firm offer other products and services, such as check-writing privileges, mutual funds, bonds, and so on?

- ▶ Does the firm offer access to research?

- ▶ Is the fee structure easy to understand?

- ▶ What is the minimum opening balance? Is there an account maintenance fee or a fee if your balance falls below the minimum?

You may have other concerns particular to your own investing style. Ask questions and don't settle for nonanswers. The brokerage business is highly competitive and you shouldn't have to settle for a firm that isn't performing.

10.5

 # ONLINE TRADING

Advantages of Online Trading
Finding a Good Online Trading Firm

When people began trading online, it took on a "high-roller" mystique for a period, until it became so commonplace that it lost its luster. This section looks at the advantages and issues of online trading and suggests ways to find a good online broker.

Advantages of Online Trading

Online trading lets you enter your trades into a system directly from your computer at home, work, or wherever you have access to the Internet. People on the go find this flexibility a wonderful convenience. Technology has expanded trading capability from personal computers to personal data assistants (PDAs) and cell phones.

For active traders, online trading offers very low commissions and access to a variety of analysis tools that help in decision-making and portfolio management. Because all of the services are web-based, it is easy to access them wherever and whenever you want.

Finding a Good Online Trading Firm

A good online trading firm should exhibit all of the qualities of a regular trading firm, but it has to have much more than a "helpful" website. Online firms use "trading platforms" to launch their services. Investors log on to these software programs and have access to tools and services that let them be better traders.

The trading platforms and all the features that go with an online brokerage account make up the online trading experience. It is possible to be an online trading customer and never speak to a human but, if you need to, because you have questions or a problem with your account, you will want to be able to connect with one quickly.

The other critical concern for online traders is connecting during peak times or when there is heavy volume in the market. If you can't connect with your online account because their system is overloaded with requests, you may miss out on a profit opportunity—or worse, you may be stuck holding a terrible investment with no way to sell. Make sure the online broker has multiple back connections and phone lines so you can phone in a trade if need be.

11

INVESTING IN MUTUAL FUNDS AND EXCHANGE TRADED FUNDS

 **MUTUAL FUND BASICS**

Fundamentals and Structure of Mutual Funds

Net Asset Value

Buying and Selling Mutual Funds

Three Ways to Make Money

Tax Consequences

Mutual funds offer a simple investing concept that may sound complicated until you grasp the fundamentals. This section focuses on the basic structure, types, and functions of mutual funds. It will help you see how the funds work, how investors buy and sell shares, and the possible tax consequences of investing in mutual funds.

Fundamentals and Structure of Mutual Funds

Mutual funds are the most popular investment instrument in the United States. More than half of all households own shares in one or more mutual funds—over 80 million accounts controlling trillions of dollars in assets. The structure of mutual funds is one of the reasons the industry has been so successful.

Investment companies are the parent organization of mutual funds and hire professional portfolio managers to manage their funds. Investors buy shares of a fund and the professionals make all of the investment decisions. Most mutual funds have a relatively low initial investment—for many $2,500 to $1,000 or less—and even lower subsequent investment minimums, often in the $50 to $100 range.

You can choose from over 8,500 different funds and they span a wide range of investment categories. Most funds fall into one of the broad categories listed in the next section. Many investment companies offer a number of mutual funds grouped together and called a "family of funds" or simply "a funds family." This combination of different types of funds lets investors move their money among the different funds as their investment objectives change, in many cases without penalty or charge.

Mutual funds have much to offer investors, especially people who don't have the time, experience, or interest in analyzing stocks or bonds for their portfolio. There are other benefits as well.

Diversification of Holdings

Each mutual fund invests in dozens of stocks, bonds, or other investments. Few individual investors can afford to diversify their holdings as broadly as a mutual fund does. **Diversification** is an important way to minimize risk, because the failure of one company or bond won't have a serious impact on a portfolio holding many stocks and bonds, whereas an individual who only owned a few stocks or bonds might suffer a serious financial setback if one of them failed. The larger the number of holdings, the smaller that impact will be.

◄ *SEE ALSO 10.4, "Asset Allocation"* ▶

WORDS TO GO . . .WORDS TO GO . . .WORDS TO GO

Diversification is the reduction of risk by spreading investment dollars over numerous stocks and or bonds to minimize the impact should one of the investments turn bad.

Reinvestment of Earnings

When the stocks held in the mutual fund pay dividends, or the fund sells a stock for a profit, or a bond or other investment makes an interest payment, those earnings accrue to the shareholders. You can take them as a cash distribution at regular times during the year, or have them reinvested in the fund to buy more shares. **Reinvesting** your earnings is a way to increase your holdings more rapidly. You will still pay taxes on the earnings, in most cases, but the money will be reinvested in the fund and earning more for you in the meantime.

WORDS TO GO . . .WORDS TO GO . . .WORDS TO GO

Reinvesting earnings from a mutual fund account automatically buys more shares of the fund. This is a way to use profits to build your stake in the fund. You do still have to pay taxes on the earnings in most cases.

11.1

Automatic Deposits and Payments

Almost all funds will accept a regular payment, usually debited from your checking or other bank account on a monthly or some other basis. This regular investment is called **dollar cost averaging** and it is discussed in detail in later sections. However, it is important to note that you pay no fee to the fund for this privilege—unlike investing in stocks where you must pay a commission to a stockbroker on every purchase or sale. Likewise, if you wish to receive a regular check from the fund, you can arrange for that service as well. If earnings on your account are not sufficient to cover your requested withdrawal, the fund will sell enough shares to meet your dollar amount.

WORDS TO GO . . . *WORDS TO GO . . .WORDS TO GO*

Dollar cost averaging is investing a fixed amount on a regular basis in a mutual fund, usually monthly and through an automatic debit to your bank account. This investment method means you buy fewer shares when prices are high and more when prices are lower, resulting in an overall lower average cost.

Retirement Accounts

Most mutual funds offer a variety of Individual Retirement Accounts (IRAs) that may have even lower initial deposit requirements than regular investment accounts. The mutual fund family concept is a convenient way to house IRAs because of the variety of funds usually offered and the flexibility of moving from one fund to another.

◁ *SEE ALSO 15.2, "IRAs"* ▷

Mutual Funds Are Transparent

Mutual funds are a registered security, which means you must receive a **prospectus** prior to investing in the fund. The prospectus and accompanying material should clearly explain the initial expenses, if any, and ongoing costs of investing in the fund. Any sales commissions should be disclosed before you invest. Once you own a fund, the daily price is available in many newspapers and on a number of Internet sites. All the information investors need to make decisions is readily available to the investing public. This makes them transparent in that there are no hidden or secret facts that only certain investors know and others don't.

WORDS TO GO . . . *WORDS TO GO . . .WORDS TO GO*

Prospectus is a legal document required by the Securities and Exchange Commission that details all the information investors need to know about an investment, including the risk of losing your money.

Net Asset Value

Mutual funds are priced differently than stocks. Most mutual funds issue as many shares as people want to buy, whereas a finite number of shares of a stock are available. These funds are known as open-end mutual funds. For example, if a fund has issued 2 million shares and has $30 million in assets, each share is priced at $15 per share. For every additional $15 invested, the fund's assets increase by that amount and the share price remains at $15 because the fund issues new shares at the current price ($15). That price is what is quoted in the newspaper and online and is known as the **net asset value.**

WORDS TO GO . . .WORDS TO GO . . .WORDS TO GO

Net asset value is the daily value of a mutual fund that includes all the assets minus the fund's liabilities converted to a per-share price. This is the price you buy and sell mutual fund shares at if you deal directly with the company.

The calculation of the net asset value is more complicated than this simple example because the fund is not just selling shares—it is buying and selling stocks and/or bonds, making and selling other investments, and redeeming shares of investors who want to sell. In addition, the market value of the fund's holdings changes every day and must be recalculated when the stock market closes and all the fund's holdings have a closing value. Here is a simple formula that illustrates the calculation of the net asset value:

Beginning value of funds assets
+
Any new investments
+
Dividends, interest, capital gains
+
Any gain in price or value of fund assets
−
Any decrease in price or value of fund assets
−
Any shares redeemed to investors (assets sold or cash diminished)
−
Dividends, interest, or capital gains paid to shareholders
−
Fund expenses
=
New Net Asset Value

If you want to buy or sell shares of the fund during the day, this is the price you will pay or receive. The fund calculates it every day after the markets close.

Another type of mutual fund called a closed-end fund works differently. A **closed-end mutual fund** issues a fixed number of shares. These shares are traded on the stock exchanges like the common stock of companies. Because closed-end funds trade on the open market, their share price is determined by supply and demand. Although closed-end mutual funds have an NAV, they may trade above or below this price based on whether investors are confident in the fund's future or not. There are many more open-end funds than closed-end funds. You'll know you are buying a closed-end fund because it must be bought through a stockbroker and you can watch the price change during the day. Unlike an **open-end mutual fund,** you can only buy or sell closed-end funds when the markets are open. More about closed-end funds can be found at the end of this chapter.

WORDS TO GO . . .WORDS TO GO . . .WORDS TO GO

A **closed-end mutual fund** is a fund that trades on stock exchanges like common stock. A fixed number of shares are issued and the value of the fund is more a function of supply and demand, unlike an open-end fund, which can issue more shares to accommodate new investors.

Open-end mutual funds make up the largest number of funds on the market. Open-end funds simply issue new shares when someone wants to buy into the fund, rather than matching an existing shareholder who wants to sell.

Buying and Selling Mutual Funds

One of the advantages of investing in mutual funds is their liquidity, meaning you can sell your shares or buy more with ease. Most funds make investing easy, with a minimum of paperwork and multiple options for payment.

Mutual fund shares are bought from the mutual fund and sold back to the fund. Except in those circumstances where a broker or sales agent is involved (more about those exceptions later), you always deal directly with the fund.

Mutual funds are not bothered with transacting fractional shares. Unlike common stock, you buy mutual funds in dollar amounts and the fund converts your investment into the correct number of shares based on the NAV at the time of your investment, even if that results in an uneven number of shares.

Most of the larger fund companies maintain extensive Internet sites and customer service phone banks to answer questions and process purchases and redemptions.

Three Ways to Make Money

Investors potentially make money three ways with mutual funds. Some funds target specific profit opportunities, while others generally participate in all three possibilities. The opportunities are:

- ▶ **Interest, dividends, capital gains from holdings of the fund passed through to the investor:** Depending on the type of fund and its holdings, investors may periodically receive their share of these earnings.

- ▶ **Capital gains from sale of profitable investments:** When the fund sells a profitable investment—a stock or bond, for example—those profits may be distributed to investors.

- ▶ **Appreciation in NAV:** As the fund makes profitable investments, the value of its assets will grow faster than new investments and the NAV will increase. Investors can sell some or all of their shares at a profit.

> **WORDS TO GO . . .WORDS TO GO . . .WORDS TO GO**
>
> **Capital gains** result when an asset is sold for a profit. In the case of a mutual fund, that asset may be a stock, bond, or a fixed income security. If the asset has been held for less than one year, it's a short-term capital gain. If it was held more than a year, it's a long-term gain.

Some mutual funds focus on generating income, while others look for capital gains, so not all funds will present all three profit opportunities.

Tax Consequences

Investing in mutual funds has personal income tax consequences. With the exception of some tax-exempt funds, most funds create taxable events during the year for shareholders. These include interest and dividend payments and may also include short- and long-term capital gains tax liabilities when the fund sells holdings during the year.

11.1

Some funds are more "tax friendly" than others. Index funds, which are explained in the next sub-chapter, are generally considered tax friendly because they seldom trade stocks or bonds. Other funds may try to avoid the higher taxed short-term gains to hold down the tax liability for investors.

Investors receive a Misc. 1099 Int. Income form after the end of the year that details the tax liability for the account.

11.2 TYPES OF MUTUAL FUNDS

Active vs. Passive Management

Index Funds

Growth Funds

Income funds

Balanced Funds

Life Cycle Funds

Bond Funds

Money Market Funds

Investors have thousands of mutual funds to choose from that are offered by hundreds of investment companies. Fortunately, most mutual funds fall into one of the categories listed in this section. There is ample room for bending definitions in the market, but most funds stay close to these broad categories.

Active vs. Passive Management

Mutual fund companies employ two basic forms of management and these forms define two distinct types of funds. Active and passive management describe the two distinctly different roles of fund managers in the day-to-day management of their respective fund's assets.

An **actively managed mutual fund** employs a manager, researchers, and stock and bond traders who are engaged daily in researching and analyzing companies for possible inclusion (or elimination) from the fund's holdings. Depending on the fund's objective, the managers will focus on those stocks and/or bonds that fit the fund's guidelines.

The managers of an actively managed fund focus on "beating the market," which is often the S&P 500 Index or another market barometer. The management team's goal of frequently buying and selling stocks and bonds is to boost the fund's return above the market index that is their gauge.

A **passively managed fund,** which means an index fund as a practical matter, does not employ a large professional staff because the funds seldom buy or sell stocks or bonds and have no need of researchers. They follow a stock or bond index and mimic its holdings.

Actively managed mutual funds are open-end funds that employ a portfolio manger who buys and sells stocks and bonds it an attempt to post a better return than the market, usually represented by some stock index, such as the S&P 500.

Passively managed funds include index funds where managers buy stocks or bonds that match the composition of popular stock and bond indexes, such as the S&P 500 and the Dow Jones Industrial Average.

Another way actively and passively managed funds differ is the stated goal. Most passively managed funds do not try to beat the index, they simply follow it.

Investors will notice a big difference between active and passive funds when they look at expenses. The costs to run an actively managed fund are much higher than those of a passively managed fund. Fund expenses are an important determinant in predicting success. The prospectus for the fund will detail the management style and whether it is actively or passively managed.

Index Funds

Index funds are passively managed funds. These funds mimic in holdings the indexes they follow. Investors find them attractive for their low expenses. Index funds track a stock or bond index by investing in the same stocks or bonds that make up the index. An S&P 500 Index mutual fund would own all 500 stocks that make up this popular stock market index. Many investors consider the S&P 500 "the market" for comparison purposes.

Although the S&P 500 index funds are the most popular, there are funds for almost any sector of the stock market, from small companies to technology stocks to foreign companies. Index funds allow investors to buy into these markets without having to research individual companies within each sector. Index funds that capture broad sections of the market move with the market, while sector index funds can be very volatile because they focus on small slices of the market.

11.2

The big advantage of index funds is their low cost. With no large professional staff, the funds keep expenses low. The only time they trade stocks or bonds is when the underlying index changes components. The trade-off for investors is avoiding the under-performance that marks 80 percent of the actively traded funds, while missing out on the 20 percent that do better than the market.

Growth Funds

Growth mutual funds focus on companies with higher than average growth and continued potential growth. The funds look for companies that reinvest profits to fund new growth rather than pay out dividends to shareholders. They target companies that are market leaders and hold dominant positions in their industry.

Growth funds invest primarily in stocks. This is important because investors consider stock investments more risky than investing in bonds. If the name or description mentions growth, the mutual fund invests in stocks.

There are several variations on the growth fund theme, which include:

Aggressive Growth Funds

These funds aim for even greater returns, but add an element of risk by looking for younger companies that may be on their way to the top spot in their industrial sector. The risk is that larger companies will thwart their efforts or will buy them out before they can challenge the market leader. You may make a profit if the company is bought out, but you lose the long-term growth potential. For example, if IBM had bought Microsoft when it was still a small company, Bill Gates, the founder of Microsoft, might be a rich man today, but he wouldn't be the richest man in the world, a title he holds because his company continued to grow.

Value Funds

Value mutual funds invest in companies that the market may have overlooked for some reason and under-priced the stock. These companies are usually fundamentally sound but may be in an industry that is not exciting or is out of favor with the market.

Value companies earn the designation by having stock prices that are below similar companies with the same general earnings and book value.

Sector Funds

Sector mutual funds carve out small (usually) pieces of the stock or bond market and focus their attention there. These funds cover everything from technology to foreign stocks to regional stocks, so you're sure to find an area that interests you.

These funds, depending on the focus, can be very volatile. Investors usually save just a small portion of their portfolio for these funds because, while the potential is high, the risk is great. However, they do offer investors the opportunity to invest in a particular part of the market without having to research individual companies.

Socially Responsible Funds

Socially responsible mutual funds put ideals about certain issues into their stock selection process. Some of the funds will not invest in tobacco or alcohol companies or firms that manufacture war materials. These funds seek out companies with good records in the environment, hiring practices, and other guidelines outlined in the prospectus.

Over the years, many of these funds have performed reasonably well, but seldom as the top performer of any grouping. By limiting their stock selections, many of the funds gave up some top performing stocks in the past such as defense contractors, tobacco companies, and others that did not pass their social responsibility screens.

Foreign Markets Funds

Foreign markets mutual funds, also called emerging markets funds, invest in companies in certain foreign countries. Some funds focus on a specific geographic area, such as the South Pacific Rim, while others are broader chartered and look for good foreign investments where they can find them.

Investing in foreign markets has occasionally been very profitable in the recent past, when developing markets in Asia have grown much faster than opportunities in the United States. Not all mutual funds that invest in foreign stocks have been successful, however. A good portfolio manager who knows foreign markets can make all the difference. Foreign markets can also be very volatile even under the best guidance. Most investors should not have more than 5 to 10 percent of their portfolio in foreign markets.

Market Capitalization Funds

Market capitalization funds invest in companies by size. There are large-cap, mid-cap, and small-cap funds. Each fund picks stocks that show leadership potential, but they're very different types of funds because size is so important in the market. The smaller the company, the higher the risk is a known factor. Smaller companies are more prone to failure and subject to market pressure from larger companies.

11.2

WORDS TO GO . . .WORDS TO GO . . .WORDS TO GO

Market capitalization or market cap is the number of shares outstanding multiplied by the per share price. For example, a company with 100 million shares on the market and a per share price of $55 would have a market cap of $5.5 billion.

Income funds

Income mutual funds appeal to investors who need current income for living expenses or to supplement a retirement plan. As the name suggests, income mutual funds often focus on investments that will yield current income in the form of dividends, such as **preferred stocks** and bonds.

> **WORDS TO GO . . .WORDS TO GO . . .WORDS TO GO**
>
> **Preferred stocks** are a special type of stock that companies issue. They have limited rights when it comes to voting on company business, but they do pay a steady dividend and that's what attracts investors. The stock's price may not rise (or fall) nearly as fast or as far as the common stock. Income investors like preferred stock from solid companies for its dependability.

The fund may not increase in share price, at least not like growth funds, because the stocks and bonds it purchases pay out current income rather than appreciate in price.

There are several variations of the income fund that involve how much of the portfolio is in stocks and how much the portfolio holds in bonds. By adjusting the preferred stocks and bonds mixture, mutual funds can increase the yield and the risk or reduce the yield and reduce the risk.

Another specialized variation is called the fixed income fund, which is another word for bond fund.

Balanced Fund

Balanced mutual funds combine stocks and bonds looking for the best from both growth and current income. Balanced funds may answer the question of what the mix of stocks and bonds should be. The balance of stocks and bonds in a portfolio is different for every individual, so finding a balanced fund that matches your stocks-to-bonds ratio may take some research.

The **stocks-to-bonds ratio** that is right for you will depend on your age, financial goals, and risk tolerance. The younger you are, the higher the ratio of stocks in your portfolio should be. Older investors should consider reducing the percentage of stocks and increasing their bond assets. A good starting place is to take your age and subtract it from 100. What remains is the percentage of stocks you should have in your portfolio.

Stocks-to-bonds ratio is the percentage of your portfolio occupied by
stocks and bonds. Because bonds are considered more conservative, investors
use a higher ratio of bonds for a less aggressive market position and a higher
ratio of stocks for a more aggressive position.

Balanced funds have a performance history that evens out the peaks and valleys
in the market. They do not rise as high as an exuberant market, nor fall as far as
a market in doubt. This makes them attractive to risk-averse investors.

Life-Cycle Funds

Life-cycle mutual funds help investors keep their stock and bond mix correct as
they move closer to retirement. Many of these funds feature a target maturity
date. People planning to retire on or near the maturity date invest in the fund,
which then automatically readjusts the stocks, bonds, and cash mix as the date
draws nearer. The closer the investor gets to retirement, the more conservative
the portfolio becomes, with a reduction in the stock percentage and an increase
in the percentage of bonds.

The targeted maturity date funds are very attractive to 401(k) participants
because they don't have to worry about making adjustments as time goes on. You
can often choose whether you want a conservative, moderate, or aggressive portfolio blend, and the fund will adjust the assets accordingly.

Life-cycle funds are designed to be your single investment, because they calculate
the proper stocks, bonds, and cash mix. Any additional funds will put your allocation out of balance and defeat the purpose of the life-cycle fund.

Bond Funds

11.2

Like pure stock funds, bond mutual funds come in a variety of configurations,
but the two major groupings are taxable and nontaxable, and by maturity of the
bonds in the portfolio.

Tax-free bond funds invest in primarily municipal bonds. Income from municipal
bonds is exempt from federal income tax. The municipal bond market isn't easy
for individual investors to navigate. Many new bonds for sale have minimum
purchase requirements of $25,000, which puts them out of the reach of many
investors. Tax-free mutual funds are a way for investors with limited means to
participate.

Many investment companies offer a variation on the tax-free bond mutual fund in many states that have a personal income tax. There "triple exempt" tax funds offer income free from city, state, or federal income tax. This is possible because many states will exempt the money raised from state and local income taxes to attract new local investors.

Taxable bond mutual funds specialize in issues of corporations. The risk is somewhat higher, but the rewards may be greater also. Corporate bonds have a higher rate of default, because the company could go out of business or not be able to repay the bond.

Other bond funds focus on investing in bonds of different maturities, such as short-term, mid-term and long-term bonds. Each has characteristics that appeal to different investors.

Bond maturities reflect matters of risk. The longer the maturity, the higher the risk to the bondholder.

◀ *SEE ALSO 13.1, "Basics of Bond Investing"* ▶

Money Market Funds

Money market mutual funds differ slightly from other funds in how they work. Unlike other mutual funds, money market funds attempt to keep the net asset value, or NAV, at a constant $1. The funds invest in short-term interest-paying securities.

The income generated by the fund is paid to shareholders in the form of additional shares. In other words, your number of shares increases. Money market funds can either be taxable or tax-free, depending on the underlying investments. **Tax-free money market funds** invest in municipal bonds and other instruments whose income is tax-free. Taxable money market funds invest in U.S. Treasury bills and notes, commercial notes, and other short-term securities.

WORDS TO GO . . .WORDS TO GO . . .WORDS TO GO

Tax-free money market funds invest in securities that generate tax-free income. In most cases, only investors in the highest income tax brackets should invest in these funds because the return is very low.

Money market funds, although not insured by the Federal Deposit Insurance Corp. like bank products, are considered very secure and safe investments. Money market funds invest in very short-term products—with maturities often measured in days rather than months. This very short-term perspective gives them the flexibility to move quickly out of difficult investments if they aren't working out. In addition, many money market funds invest in U.S. Treasury securities, which are considered among the most secure investments on the market.

◀ *SEE ALSO 13.2, "Types of Bonds"* ▶

11.2

11.3 MUTUAL FUND EXPENSES

Load and No Load Funds

12b-1 Fees

Expense Ratio

Management Fees

Expenses are a major factor in the performance of mutual funds. In most cases, funds with lower expenses will provide investors with a better return than funds with higher expenses. This section explains the different expenses and types of funds that charge expenses.

Load and No-Load Funds

Open-end mutual funds are sold either directly by the fund itself or through a broker. If the fund is sold through a broker, it will most likely charge a sales fee called a "load" to pay the broker's commission. Mutual funds that investors buy directly from the fund company usually do not charge a sales fee and are called "no-load" funds.

The loads come off your investment dollars and many financial advisers urge investors to avoid mutual funds that charge a load. A $5,000 investment in a loaded mutual fund, if the load is the typical 5.75 percent, means only $4,712.50 of your money is actually invested in the fund. You have, in effect, lost money before you start. That loss gets magnified to $1,935 if you hold the fund for 20 years and it earns 10 percent.

Loads come in three types:

The Front-End Load

Front-end loaded funds, also known as Class A shares, charge a fee that comes out of your investment before it begins earning for you (this is the illustration above).

The Back-End Load or Deferred Load

These funds charge a declining fee based on how long you leave money in the fund. For example, you might pay 5 percent if you withdraw money the first year, 4 percent in years two and three, and so on. These shares are called Class B.

Level Load

These fees include a marketing fee and an exit fee that is usually around 1 percent. These shares are called C shares.

Loads pay sales commissions and do not add any benefit to the mutual fund. There is a negative correlation between paying a load and fund performance, which means loaded funds historically under-perform no-load funds.

Like all financial decisions, outright rejection of all loaded mutual funds would be a mistake; sometimes a loaded fund may be the better choice. Just because no-load funds don't charge a sales fee doesn't mean they don't have other expenses. These expenses are discussed in detail below.

A loaded fund may have very low operating expenses, which could make it a better buy for a long-term investor than a no-load fund with higher operating expenses. Only a check of the numbers will reveal the best choice.

A no-load fund does not charge a sales fee and, in most cases, is sold directly by the mutual fund. The advantage is that more of the investor's money is put to work earning a return, rather than paying a sales commission. This is not to say that no-load funds have no expenses, they just don't have a sales expense. Historically, funds with lower expenses have better returns than funds with higher expenses.

12b-1 Fees

All loaded funds and many no-load funds charge a 12b-1 fee, which goes to marketing and advertising the fund. Brokers may be paid out of this fee. The 12b-1 fee is controversial because it is also charged by many no-load funds, but if the fund charges more than 0.25 percent, it may not call itself a no-load fund.

Do not automatically reject a fund that charges a 12b-1 fee. Look at the total expenses, both immediate and ongoing, to make your evaluation.

11.3

Expense Ratio

A mutual fund's expense ratio is the single most important number to consider when looking at the ongoing cost of holding the fund. The expense ratio captures all the operating expenses of the fund and is expressed as a percentage of the fund's assets. Investors use the expense ratio to compare funds. Historically, a lower expense ratio has meant better performance.

The expense ratio captures all the costs of operating the fund except for the sales loads. These expenses are charged back to the mutual fund.

Management Fees

Management fees cover the operations of the fund and pay the investment professionals for their expertise in making investments for the fund. The fee must also cover the typical costs of doing business such as rent, utilities, and so on. Management fees range from 1.5 percent to 0.25 percent in typical funds. One of the main differences in mutual funds that affects the amount of the management fee is whether the fund is actively managed or passively managed.

An **actively managed fund** is one where the portfolio manager frequently buys and sells stocks and bonds in an attempt to meet or exceed the fund's goals. Frequent trading drives up the cost of trading fees and requires more professional staff to conduct research and analysis.

A **passively managed fund** is like an index fund. These funds buy and sell stocks and bonds infrequently. This keeps the management fee low.

WORDS TO GO . . . WORDS TO GO . . . WORDS TO GO

An **actively managed fund** manager believes in beating the market through careful stock selection and bargain hunting. The manager of an actively managed fund will often trade actively in pursuit of a better return than a major index can provide.

The **passively managed fund** relies on the natural returns of the underlying index and doesn't tinker with the established system. Passively managed funds are almost always index funds.

The expense ratio can range from a very low 0.1 percent to more than 2.5 percent. You can find a fund's expense ratio in the prospectus or online at several Internet sites, including www.morningstar.com.

The lower the expense ratio, the less drag there is on earnings of the fund. All other considerations being equal, a fund with a lower expense ratio will perform better over the long term than a fund with a higher expense ratio.

As always, there are exceptions. Management fees pay for professional expertise. In some situations, funds that invest in foreign stocks for example, it might make sense to pay a higher management fee to a portfolio manger with a successful track record in the complicated field.

Following are guidelines for expense ratios for mutual fund types.

Fund Type	Highest Expense Ratio You Should Pay
Index funds	0.25% or less
Bond funds	0.75% or less
Actively managed funds	0.75% or less
Growth funds	1.0% or less
Specialty funds*	1.5% or less

Small cap funds, sector funds, foreign funds, and such

The differences in expense ratios reflect the degree of difficulty in managing the various funds and the amount of trading that the fund does.

Because expense ratios are regularly deducted from your assets, it is important to consider funds with the low ratios before paying more for future potential gains. There is ample historical evidence that funds with lower expense ratios outperform funds with high expense ratios, especially for long-term investors.

11.3

FINDING GOOD MUTUAL FUNDS

Investment Objectives Come First
Performance Expectations
Performance Determinants
Historical Perspective
Management Experience
Investment Strategy

Finding the right mutual fund for your financial needs is a process of elimination beginning with reducing the 8,500 plus mutual funds to a manageable number for further analysis. This section explains how that process works.

Investment Objectives Come First

The first step is to find mutual funds that have the same investment objectives as your own. You can narrow the list down quickly to those funds in a category compatible with your objectives. If you are looking for rapid growth and are willing to bear some risk, an aggressive growth fund will match up nicely with your goals. An investor with a more moderate objective might want to stick with a growth fund.

Thanks to regulations by the Securities and Exchange Commission, funds can't use a phrase in their names that might lead an investor to believe the fund is in one category, when its investment style is more like another.

You can discover a fund's investment objective several different ways. It will be part of the prospectus you should receive before you invest in the fund. However, many investors need a way to identify a larger set of funds that match their needs. One of the more convenient ways is to use a **stock screener.** You can find these handy tools on many different Internet sites, and most are free. Morningstar.com offers a mutual funds screener that lets you select by category and other criteria, if you want.

WORDS TO GO . . . WORDS TO GO . . . WORDS TO GO

Stock screeners are online tools that investors use to narrow down possible investment candidates. Despite its name, you can also use the tool to sort through mutual funds and find those that match a set of criteria you select.

The stock screener will scan all available mutual funds and find the ones that match your requirements. This free service lets you sort through thousands of funds and pick out only those that meet your needs.

The **prospectus** will reveal the fund's objectives. In this document, which you can receive by asking for one from the mutual fund company, is detailed information about the fund and its objectives along with other important data.

WORDS TO GO . . .WORDS TO GO . . .WORDS TO GO

A **prospectus** is a legal document that must accompany any request for information about purchasing a mutual fund. The Securities and Exchange Commission requires fund companies to use "plain English" in composing the prospectus so people can understand what it is saying without an accounting or law degree.

The prospectus is a legal document that requires the fund to state the amount of risk it plans to take in order to meet its investment objectives. This level of risk should match your own. In general, the more risk in a fund's strategy, the higher the potential return and the lower the likelihood that it will achieve its goal.

◀ *SEE ALSO 10.3, "Risk and Reward Relationship"* ▶

A further refinement of investment objectives is to describe the types of securities the fund buys. This is especially important for mutual funds that buy primarily stocks. There are a number of ways to classify different types of stocks. Two basic ways involve the size of the companies and whether the companies are growth or value stocks.

Market Capitalization

Size matters when investing in companies. Large companies react to market conditions differently than small companies. Large companies are more often older and more established. These companies may weather bad economic news because of strong financial reserves. Small companies, on the other hand, are capable of very rapid growth and can post very impressive gains if their products catch on in the market. Small companies are also vulnerable to larger competitors and may not have the financial resources to sustain growth or survive an economic downturn. Mid-size companies may fall either direction depending on the circumstances. They, too, are vulnerable to larger competitors, but are more likely to survive a bad economy.

11.4

The investing community categorizes companies using a tool called **market capitalization,** which makes it relevant to compare companies even if they are not in the same industry. Market capitalization is a way of measuring a company's size using the stock price and outstanding shares.

> **WORDS TO GO . . .WORDS TO GO . . .WORDS TO GO**
>
> **Market capitalization,** or market cap, as it is known, is calculated by multiplying all of a company's outstanding shares (those shares available for trade on the stock exchanges), by the current per share price.

The general rule is this for size:

Size	Market Cap
Large	$10 billion plus
Mid	$1—$10 billion
Small	$1 billion and less

It is important to know whether the fund invests in just one size company or more than one size and in what proportion.

Growth, Value, or a Mix

Another way to look at stocks, and mutual funds that invest in them, is whether they are growing (and how rapidly) or whether they are under-priced value stocks.

Growth funds focus on stocks that show consistent patterns of growth and the fund managers expect that growth to continue. Growth funds can be further refined as aggressive growth funds that invest in younger companies that may be poised for a burst of growth thanks to a new product or technology. Aggressive growth funds look for higher returns because the risk is higher in investing in smaller firms that may not achieve the expected spurt of growth.

Value funds seek out stocks that the market has under priced for some reason. The company may have gone through a management shakeup, or the general market for the company's products may be temporarily depressed. For whatever reason, the fund believes the stock will bounce back when the market realizes it is trading at a price lower than its true value.

Blended funds will use both growth and value investing styles in an attempt at receiving the best returns from both.

◀ *SEE ALSO 12.4, "Finding Good Stocks"* ▶

Putting Size and Growth Together

One of the more popular ways to categorize stock mutual funds is by combining size and growth parameters. With three size parameters (large, mid, small) and three growth parameters (growth, value, blend), you come up with a nine-square grid.

The grid is as follows:

Large growth	Large blend	Large value
Mid growth	Mid blend	Mid value
Small growth	Small blend	Small value

Morningstar.com has its own proprietary grid system and they pioneered this concept. It is a helpful way of fitting stock mutual funds into a category that makes sense based on investment objectives. Of course, there will be funds that fall into the "hybrid" category, meaning they don't fit on this grid.

Investment Objectives of Other Funds

Stock funds may be the most complicated in defining objectives. Other funds, such as balanced funds, small cap funds, global funds, and bond funds almost define their objectives by their names. Regardless of any fund's name, the actual objectives are defined in the prospectus and that's where investors should check for the details.

Bond funds may be among the easiest to get a good idea about the objectives of the fund from the name. Many bond funds put the type of bonds right in the name of the fund. For example, Acme Long-Term Corporate Bond Fund tells you that this mutual fund invests primarily in long-term corporate bonds.

Two mutual funds with the term "balanced" in the name may have very different ideas of what that means. Labeling and categorizing funds is only a tool to narrow the selection process down to a manageable level. Investors must still ferret out the details of each fund.

11.4

Performance Expectations

Mutual funds set a standard as a performance goal. Quite often, funds use the **S&P 500 Index** as a proxy for "the market" and use it as the benchmark to beat. For some stock funds, this measure may make some sense, but a number of funds use the index for no logical reason other than it is an industry standard.

In many years, beating the S&P 500 index was not a great accomplishment, because the index closed with modest annual gains. Over the years, stock mutual funds have returned about 10 percent on average. However, remember that mutual funds are long-term investments and you should not invest money in them that you'll need in the next three years or so.

Returns on bond funds have averaged less than stock funds, especially tax-free funds, which invest in low-yielding tax-free bonds.

Specialty funds such as sector funds, small cap funds, and such may return spectacular numbers one year and be down the next. Because of their extreme volatility, these funds should only occupy a small percentage of your portfolio.

Most funds will also compare their performance to a composite performance of others funds with similar investment objectives. A large growth fund might set the S&P 500 Index as its objective to match or beat, but it is important to see how it did compared to its peers. If all large-cap growth funds were down for the same period for the same amount, one could conclude the fund performed as best as could be expected under the circumstances. However, if all the other large-cap growth funds were up by considerably more, it suggests the fund is under performing, regardless of how it did against the S&P 500 Index.

Rationale for Index Fund Returns

Investors pay management fees to professionals so they can achieve a better return than the market or the S&P 500 Index. If the fund cannot beat the index, it is reasonable to ask why pay the fee?

This is the rationale for index funds. Index funds have simple expectations: they seek to match the return of the underlying index by buying the same stocks or bonds. Index funds still have expenses, but they are typically very low and do not significantly drag down the earnings of the fund.

Investors can choose an actively managed mutual fund where the manager is constantly buying and selling stocks and bonds in an attempt to beat the index, or go with the index fund and accept that return regardless of how it is faring. This is a common strategy and may be the smartest for the long-term investor, because index funds outperform approximately 80 percent of the actively managed funds. It does, however, preclude the possibility of beating the index's return, which 20 percent of the actively managed funds do on an annual basis.

Total Return

Investors want to know how much they are making with their mutual fund. One way to look at your investment is to take the price at which you bought in and the current price and compare the two, but this isn't a completely accurate way to measure your return.

The **total return** of the fund, which takes in share appreciation, dividends, interest, capital gains, and other income generated by the fund, is the most important measurement of return. How you calculate your personal rate of return is determined by when you bought the fund, when you sold the fund, and whether you reinvested dividends and capital gains or not.

WORDS TO GO . . .WORDS TO GO . . .WORDS TO GO

Total return of an investment in a mutual fund includes any dividends, capital gains distributions, and interest income. This is the appropriate number to consider. It should be noted that this is also a pre-tax return.

The quarterly and annual reports from the mutual fund will stress total return and direct you to the area of the publication for reference. Morningstar.com and other websites also report performance data.

Performance Determinants

One of the most important factors in predicting the success of a mutual fund over the long term is its expense ratio—that ongoing cost of owning the fund. The higher this fee, the less likely the fund will meet its investment objectives over a long period.

11.4

Although a load or sales fee may be an immediate drag on earnings, the total expense ratio will ultimately decide how much you pay in fees. These ongoing fees are charged against fund assets month after month. The lower these fees, the better the fund's chance of meeting performance expectations.

The expense ratio takes on different significance for different types of funds. For example, money market mutual funds operate on a razor-thin margin between the cost of funds and the payout to investors. In this scenario, there is not much room to maneuver. The best performing money market mutual funds have the lowest expense ratios. Bond funds also suffer from high expense ratios, because they don't typically deliver high returns.

Stock mutual funds, on the other hand, have operated with relatively high returns compared to money market funds. While a higher expense ratio might drag the sock fund some, it is less of a problem. Still, higher expense ratios are money not invested or earning a return for the investor.

◀ *SEE ALSO 10.4, "Asset Allocation"* ▶

Because expense ratios can buy investors value (professional fund management), it is reasonable to consider the value added for the expense. Some fund managers have lengthy track records of operating successful mutual funds. Many investors might consider a higher expense ratio money well spent for that expertise and an investment strategy.

Historical Perspective

One of the biggest mistakes investors make is chasing currently hot mutual funds. The list of hot mutual funds changes frequently and depends on what investment style is particularly successful given market conditions at that moment. When market conditions change—and they always do—the hot fund frequently fades away because its investment style no longer works for the new market conditions.

In evaluating mutual funds, don't consider any performance information less than three years old. The farther back performance information goes, the better, because it tells you how the fund did in all types of market conditions. Many funds did well in the bull market of the late 1990s, but how did the fund do in the bear market of 2000–2002?

Look for comparisons to other funds of the same type and see how the fund did. This will tell you whether the fund is a superior performer or an also ran under different market circumstances. Most stock funds, for example, will not do well in bear market conditions, however a good fund will hold its own and find ways to stay at the market or slightly better.

◀ *SEE ALSO 10.2, "Investment Objectives"* ▶

This performance information is in the prospectus or you can find it online at Morningstar.com.

Management Expertise

Professional management is one of the main advantages of investing in mutual funds. Investors pay for this expertise through management fees that are included in the expense ratio. Not all fund managers are created equal. Some are markedly better than others, and the funds they manage consistently do better than other funds.

Investors follow fund managers with records of high achievement. If the manager moves to a different mutual fund company, some investors will move their money also.

The investment expertise of the fund manager is particularly important in specialty funds. Sector funds that invest in narrow industry sectors require investment managers with a deep knowledge of the industry and intimate contacts within the companies. Foreign or global funds are another example where fund managers must have specialized knowledge and expertise to be successful.

When looking at the performance of a mutual fund over time, see how long its current manager has been in place. This will tell you how much responsibility this manager can claim for past performance. A fund with a good past track record but a new fund manager, may not be continuing the same practices that produced good results in the past.

Investment Strategy

A consistent and focused investment strategy contributes to successful performance. Mutual funds are a long-term investment and an investment strategy that capitalizes on that commitment will help performance.

Over time, the stock and bond market will rise and fall. You want a mutual fund that holds up well under all conditions, and you need an investment strategy to match the predictable ups and downs of investing.

11.4

One of the easiest and most successful forms of investing for the long term is dollar cost averaging. This strategy takes most of the decision making of investing and provides the opportunity for a better return than trying to guess when the best time to invest is.

Dollar cost averaging is simply investing a fixed amount of money in a mutual fund on a regular basis, usually monthly. Almost all mutual funds will help you set up a debit to your checking or other bank account for the fixed amount at a certain time each month. The money is automatically withdrawn from your bank account and deposited in your mutual fund account where it buys shares of the fund at the current NAV. This automatic investment plan removes the emotion of investment decision making, because the money is invested regardless of the current share price.

Dollar cost averaging works because when the share price is high, your fixed investment buys fewer shares, and when the share price is lower, it buys more shares. The result is you own shares at a low average cost per share.

If you belong to a 401(k) or 403(b) retirement plan at work, you are using dollar cost averaging already.

◀ *SEE ALSO 15.3, "401(k) and 403(b) Plans"* ▶

11.5 EXCHANGE TRADED FUNDS (ETFs) BASICS

Fundamentals

Market Price

Buying and Selling ETFs

Tax Consequences

Exchange Traded Funds (ETFs) are relatively new investment vehicles that combine the simplicity of index funds with the liquidity and trading action of stocks. This section explains ETFs.

Fundamentals

Exchange Traded Funds are very much like index mutual funds in that they track an index of some types. Some track well-known indexes such as the Dow or the S&P 500, while others track lesser-known indexes. ETFs are a fixed portfolio of stocks or bonds that mimics the index it tracks. For example, one of the most popular ETFs is the QQQQ that tracks the Nasdaq 100, which includes the largest 100 stocks on that exchange. Some ETFs track obscure indexes like the price of gold or the market in a foreign country.

One of the main differences between ETFs and mutual funds is ETFs are traded like stocks, mainly on the **American Stock Exchange**. You can buy or sell an ETF any time the market is open through a broker. Like stocks, you will pay a commission to buy or sell an ETF.

WORDS TO GO . . .WORDS TO GO . . .WORDS TO GO   **11.5**

American Stock Exchange is one of the three major national exchanges, although it doesn't get as much attention from the general public as the New York Stock Exchange or the Nasdaq. The exchange trades ETFs, options, and other sophisticated securities in addition to shares of common stock.

When you buy an ETF, you are buying a partial unit in a trust that holds shares of stock or bonds. The price of the ETF rises or falls as the value of the stocks or bonds changes.

Market Price

The market price of ETFs is driven by supply and demand forces in the market just like stock prices. However, ETF companies keep the fund's net asset value close to the market price by adding units to the fund if there is heavy buying pressure. These units are large blocks of the underlying security. If there is selling pressure that may drive share prices significantly below the NAV, large investors step in and buy units of the fund, which typically are valued at $50,000 and more at bargain prices. This reduction in assets reduces the NAV to be closer to the market price.

Buying and Selling ETFs

You need a broker to buy and sell ETFs. This presents a problem if you want to use dollar cost averaging as mentioned above because of the commissions you must pay. Although some ETFs are very popular and trade heavily, that is not true of all the funds. Care must be taken when investing in lightly traded ETFs because it may be difficult to get the price you want when you want to sell.

An advantage ETFs have over mutual funds is the ability to employ sophisticated trading techniques. With mutual funds, it is mainly a buy or sell. ETFs allow you to trade on margin which means borrowing from your broker so you can buy more shares. You can use limit orders that will result in an immediate sell order if the ETF price hits a level you set and other techniques. This flexibility adds another dimension to the benefits of owning ETFs over mutual funds.

◀ SEE ALSO 10.6, *"Online Trading"* ▶

Tax Consequences

ETFs are considered more tax efficient than mutual funds. They don't buy or sell stocks or bonds often because they mimic an index and there is minimal dividend income from most ETFs. You are not taxed until you sell the ETF and then only if you earned a profit.

When investors in a mutual fund want to redeem their shares, the fund must buy them back. That may mean selling stocks or bonds in the portfolio for a profit, which creates a taxable event for the other mutual fund shareholders. When the fund sells an asset for a profit, it creates a capital gains distribution (tax) that is passed on to the shareholder in proportion at the end of the year. Shareholders have no control over these tax events and may be surprised at the tax bill they receive from the mutual fund.

With ETFs, all the trading is done among shareholders on the stock exchange, so the fund does not have to sell stocks to redeem shares. This means few if any capital gains distributions at the end of the year.

11.5

11.6 TYPES OF ETFs

Market Index ETFs

Market ETFs

Sector ETFs

Exchange Traded Funds cover a wide variety of indexes and markets. This section looks at the major types of ETFs and the markets they cover.

Market Index ETFs

The most popular ETFs track well-known indexes such as the S&P 500, the Nasdaq 100 Composite Index, the Dow, and other indexes. These ETFs are pure index funds and follow the movement of the index. If investors believe an index is going to rise, they will buy the corresponding ETF in anticipation of the gain. Likewise, an anticipated drop in the index may send investors a sell signal and the price of the ETF will fall.

Index ETFs cover not only stock indexes but bond indexes as well. Bonds are sensitive to interest rates, so anticipated changes in market interest rates will affect bond ETFs.

Market ETFs

Market ETFs are typically broader in scope than most popular indexes. The Russell 5000 index and several total market indexes are covered by ETFs that give investors the opportunity to buy the broadest possible market coverage. This is useful as a strategy to balance more aggressive and narrowly focused holdings.

◀ SEE ALSO 12.2, *"The Stock Markets and Indexes"* ▶

Sector ETFs

Sector ETFs focus on particular industry or geographical sectors and are typically the highest risk ETFs. Sector ETFs are risky because they are not diversified and, if the area of investment is troubled—remember Internet stocks in 2000 took a horrible beating in the stock market—the fund could suffer dramatic losses.

Sector funds also invest in geographic areas, such as overseas markets, which are also risky because of potential economic and political disruptions in some countries. Because of their risk, sector funds should only be a small portion of your holdings.

11.7 FINDING GOOD ETFs

Matching ETFs to Objectives
Using ETFs to Diversify

Exchange Traded Funds are still new on the market and more are being added all the time. Because most ETFs are passively managed index funds, performance of the fund is not the issue as much as how the ETF fits into your investment objectives.

Matching ETFs to Objectives

ETFs, like any other investment, must meet an investment objective to be considered for inclusion in an investor's portfolio. Depending on which ETFs you consider, you could select a very conservative or very aggressive investment.

The broad market and market index ETFs make good **core holdings** for long-term investors as long as you don't plan on making regular investments like dollar cost averaging. Dollar cost averaging is a systematic way to make investments that results in a lower average cost. It works well with mutual funds where the investor can buy directly from the fund with no transaction fee. The commissions you pay a broker for buying ETF shares defeat the purpose of dollar cost averaging by adding extra cost to each transaction. For a lump sum deposit, the ETF is probably the better choice because most offer lower expense ratios than mutual funds.

WORDS TO GO . . .WORDS TO GO . . .WORDS TO GO

A **core holding** is a mutual fund or exchange traded fund that is broad based and central to an investor's investment strategy. The investor will plan an investment to hold and not trade.

11.7

Sector ETFs may be used to gain exposure in special market niches where an investor may believe there is growth potential, but it's unclear which companies will emerge as leaders. The sector fund will give exposure to that market without having to pick a winner out of hundreds of contenders.

Using ETFs to Diversify

Investors can use exchange traded funds to diversify their holdings without buying a large number of individual securities. ETFs that track bond indexes are popular for this function, because many investors are unfamiliar with selecting and investing in individual bonds. The liquidity of ETFs let you move in and out of different funds as your diversification needs change and the many narrow and broad indexes represented give you a wide selection.

Indexes are significant diversification tools because they represent either whole markets or large parts of markets. ETFs allow investors to be precise in establishing a diversification plan that touches all their needs.

◄ *SEE ALSO 10.4, "Asset Allocation"* ►

11.8 OTHER KINDS OF FUNDS

Closed-End Funds

Unit Investment Trusts

Closed-end funds and unit investment trusts are types of funds that are close relatives to mutual funds and exchange traded funds but have some unique characteristics of their own. In this section, you'll learn about these two hybrid investment vehicles.

Closed-End Funds

Closed-end funds raise an initial sum of money through a public offering and then close the fund to new investment. Shares of the fund then trade on stock exchanges like stocks. The price of the fund may be at a discount or premium to the net asset value.

The funds specialize in certain investment areas such as real estate stocks, foreign markets stocks from a single country, and so on. Whether the fund is trading at a premium or discount may depend on how investors view the assets held in the trust. Expenses are important, just like in open-end mutual funds, and expense ratios greater than 1.5 percent should be viewed with caution.

Because closed-end funds can swing from a discount to a premium, investors should watch prices carefully before buying. It is usually not a good idea to pay a premium for a closed-end fund. You can find information on prices and whether the fund is selling at a premium or discount at Morningstar.com.

Unit Investment Trusts

11.8

Unit investment trusts are sold by brokers and should be viewed with caution, not because brokers are untrustworthy, but because there is no easy way for consumers to compare performance. A unit investment trust is a collection of securities—stocks, bonds, mortgage-backed securities, and so on—that is put together as a package and then sold in units.

There is no management of the assets. The unit is usually left to generate income through interest or dividends, which are distributed to investors. If it is a bond unit, it will dissolve when the bonds mature and the investors will be paid the principal. Unit investment trusts are a popular way to hold bonds because investors can buy units in increments of $1,000 instead of the much larger commitment that individual bonds may require. Since the trust holds the bonds, investors know they will provide a steady income stream.

◄ *SEE ALSO 13.1, "Basics of Bond Investing"* ►

The main concern with unit investment trusts may be the sales pressure of brokers who want to sell out the units quickly and the lack of comparison data.

12

INVESTING IN STOCKS

12.1 BASICS OF STOCK INVESTING

Fundamentals of Stock Investing

Initial Public Offering

How Market Price Is Determined

Stocks represent a share of ownership, which allows you to participate in the profits or experience the losses of a company. The profits and losses are, for the most part, reflected by the share price of the company's stock. This section looks at how stock investing works and how prices are set.

Fundamentals of Stock Investing

The fundamentals of stock investing are simple to explain, but not so simple to execute. You buy a stock at one price, wait until the price has risen as high as you think it will, and sell for a profit. Unfortunately, executing this strategy is more difficult than it seems. Stocks can also fall in price or, in some cases, not move in either direction for long periods.

A good investing strategy makes the difference, and that involves looking at the company behind the stock. Picking a good investment candidate involves examining the company for future growth potential, because the market always pays for future **earnings** and growth. If a company has continued growth in earnings, the stock price will generally continue to rise. As you investigate potential investment candidates, consider not only the current financial health of the company, but also the future prospects, because this is what will fuel increases in share price.

WORDS TO GO . . . WORDS TO GO . . . WORDS TO GO

Earnings is a word that can have several meanings when used to describe accounting activity, but it generally means profits when used without a modifying term to describe some other function.

There are many different investment strategies, but two distinguish themselves based on their approach. The first is a buy-and-hold philosophy and the second is the active trader approach.

Buy-and-Hold Investors

Buy-and-hold investors look for quality companies that have products and market position that will make them good investments for years to come. You're looking for continued growth in share price and dividends over many years, and these companies are typically market leaders in their industry sector with little chance of being replaced.

Active Traders

Active traders believe they can spot short-term profit opportunities and buy companies that are about to move sharply in price. They will buy and hold the stock for a short period, then sell when they feel the profit is out of the stock and move on to the next deal. This may mean a holding period of a few days, weeks, or months. Active traders feel they can beat market indexes by picking smart buys, taking quick profits, and moving on.

The extreme example of this strategy is the day trader who sits in front of multiple monitors every day trading stocks for small profits. A day trader may do 25-75 or more trades a day, each for a small profit or small loss.

Initial Public Offering

Companies start out privately owned, with a few investors contributing the money to get the business started. As a business grows, it needs more money to fund expansion. Companies can borrow some of the money, but it must be paid back with interest, which can slow growth down. If the company wants to expand beyond its local market, more capital will be needed—usually much more than the company could borrow.

The way many companies choose to raise this capital is by offering shares of their stock to the public. The initial public offering or IPO is a highly regulated event. The **Securities and Exchange Commission** has a stringent set of guidelines that the company must follow during the process.

One of the documents the company produces is a prospectus, a legal summary of the business, its principal officers, its competitors, and detailed financial records of the company's history to date. One major feature of the prospectus is a listing of all the risks involved in investing in the company.

12.1

When all the legal paperwork is complete to the regulatory authorities' satisfaction, a date is set for the offering to the public. An **investment-banking firm** is responsible for bringing the stock to market and setting the initial price. Once shares are offered on the market, supply and demand for the IPO drives the price up or down.

IPOs have a mythical quality on Wall Street because of all the stories of stocks coming out and being bid up several hundred percent in price the first day. That was the case during the tech stock boom of the 1990s; however, with a few exceptions, that fever has died down in the recent past.

WORDS TO GO . . . *WORDS TO GO . . .WORDS TO GO*

The **Securities and Exchange Commission** is the main regulatory agency responsible for monitoring the stock markets and securities industry. It must approve all IPOs and requires frequent and regular filings from publicly-traded companies. It is a watchdog for investors to protect them against unethical investing practices.

Investment-banking firms are large financial institutions that handle the initial distribution of shares during an IPO. They sell shares to national and regional brokerage firms who in turn sell them to their best client.

How Market Price Is Determined

The basic rule of stock pricing is that the market values a stock based on its stream of earnings. If a company's earnings continue to grow, the stock price will generally follow. If the company falters in earnings growth, the stock will drop in price.

Stated another way, a company's stock price is the value investors place on a company's ability to generate future profits. Investors vote on that value every day the market is open by bidding up or down on the stock's price. That vote is illustrated not as a dollar-for-dollar change in earnings and stock price, but through a multiple known as the Price/Earning ratio or P/E.

The P/E ratio is the single most important number you need to know about a stock. It tells you how much investors are willing to pay in share price for a company's earnings. You calculate the P/E ratio by dividing the share price by the company's earnings per share. Fortunately, there's no need to do the math, the P/E ratio is widely available on any number of Internet sites.

If a company has a P/E of 15, it tells you that investors are willing to pay $15 for every $1 in earnings. The higher the P/E, the more investors are willing to pay, but the higher the risk that—if the company fails to meet earnings expectations— the market may drive the stock price down in a hurry.

12.2 THE STOCK MARKETS AND INDEXES

The New York Stock Exchange

The Nasdaq

The American Stock Exchange

The S&P 500 Index, The Dow, and Others

The major stock exchanges handle most of the transactions during the trading day. They each operate differently, but accomplish the same thing: they create an efficient market for buyers and sellers of securities. In this section, we'll look at how the markets work and some of the major market indicators.

The New York Stock Exchange

The New York Stock Exchange (NYSE) is the second oldest (the Philadelphia Exchange beats it by two years) stock exchange and arguably the most prestigious. The exchange began on a corner of Wall Street in New York City in 1792. The exchange is home to the oldest and most of the largest companies on the market. Several billion shares of stock may trade on the exchange in an average day.

A **specialist** represents each stock listed on the NYSE. The specialist is responsible for maintaining an orderly market for the stock and matching buyers and sellers. If you put in a buy order for a stock at $50 per share, the specialist finds someone with a sell order at $50 per share. If there are no takers at $50 per share, you will not get your order filled. However, if you want to sell your stock and don't care about the price, the specialist must find you a buyer or buy it for the specialist's account. You may not like the price, but you will sell your stock.

WORDS TO GO . . .WORDS TO GO . . .WORDS TO GO

A **specialist** is an employee of a member firm of the NYSE. This investment professional is responsible for maintaining a market in a particular stock. The specialist matches buy and sell orders but, if the market gets out of balance, may step in and buy or sell out of the company's account to regain balance.

12.2

The Nasdaq

The Nasdaq (an acronym) is the name of the fastest growing stock exchange and home to thousands of smaller companies where the listing requirements are not

as high as the NYSE. The Nasdaq is also home to a number of high-tech companies. A few grew up to become giants, including Microsoft, Intel, and others.

The Nasdaq has no physical presence, unlike the NYSE. It exists as a computer
network of **market makers,** companies who specialize in a particular stock.

WORDS TO GO . . .WORDS TO GO . . .WORDS TO GO

Market makers on the Nasdaq make a market for a stock they cover by providing a quote at which they would buy or sell the stock. They enter customer's
orders and the computer system places the best buy order and the best sell
order at the top of their respective quote lists.

You will see two stock prices on Nasdaq quotes: the "bid and ask" prices. Here's
how it works. The price is quoted at bid: $25.50—ask: $25.75. If you are the
buyer, you'll pay $25.75 and the seller receives $25.50. The difference ($0.25) is
the spread and that is what the market maker keeps for their fee.

The Nasdaq computer system matches buy and sell orders with the best prices
going to the front of the line to be filled first. This feature of moving the better
orders in front of other orders is known as a negotiated market and it is another
distinctive feature of the Nasdaq.

The American Stock Exchange

Not that many years ago, the American Stock Exchange (AMEX) was in danger
of losing a place of any prominence in the financial world. It had not kept up with
the technology and was not considered a major player on the financial scene.

The emergence of **exchange traded funds (ETFs)** and some key alliances with
Nasdaq have changed the exchange's fortunes. ETFs are very popular with investors and new ones are being added all the time. AMEX has a lock on the ETF
business, and that has brought it back to the forefront of the financial scene.

WORDS TO GO . . .WORDS TO GO . . .WORDS TO GO

Exchange traded funds (ETFs) are similar to mutual funds in that they are
baskets of stocks or bonds, but they are traded on the open market like stocks.

◀ SEE ALSO 11.5, *"Exchange Traded Funds (ETF) Basics"* ▶

The S&P 500 Index, The Dow, and Others

The major stock market indexes the movement of investor dollars in to and out of the market. They are key measures of the overall health of certain segments of the market, although most acknowledge that the important indexes represent "the market."

What Is an Index?

We use an index to measure the change in a particular set of numbers. Indexes start with a base number, which represents the value of the set of numbers you are following. As the numbers change in value, the base number changes and that change in the base number is the index. The index number itself usually has no meaning relative to the numbers it is tracking—what is important is the change from one period to the next in the index.

Stock market indexes tell us whether there are more buyers or sellers at a given point in time in a segment or the whole market. There are three major market indexes:

▶ The Dow Jones Industrial Average (the Dow)

▶ The S&P 500

▶ The Nasdaq Composite

The Dow Jones Industrial Average (Dow)

The Dow is the oldest and the most widely known stock market index in the world. Although it is not the most representative (it only contains 30 stocks), it carries a lot of weight in the investing community. The Dow tracks some of the most prestigious companies in America, and all have annual revenues in excess of $7 billion. Together, they make up 25 percent of the total market.

The Dow is considered by many as the market proxy and, if it lacks the breadth of coverage to legitimately earn that title, it certainly owns the emotional crown. The Dow does not include any smaller companies, which make up the bulk of companies in the market.

12.2

The Dow is the only index that is price weighted, which means if a $25 stock increases in value by $2, it has the same affect on the index as a $50 stock that increases $2.

The S&P 500

The S&P 500, compiled by the Standard & Poor's company, includes 500 of the leading and largest companies in the market. Although it is not exclusively large companies, it is heavily weighted that way. The index covers some 70 percent of the total market's value. The S&P 500 is weighted by company size (as are most indexes with the exception of the Dow), which means a change in the price of a large stock has more influence on the index than the change in price of a smaller stock.

The S&P 500 is "the market" when many financial professionals measure the performance of an investment. This is especially true in the mutual fund business.

The Nasdaq Composite

The Nasdaq Composite tracks some 5,000 plus stocks, many of which are small technology companies. The Nasdaq is weighed by size. Even though it is home to technology giants like Microsoft, Intel, and others, most of the companies are much smaller. In addition, many survivors from the dot.com boom (and bust) remain on the Nasdaq, including Amazon.com.

The Nasdaq is the most volatile of all the major indexes and doesn't come close to representing "the market," but it does give you a good idea about where smaller companies and technology stocks are headed.

12.3 TYPES OF STOCKS

Growth Stocks

Income Stocks

Value Stocks

Small, Medium, and Large Cap Stocks

American Depository Receipts

Investors classify stocks using several different means. One measure is the expectation investors have when they invest in a stock; another is the more quantifiable measure of size.

Growth Stocks

Growth stocks grow and keep growing. When they stop growing they aren't growth stocks anymore and their share price is likely to drop dramatically unless the slowing is seen to be the natural process of a maturing company. Growth investors focus on share price appreciation and are not concerned with dividends, because few growth stocks pay any.

Investors choose growth stocks for their above-average growth rates and hope the stock price follows the growth. This is always a judgment call, because growth in revenue doesn't always translate into growth in earnings. In fact, some growth companies reinvest all their earnings back into the company to fund more growth. This is a good strategy if growth continues. When growth begins to slow because competition is catching up or the company has grown so big that huge growth isn't possible, growth investors may move on.

Income Stocks

Income stocks represent mature, stable companies that pay consistent **dividends.** These companies often don't have much growth room, but are steady income producers. Utilities are considered income stocks because they aren't usually expanding and often pay attractive dividends.

12.3

Companies that have income stocks often issue a special type of stock, called **preferred stock,** that has limited rights but pays consistent dividends. The only reason to own preferred stock is for the dividends.

People who own income stocks should do so in a tax-qualified account, such as an IRA, so the income is not immediately taxed. However, many retired people use income stocks to help pay for retirement expanses.

WORDS TO GO . . .WORDS TO GO . . .WORDS TO GO

Dividends are cash payments (usually, but not always) to shareholders by companies. Dividends are a distribution of profits to the owners. Companies that pay regular dividends are valued for that extra return they provide shareholders.

Preferred stocks are a special type of stock that companies issue. They have limited rights when it comes to voting on company business but they do pay a steady dividend and that's what attracts investors. The stock's price may not rise (or fall) nearly as fast or as far as the common stock. Income investors like preferred stock from solid companies for its dependability.

Value Stocks

Value stocks represent companies that have been incorrectly valued by the market. For some reason, the stock price is lower than it should be to accurately reflect the value of the company. Maybe other companies in the same industry sector are having trouble and this company's stock is suffering guilt by association. Whatever the reason, value investors look for these types of stocks, betting that the market will someday realize the company's true value and the stock price will rise. This is a true buy-and-hold strategy that may take some time to work out. However, if you have done your homework, the rewards can be excellent.

Small, Medium, and Large Cap Stocks

Market capitalization or market cap is simply a way of referring to the size of a company in a manner that allows you to compare companies in different industries. Annual sales would not be a good way to compare companies, because they have little to do with the value of the company. Market cap gives you the total market value of the company.

You compute market cap by multiplying the number of outstanding shares by the current stock price. For example, if a company had 100 million shares of common stock outstanding and a current stock price of $45 per share, its market cap would be $4.5 billion (100 million × $45).

You can find the market cap of any stock reported on dozens of Internet sites such as Yahoo! Finance. Simply enter a symbol and the market cap will be among the data reported.

Investors categorize companies under one of these labels—although there is not universal agreement on the exact cutoffs.

- ▶ Micro cap: $300 million and under
- ▶ Small cap: $1 billion and under
- ▶ Mid cap: $8–$1 billion
- ▶ Large cap: $100–$8 billion
- ▶ Mega cap: Over $100 billion

These rankings are completely arbitrary and other sources may use different numbers. Size matters in the market place. Small companies are more risky than larger companies are. They have shorter life spans unless they grow or merge with a larger company. However, with risk comes the potential for reward. Small cap stocks can out-perform all other size stocks under certain market conditions, so many investors carry a small portion of them in their portfolio.

Small companies that grow to be big companies (like Microsoft and Apple) can make early investors very wealthy, but most don't. Large companies can protect their market share and fend off competitors more easily. They may not grow as rapidly, but they may also pay consistent dividends. You invest in small companies expecting rapid and large growth, while an investment in a large company is more secure and done with the expectation of reasonable growth and dividends.

American Depository Receipts

American Depository Receipts (ADRs) are a way for U.S. investors to own foreign stocks without investing directly in a foreign exchange. U.S. financial institutions bundle foreign stocks to create ADRs and then sell shares of the bundle on U.S. stock exchanges. The stock will have "ADR" after the name to indicate it is a foreign stock.

ADRs are bought and sold in U.S. dollars, although there is still some currency risk related to the country where the stocks originate. If the country experiences rapid inflation or **deflation,** your shares of ADR will decrease in value.

12.3

WORDS TO GO . . .WORDS TO GO . . .WORDS TO GO

Deflation is a marked decline in the prices of goods and services, usually accompanied by high unemployment and a drop in the output of a nation's economy.

Investing in foreign stocks is a reasonable use of a small portion on your invest-ing assets (no more than 10 percent). Foreign stocks react to a different economy than U.S. stocks and may do well when domestic stocks are down or stagnant. With globalization, business is happening all over the world and ADRs allow you to participate in growing markets outside the United States.

12.4 FINDING GOOD STOCKS

Growth Investors

Value Investors

Income Investors

Finding good stocks for investment is a process of sifting through the opportunities to locate those that fit a profile of what you what. This section looks at some of the factors investors should consider when looking for good stocks.

Growth Investors

Growth investors care nothing about history or even the present: they are always looking to the future. The type of investment they are looking for is a company that will show sustained growth quarter after quarter. They look for companies that can capitalize on a consumer or business need that is significant enough to allow the company to capture a large share of the market. Growth investors willingly pay for growth, but will quickly dump an investment that fails to meet expectations.

Finding good candidates requires some idea about what markets or technologies will be important in the future. The growth investment community is drawn to new technology, such as information, biotech, healthcare, and so on. The problem for all growth investors who want to get in on the early stages of a company's growth is identifying which ideas will mature into markets, because much technology doesn't prove commercially viable or only applies to a small market.

◀ *SEE ALSO 10.3, "Risk and Reward Relationship"* ▶

The fate of all growth stocks is to slow down. Microsoft was a growth stock, and so was Intel, and so was Apple. Once companies reach a certain size, it is almost impossible to sustain high growth rates.

12.4

Value Investors

Value investors are very concerned with knowing the precise value of companies they consider for investment. What makes value investing work is finding companies that have a higher value than the market assigns through the stock price. This places the value investor's focus on the present financial records of the company. It is a mistake to focus on low price alone, but the price of the stock is important to the value investor as it relates to the company's earnings. You are looking for companies with high earnings and low stock prices. One major measure of this relationship is **earnings per share** or EPS. You calculate earnings per share by taking the net earnings and dividing by the outstanding shares. A high EPS is a good sign for the value investor.

Earnings per share (EPS) is a way of reporting earnings or profits on a per share of stock. The number is found by dividing the annual earnings by the number of shares.

Another measure of value is the assets on the company's books. Value investors spend a lot of time looking at the balance sheet to determine the book value of the business. A good value candidate will have a high book value.

In the end, the value investor needs to make a judgment about the price of the stock. Is it depressed because all other stocks in this sector are depressed, or is this company poorly managed and not going anywhere? Will the market recognize the value of this company at some point and bid up the stock to a higher level?

Income Investors

Income investors have an easier time finding good stocks than value or growth investors, because history is a decent indicator of future performance. Income stocks, which tend to be older, more stable companies, including utilities, are easier to identify. Another source of current income is **real estate investment trusts** (REITs), which must return 90 percent of their profits to investors. These investments are more risky than income stocks, but can pay a nice current income.

Real estate investment trusts are closed-end funds that invest in real estate and mortgages. They must pass 90 percent of all profits on to the shareholders, which makes them well-suited for people looking for current income.

◄ SEE ALSO 10.1, *"Defining Investment Options"* ►

12.5 DIVIDENDS

Paid Quarterly

Reinvestment Plans

Corporations pay out part of their profits to owners in the form of dividends. This section looks at that process and how you can reinvest dividends to buy more shares.

Paid Quarterly

Dividends are profits that the company pays out to shareholders. The board of directors declares the dividend payment (which is usually quarterly, but doesn't have to be), and owners of stock on a certain date receive the dividend. Most quarterly dividends are paid on the first day of January, April, July, and October, but some companies may pay on a different schedule, or semiannually or annually.

Paying dividends follows a sequence of four important dates, and when you buy stock in the sequence determines whether you will receive the dividend. The important dates are:

▶ The declaration date is when the board sets the dividend and announces when the stockholders will get their checks. The board also announces the ex-dividend date, which is a very important date to know.

▶ The record date is when the company sets the list of shareholders to receive the dividend. You must own the stock before this date to get the dividend, but the ex-dividend date is more important.

▶ The ex-dividend date usually falls two to four days before the record date to allow for the completion of all pending transactions; it usually takes three days to settle a regular stock sale. The ex-dividend date is the most important date as far as owning the stock if you want to receive the dividend.

▶ The payment date is when the company mails the checks, often two weeks or so after the record date.

On the ex-dividend date, the market discounts a stock's price, because the dividend is no longer available to buyers.

12.5

Reinvestment Plans

A dividend reinvestment program, or DRIP, is a service that lets you build your position in the company by reinvesting your dividends in more company stock. Companies that offer DRIPs usually inform shareholders or have a place under "investor relations" on their website with information on getting started. Your dividends are reinvested in new stock through the program, even if the amount is not large enough to buy a single share. For example, if your quarterly dividend payment is $25 and the current per share price of the stock is $50, you purchase 0.5 shares. You can't buy fractional shares through a stockbroker.

Most DRIP programs allow you to have additional money regularly withdrawn from your checking account and deposited into your DRIP. Most DRIPs charge very low or no fees, which increases your odds of earning a better return.

Check with the company for details on how its DRIP works. If you don't need the dividend income, this is a low-cost way to increase your holdings. Remember, however, that even though you don't receive the dividend, you are still liable for the taxes due on it.

12.6 BUYING AND SELLING STOCKS

Avoiding Mistakes

Stopping Losses/Protecting Profits

One way to make money investing is to avoid losing it. This section looks at common investing mistakes and how you can to avoid them.

Avoiding Mistakes

Investors are prone to making the same mistakes, so watch out for these situations:

▶ **Loving a stock:** Investors become emotionally attached to a stock and overlook the company's shortcomings. Maybe your father worked for the company and you inherited the stock, or you're retired from the company yourself. Whatever the reason, separate your emotions from the hard reality that it may be time to sell.

▶ **Hot tips:** Acting on hot tips is almost always a recipe for overpaying. By the time you hear about a "hot tip," the professional traders have bought and sold the stock and made their profit. You will buy at the top of an inflated price that will almost certainly fall well below what you paid.

▶ **Forgetting trading costs:** It's easy to forget that it costs money now and in the future to make a profit on a stock trade. In the present, there are commissions to pay; in the future, you will pay a commission when you sell *and* taxes on any profits. Which taxes you pay will depend on how long you held the stock before you sell it. A stock must rise enough in price to cover all the past trading cost, future trading costs, the anticipated taxes, and still have a nice profit for you.

◀ *SEE ALSO Chapter 8, "Taxes"* ▶

▶ **Poor diversification:** If you fail to properly diversify your holdings, you're setting yourself up for a major setback. An economic move against the stocks you are holding can cause an across-the-board drop in price if you are not diversified. Diversification lowers your risk by spreading your investing dollars over industries and **asset classes.**

12.6

WORDS TO GO . . .WORDS TO GO . . .WORDS TO GO

Asset classes are tangible assets such as stocks, bonds, cash, real estate, and other types of assets. These different classes form the basis of active diversification.

▶ **Speculating:** Investors can easily forget they are investing for the long-term and be lured into the excitement of trading for the short-term. Traders buy and sell stocks over short periods: hours, days, weeks. It takes a great deal of experience and nerve to be an active trader. Most long-term investors don't have the experience or risk tolerance for speculating and are lured into trading by the potential for gain, only to find it is hard work and not an easy way to make money.

▶ **Inability to sell:** Investors sometimes have a difficult time admitting to themselves that an investment isn't working out. They hold on irrationally, hoping the company is going to bounce back from the brink of bankruptcy. Investors should set a loss limit and sell when the stock hits that mark.

▶ **Giving up too soon:** Investing in stocks is a long-term commitment: at least three years, and preferably five or more. Even companies with good fundamental economics may stall in stock price. If you had a logical reason for investing in the company in the first place, be patient and let the market catch up with your thinking.

Stopping Losses/Protecting Profits

You can use special orders with your broker to ensure you cut your losses and/or protect your profit in a stock. Generally called **stop-loss orders,** they instruct your stockbroker to sell when the stock hits a certain price. These orders are placed as a "floor" under the current market price of the stock, so if the stock drops to this point, the order becomes a "sell" order and your broker sells at that price or close to it. This strategy prevents you from losing too much money if the price starts to fall and you aren't aware of it. The order happens automatically, so once you put it in place, it stays until you cancel it.

If you own a stock that is rising rapidly, you may want to use what are known as **trailing stops.** Trailing stops follow the price of the stock up by a certain percentage—say 12 percent. As the stock rises, the trailing stop also rises, following 12 percent (or whatever percentage you set) behind. If the stock runs into trouble and begins to fall, the trailing stop will be activated when the stock price retreats 12 percent or more.

Decide in advance how much of a loss you're willing to take before selling a stock. Some stocks regularly fluctuate in price, so you want to stay outside that range. However, you do need a price or a percentage drop that is your limit and if the stock drops that far, you sell.

WORDS TO GO . . .*WORDS TO GO* . . .*WORDS TO GO*

Stop-loss orders tell your stockbroker to execute a sell order when the price of a stock drops to a specific level. When the price falls to this level, the broker sells the stock at the current market price. This strategy prevents you from losing more than a specific amount.

Trailing stops are similar to a stop loss order, but they are used by investors to protect a profit. Investors place a trailing stop behind a profitable stock so that if the price begins to fall, the broker will sell while the price will still produce a profit. If the stock continues to rise, the trailing stop rises with the stock's price, usually following by a percentage.

12.6

12.7 EMPLOYEE STOCK OPTIONS

The Basics

Nonqualified

Qualified or Incentive

Stock options are a way for companies to offer an incentive to employees, either to stay with the company or as a recruiting tool to attract new employees. This section covers the basics of employee stock options.

The Basics

Employers use employee **stock options** as an incentive to retain key employees or attract new ones. Unlike other benefits, employers can choose who gets stock options and who doesn't.

WORDS TO GO . . . WORDS TO GO . . . WORDS TO GO

Stock options give the owner the right but not the obligation to buy a certain number of stock shares at a fixed price on or before a certain date regardless of the current market price. Employers often use stock options as incentives for employees.

A stock option gives the owner the right, but not the obligation, to buy a designated number of shares of company stock at a fixed price. If the market price of the stock is higher than the fixed price, the employee can exercise the option and buy the stock at the lower price, then sell it on the market at a higher price for a profit. That is the simple way the transaction can work, although it is not always the best way because of the tax consequences.

The employer controls the details of the employee stock options. The **strike price** is the preset price of the stock that the option grants the owner. It is the price the owner of the option pays when they exercise the option. For example, an option may have a strike price of $25 per share. This grants the owner the right to buy the stock (usually 100 shares) at $25 per share, no matter what the market price of the stock is. If the stock is selling on the open market for $35 per share, the owner of the option can make a profit of $10 per share by exercising his option and selling the stock (ignoring commissions).

WORDS TO GO . . . *WORDS TO GO . . .WORDS TO GO*

Strike price is the price specified in the option that the owner can pay for shares of stock. If the market price is higher than the strike price, the options are valuable; however, if the market price is lower than the strike price, the options are worthless.

Employee stock options have an expiration date. The option must be exercised on or before this date or it expires, worthless. If the stock option has a strike price of $25 per share, but the market price drops to $20 per share and stays there, the option will expire. Ten years is a common length for employee stock options. Many employee stock option programs have a **vesting schedule** that requires the employee to own the option for three to five years before they can fully exercise all their options.

WORDS TO GO . . . *WORDS TO GO . . .WORDS TO GO*

Vesting schedule is a period set by management for the options to become valid. For example, 20 percent of the options might become valid after one year; 40 percent after two years; and so on. This is known as stepped or phased vesting. Another type of vesting is cliff vesting, which declares 100 percent of the options valid after three years, for example.

There are two different types of employee stock options:

▶ Non-qualified

▶ Qualified or incentive

Nonqualified

Nonqualified employee stock options are most often used when a large group of employees is covered by the same plan. This type of employee stock option may have a strike price slightly above or slightly below the current market price.

Employees do not owe tax when the options are granted, but only if they are exercised for a profit. The profit is treated as ordinary income for tax purposes. You pay tax on the difference between what you pay for the stock (the strike price) and the market price. That difference is known as the spread and is subject to ordinary income tax. This is important because you owe this tax even if you don't convert the stock into cash.

12.7

For example, if the option has a strike price of $15 and you exercise the option when the market price is $25 per share, you owe ordinary income tax on $1,000 ($25 – $15 = $10 × 100 shares = $1,000), even if you don't sell the stock. If the market value of the stock drops to $20 per share before you sell, you still owe the $1,000 ordinary income tax. You may be able to claim a capital loss of $500 ($2,500 – $2,000 = $500), depending on how long you held the stock before selling.

If you are unsure about the tax consequences of exercising nonqualified employee stock options, check with a competent tax advisor to clarify your particular situation.

Qualified or Incentive

Qualified or incentive employee stock options are usually reserved for senior management or stellar employees the company wants to retain or attract. Qualified employee stock options receive special tax breaks because they are not taxed until the stock is sold. When stock from a qualified employee stock option is sold, the proceeds are treated as long-term capital gains, assuming the options have been held for at least one year.

The employer does not benefit from these options with any tax reduction, which explains why they are reserved for top management and highly paid employees. To retain the tax benefits, the employee must hold the option for at least two years after the company grants it and one year after the exercise. The employee pays long-term capital gains tax on the spread between the option strike price and the price the shares sell for on the open market. If you violate the holding period requirement, qualified options are then considered non-qualified and taxed that way.

Exercising qualified employee stock options can trigger the Alternative Minimum Tax.

◄ SEE ALSO 8.5, *"Alternative Minimum Tax"* ►

Exercising Options

You can exercise employee stock options one of three ways:

> ▶ **Cash:** This is the simplest method. You write a check to your employer for the exercise. If you hold an employee stock option for 100 shares of company stock at a strike price of $20, you need $2,000 to exercise the option.

▶ **Cashless:** If you don't have the cash on hand to exercise the option, you can borrow the money from your broker and exercise the option. You immediately sell the stock and pay back the broker, plus interest. This is a popular method for people short on cash, but you are still responsible for the taxes on the sale.

▶ **Swap stock:** You can swap company stock you own for option stock. If you own company stock that is worth quite a bit more than option stock, you may be able to swap shares to receive more shares without paying much out-of-pocket.

If you have a large number of employee stock options, it would make sense to discuss how and when to exercise them with a competent financial advisor who knows your complete financial situation.

12.8 RETURN ON INVESTMENT

Calculating Return on Investment

Do you know how much you made on your investment? There are more factors to consider than just share prices. This section looks at the way to calculate returns on investment.

Calculating Return on Investment

You need to know how much, if anything, you made on an investment. You can do some simple math that will give you this answer—you can also do this as a "what if" exercise before selling to see where you are. The first formula is known as the Simple Return and it gives you a quick number, but it has some limitations.

The formula is:

Simple Return =
net proceeds + any dividends / what you paid – 1

For example: if you bought 200 shares at $30 per share and paid an $18 commission, the total cost would be $6,018 (200 × $30 = $6,000 + $18 = $6,018).

You sold the stock for $36 per share and paid an $18 commission. If you received dividends of $1 per share, that equals $200.

Plugging those numbers in: $36 × 200 = $7,200 – $18 = $7,182 for net proceeds.

Simple Return = $7,182 + $200 / $6,018 – 1

Simple Return = $7,382 / $6,018 – 1

Simple Return = 1.23 – 1

Simple Return = .23 or 23%

This number has limited use and is really only valid for investments held for very short periods, because it does not consider the time value of money. To get a valid picture of how a stock or other investment has done over time, you need to calculate the compound annual growth rate.

The compound annual growth rate takes into account the time value of money and evens out the ups and downs so you can see the growth as a single number. To get the compound annual growth rate, you use the Simple Return with the adjustment of eliminating the subtraction of 1 at the end of the calculation.

From our previous example, the Adjusted Simple Return would be 1.23.

The next step is to factor in the length of time you have held an investment. Let's assume you held the stock for four years.

Divide 1 by the number of years the investment has been held (4) and this will give you the factor to adjust the return:

$\frac{1}{4}$ = .25 power or exponent

Compound Annual Growth Rate = Adjusted Simple Return $^{\text{(raised to the power)}}$ − 1

Compound Annual Growth Rate = 1.23 $^{(.25)}$ − 1

Compound Annual Growth Rate = 1.05311 − 1

Compound Annual Growth Rate = .05311 or 5.31 percent

You will need a calculator that allows you to enter the exponent or power. You can also make the calculations using Microsoft Excel. In the "Insert Function" under the "Insert" menu, pick "Math & Trig" from the drop down box and scroll down to "POWER." This function allows you to enter the number and the power you want to raise it to.

As you can see, our 23 percent Simple Return looked good until we factored in the time you held the stock. The Annual Compound Growth Rate of 5.31 percent is nothing to get excited about. After you pay taxes and factor in inflation, this investment may have lost money. If you want an after-tax calculation, substitute after tax proceeds and after-tax dividend numbers.

12.8

13

INVESTING IN BONDS

13.1 BASICS OF BOND INVESTING

Bond as a Debt

New Issue vs. Secondary Market

Interest Rates

Inflation

Bonds vs. Certificates of Deposit

Call Feature

Bonds represent a debt owed by a governmental unit or a corporation. Bond-holders are the creditor and earn interest, but take the credit and interest rate risk. This section is a general overview of bonds and their key features.

Bond as a Debt

Bonds represent a debt. They are a legal obligation to repay to bondholders a specific amount at or by a specific date and at a stated rate of return. They are different from a loan because in most cases the **face value** or principal amount of the bond is paid in a lump sum at the bond's **maturity.** Most loans pay down part principal and interest with each payment.

WORDS TO GO . . . WORDS TO GO . . . WORDS TO GO

Face value is the amount the bond pays at maturity. It is usually the amount the investor pays for a newly issued bond, but may not be the price an investor pays on the open market.

Maturity is when a bond reaches the end of its financial life and the face value or principal is returned to the owner. Bonds may have maturities of just a few years or may stretch out for many years.

Bonds are issued for various maturities ranging from 1 to 100 years. Governmental agencies and corporations use bonds rather than commercial loans because the interest rates are usually better and the terms longer.

New Issue vs. Secondary Market

Governmental agencies and corporations issue new bonds when they need to raise money to finance some aspect of their responsibility or business. These new issues are sold either directly to the public in the case of U.S. Treasury bonds, for example, or through stockbrokers that specialize in bonds. Newly issued bonds have a stated interest rate and maturity.

Once a bond has been issued and bought, it can be resold on the secondary market through stockbrokers who handle bond business. In most cases, the stockbroker tries to match buyers and sellers. Some bonds are listed in major daily newspapers, but many are not, which is why investors must rely on brokers to find or sell bonds.

Interest Rates

Bonds, for the most part, have fixed interest rates, which makes them very vulnerable to changing interest rates. If interest rates go up, the bond's value goes down because it does not pay as much as newly issued bonds. Likewise, if interest rates go down, bond values go up, because their fixed interest rate is now higher than the prevailing market interest rate.

Because bonds are so sensitive to interest rates, the longer the term of the bond, the riskier the investment, because there is more time for interest rates to rise with long term bonds. For this reason, long-term bond rates should always be higher than short-term bond rates. This doesn't always happen because interest rates can fluctuate in the short-term and end up higher than long-term rates. This drives money out of the long-term market and makes those bonds worth less. Long-term bond rates that don't compensate investors for the risk should raise a flag with investors.

Inflation

Inflation is another serious problem for bond investors, because it reduces the value of future payments. Most bonds have no way to adjust for inflation, so the return over time suffers in an inflationary environment. There are U.S. Treasury bonds that offer some protection from inflation, but most do not. There are investment strategies that address inflation dangers, but bonds themselves offer no protection.

WORDS TO GO . . .WORDS TO GO . . .WORDS TO GO   **13.1**

Inflation is a rise in the cost of goods and services with a corresponding decrease in the value of money.

Bonds vs. Certificates of Deposit

Bonds behave very much like bank certificates of deposit, with several major exceptions:

▶ Not all bonds are as safe as bank CDs. Municipal and corporate bonds, in particular, do experience default where you can lose your investment.

▶ Bonds, with the exception of U.S. Treasury issues, can be called, which means you may have the bond redeemed early (see the following section for more information).

▶ Bonds allow you to take a measured risk in return for a higher interest rate.

Bonds may not be a good substitute for bank CDs depending on interest rates and maturities.

◀ SEE ALSO 3.3, "Savings Accounts" ▶

Call Feature

Most corporate and municipal bonds contain a call provision, which gives the issuer the right to **redeem** the bonds if interest rates fall. The issuer would want to call or redeem the bonds if they could refinance the debt at a lower rate. It is no different from a homeowner wanting to refinance their mortgage if interest rates fall.

WORDS TO GO . . .WORDS TO GO . . .WORDS TO GO

Redeem, in bond parlance, means for the issuer to pay the owner the full face value of the bond. Bonds are usually redeemed at maturity, but can be redeemed earlier through a call provision.

If the issuer does redeem or call a bond, the bondholder receives the interest they are due up to that point plus the face value of the bond. Some bonds with call provisions state the bond can't be called in the first two years or some other window. Bonds that have a call provision should pay a slight premium for this risk to the bondholder.

The risk to the bondholder is that interest rates will fall, making the bond they own more valuable. The issuer will then call the bond, because they can refinance the debt with new bonds at a lower interest rate. The bondholder, however, must now find a new investment for the proceeds, which will be at a lower interest rate. The risk to the bondholder is the difference between what the original bond paid and what the bondholder will earn on a new bond.

13.2 TYPES OF BONDS

U.S. Treasury Bonds
U.S. Agency Bonds
Municipal Bonds
Corporate Bonds
Zero Coupon Bond
Junk Bonds

The variety of types of bonds makes it possible for investors to find one to suit their investment objective. This section covers the different types of bonds.

U.S. Treasury Bonds

U.S. Treasury issues are not only the most secure bond, but also the most secure investment you can make. They are backed by the "full faith and credit" of the U.S. government. For this safety, investors earn a very low return.

The interest on U.S. Treasury issues is exempt from state and local taxes, but not federal income tax. Here are the different types of U.S. Treasury issues:

Treasury Bonds

These bonds have a maturity exceeding 10 years. They are issued in denominations ranging from $1,000 to $1 million. Due to popular demand, the 30-year bond was brought back in 2006 after the Treasury took them off the market for a number of years. They pay interest every six months.

If you buy the older bonds from another investor or organization other than the U.S. government, Treasury Bonds are still backed by the "full faith and credit" of the U.S. government.

Treasury Notes

Notes have maturities of 2, 3, 5, or 10 years and denominations of $1,000. The U.S. Treasury sells notes at frequent public auctions. You bid for notes by placing a competitive or a noncompetitive bid.

A noncompetitive bid guarantees you will get the note because you will accept whatever rate is set at the auction. A competitive bid states what interest rate you will accept. If that happens to be the rate set at the auction, you get the

13.2

note. If not, you don't get the note. You do not have to attend the auction, which is all done electronically. You submit your bid online or through a participating bank or broker.

TIPS or Treasury Inflation Protected Securities

TIPS are bonds with maturities of 5, 10, and 20 years. They are sold in $1,000 denominations at auction just like Treasury notes. TIPS are adjusted for inflation. Every six months the Treasury adjusts the principal by the **Consumer Price Index** for inflation. The fixed rate of interest paid by the bond is applied to this inflation-adjusted principal. In an inflationary environment, each six-month interest payment would be higher than the next. At maturity, the TIPS pay the inflation-adjusted principal or the original face value, whichever is greater.

How could the principal be less than the face value? During a period of **deflation,** your principal would be reduced and subsequent interest payments less. Under these circumstances, it is possible that the deflation-adjusted principal could be less than the original face value, but you will be paid the original principal if that is greater.

WORDS TO GO . . . WORDS TO GO . . . WORDS TO GO

The **Consumer Price Index** is a basket of goods and services tracked by the Bureau of Labor Statistics for the relative price change from month to month. This change is the rate of inflation.

Deflation is a marked decline in the prices of goods and services, usually accompanied by high unemployment and a drop in the output of a nation's economy.

I Bonds

I Bonds offer a measure of protection from the eroding effects of inflation. I Bonds are sold at face value through financial institutions and directly from the U.S. Treasury in denominations ranging from $50 to $10,000. You can buy up to $30,000 in paper I Bonds per year. In addition, you can purchase up to $30,000 in electronic I Bonds through **Treasury Direct.**

I Bonds have a two-part interest rate. The first is a fixed rate set when you buy the bond. The second rate is variable and tied to the **Consumer Price Index for Urban Consumers.** This rate changes twice a year according to changes in the CPI-U.

You can hold I Bonds up to 30 years. You will pay a penalty for cashing them in the first five years; it will cost you three-months worth of interest.

Interest is credited monthly and compounded semiannually, but you don't receive any interest payments until you redeem the bond.

I Bonds are exempt from state and local taxes. You don't owe any federal income taxes until you redeem the bond. If you use the I Bond to fund eligible college expenses, the interest income is exempt from federal income taxes.

If we should enter a deflationary environment, the variable interest rate would be negative so your bond would not increase in value. However, the I Bond would never fall below its face value regardless of the rate of deflation.

Treasury Bills

Treasury bills or T-bills are not bonds in the strict sense because their maturities range from 4 to 26 weeks. T-bills belong in a cash management category, rather than strictly bonds. You buy them at a discount from face value and collect the full face value at maturity. The difference is the interest earned.

For example, a $1,000 13-week bill may sell at auction for $970. When the bill matures, you redeem it for $1,000. The $30 difference is your interest.

U.S. Agency Bonds

Agency bonds refer to a group of bonds issued by organizations related to the U.S. government. These agencies typically do not have the explicit backing of the U.S. government behind their bonds, but it is assumed that the government would not let these agencies default on their bonds.

13.2

Most belong to a category of collateral-backed mortgages or loans, meaning some asset, usually real estate, is tied to the loan. These bonds pay higher rates than strictly U.S. Treasury issues for the somewhat, although not much, higher risk. Following are some of the better-known agency bonds.

▶ The Government National Mortgage Association, or Ginnie Mae, buys mortgages from lenders and pools them into securities. Its bonds are backed by the full faith and credit of the U.S. government.

▶ The Federal National Mortgage Association, or Fannie Mae, buys mortgages on the secondary market and resells them to investors. Some of the mortgages may be insured by the Federal Housing Authority (FHA).

▶ The Federal Home Mortgage Corporation, or Freddie Mac, is similar to Fannie Mae, but they don't contain any mortgages guaranteed by FHA.

▶ The Student Loan Marketing Association, or Sallie Mae, pools student loans instead of mortgages. These are more risky than mortgaged back bonds.

Securities issued by agencies are sold by brokers. Many of the bonds and mortgage-backed issues are only sold in very high denominations. For many investors, it may make more sense to find mutual funds that specialize in agency bonds.

◀ *SEE ALSO 11.2, "Types of Mutual Funds"* ▶

Municipal Bonds

Municipal bonds fund projects for local governmental entities like states, counties, townships, cities, utility districts, and so on. Municipal bonds, often called munis, fund new roads, schools, sewers, and other projects; in some cases, fees collected from the project go to retire the bonds, in other cases tax money is used or a combination of both.

Although not as safe as the U.S. Treasury issues, munis have a good record of security. One of the key features of these bonds is that the income is free from federal income tax. If you buy a muni, in the state where you live, the bond will likely be free from local, state, and federal income taxes. Mutual funds that are state specific specialize in these types of municipal bonds.

◀ *SEE ALSO 11.2, "Types of Mutual Funds"* ▶

This tax-free feature, combined with relative security, makes municipal bonds attractive to conservative investors. You buy munis from a broker either at new issue or existing bonds. They range in maturity from five to 30 years. Municipal bonds fall into one of two categories:

▶ **Revenue bonds:** These bonds are tied to a project that generates fees or revenue of some type, a toll road, for example. This revenue is used to pay off the bonds. A risk for revenue bonds is the project will fail to generate enough revenue to cover the repayment of the bonds.

▶ **General obligation bonds:** These bonds are backed by the taxing authority of the governmental unit issuing them. They are considered less risky because taxes can be raised to cover bond repayment if necessary.

Three major rating companies judge the creditworthiness of municipal bonds. There is a very low default rate with bonds given high marks by the rating firms.

Corporate Bonds

Corporations use bonds to fund large projects such as new plants and equipment that has a long, useful life. Corporations issue bonds to finance large projects they can pay off over time. Rather than issue new stock, which dilutes the value of existing shareholders' stock; or use short-term credit, which carries higher interest rates, companies use longer-term bonds to finance new facilities, acquisitions, and other needs.

Corporations, even the most creditworthy, do not carry the same degree of safety as governmental issuers; therefore, their bonds pay higher interest rates to compensate investors for the extra risk. There are two types of corporate bonds, one more risky than the other. **Secured bonds** are tied to a lien on some asset such as real estate, a plant, or equipment. If the corporation defaults, the assets can be sold to repay the bondholders. **Debentures** are unsecured bonds issued on the credit rating of the company. If the company goes into bankruptcy, any assets will go to pay off secured creditors first and, if there is any money left, the unsecured creditors then are paid.

WORDS TO GO . . .WORDS TO GO . . .WORDS TO GO

Secured bonds are issued by corporations and are tied to a physical asset such as real estate or equipment. These bonds typically are more secure because of the collateral of the asset linked to the bond.

Debentures are unsecured bonds offered on the credit of the corporation. With a well-known, established company, this may not be a risky bond, but these are very risky investments with less financially secure companies, because they are unsecured by any corporate asset.

Corporate bonds offer two features not common in other bonds:

13.2

▶ **Convertible bonds:** This feature allows the bond to be converted into common stock under certain conditions. Those conditions are spelled out when the bond is issued.

> ▶ **Callable bonds:** These bonds may be called or redeemed by the company before maturity. A company would call or redeem the bond if interest rates have fallen significantly since they issued the bond. By calling the high interest bond, the company can refinance the debt at a lower interest rate.

Look to the rating companies for guidance on buying corporate bonds. The higher the rating, the safer the investment, but no investment in corporate bonds is as safe as a U.S. Treasury issue.

Zero Coupon Bond

Zero coupon bonds exist because a financial institution has taken a regular bond and created a "zero." The other bond types discussed differed by issuer. This bond type is issued by many entities, but because it is so different from traditional bonds, it is set apart. Zero coupon bonds, or zeros, pay no regular interest. You buy the bond at a deep discount and redeem it at full face value, receiving all the interest in one lump sum when the bond matures. The difference is the interest that has accumulated over the years.

Zero coupon bonds come in maturities from one to forty years. The U.S. Treasury issues are the most popular zeros, although zeros are offered for both municipal and corporate bonds.

Here are some general characteristics of zero coupon bonds:

> ▶ Issued at deep discount and redeemed at full face value
>
> ▶ Some issuers may call zeros before maturity
>
> ▶ You must pay tax on interest annually even though you don't receive it until maturity

Treasury bonds are the most popular. However, the U.S. Treasury doesn't issue them directly; you buy "STRIPs" from qualified financial institutions or brokers. STRIPs stands for Separate Trading of Registered Interest and Principal of Securities and it means a financial institution has taken a regular U.S. Treasury issue and separated the principal and interest payments into two separate securities. The normal income is packaged into a separate security and sold to investors who need a reliable cash flow and the principal becomes a zero coupon bond.

Although you buy the STRIPs (they come in other names also) from brokers and financial institutions, they still carry the full faith and credit of the U.S. government. Municipalities and corporations also issue zero coupon bonds. They are also sold at a deep discount and redeemed in the future at full face value.

However, some of these issues may have call features allowing the issuer to redeem them before maturity. Be sure to check for those provisions before you invest. Municipal zero coupon bonds are exempt from federal income tax like regular municipal bonds. The major credit agencies rate most zero coupon bonds for credit worthiness. This rating can change during the life of the bond, which can affect the price.

There is a secondary market for zero coupon bonds, although not as robust as for regular bonds. If you need to get rid of a zero coupon bond, its value will be determined by prevailing market rates, years remaining, and credit worthiness of issuer. The advantage of zero coupon bonds is in keeping them until maturity. Many investors use them to provide a solid base against a volatile stock market.

For example, suppose you had $100,000 to invest. You might take $25,000 or so and buy a $100,000 STRIP (U.S. Treasury issue) maturing in 20 years. You might then take the remaining $75,000 and invest it in stocks appropriate for your financial goals. The worst that can happen is in 20 years, you'll get your money back. (Fees and taxes would have to be paid.)

Zero coupons are taxed just like regular bonds even though they don't pay interest until maturity. Every year the issuer will send a statement telling you how much interest accrued to the bond that year. There are some things you can do to offset the tax on "phantom" interest. Municipal zero coupon bonds are free of federal income tax and may be free of state and local tax where issued, but are difficult to find. Zero coupon bonds work best in retirement accounts where they can grow free from tax on current interest.

Junk Bonds

Junk bonds, as the name implies, are just like regular bonds except they carry a very low creditworthiness rating. This makes them an extreme risk for default, but they also pay from 4 to 6 percent more than U.S. Treasury bonds.

The junk bond market is very speculative and not for beginners. If you are interested, your best approach is through a mutual fund run by professionals who spend their days studying this particular investment.

13.2

13.3 BOND MUTUAL FUNDS

Mutual Funds Differ from Individual Bonds
Tax Consequences Different

You can own bonds either individually or through a mutual fund that focuses on bonds of various kinds. You may want some of both in your portfolio, because owning individual bonds is not the same as owning a bond mutual fund. This section looks at the differences.

Mutual Funds Differ from Individual Bonds

Owning individual bonds assures you (barring default) that when the bond matures, you will receive the face value of the bond back. Along the way, you have been receiving (for most bonds) interest payments on a regular basis. If your plan was to hold the bond to maturity, you don't care what happens to interest rates or other market circumstances. You are interested in your twice a year coupon payments and knowing that your face value will be there when the bond matures.

◄ *SEE ALSO 10.1, "Defining Investment Options"* ▷

When you buy a bond mutual fund, the manager has a different set of priorities. The manager must constantly buy and sell bonds, which means the fund has no maturity date or set interest rate. What happens when interest rates begin to drop?

The individual bondholder's income is higher than the market rate because it is fixed to the bond, but the mutual fund will see the collective rates begin to fall as maturing bonds must be replaced with new, lower-interest bonds, and any new bonds will be at the lower interest rate.

If interest rates rise, the bond fund loses again because the value of existing bonds drops (because they pay lower interest), which means the fund's **net asset value** drops. The individual investor, intent on holding on until maturity, is unaffected by rising or falling interest rates.

WORDS TO GO . . .*WORDS TO GO* . . .*WORDS TO GO*

Net asset value is the daily value of a mutual fund that includes all the assets minus the fund's liabilities converted to a per share price. This is the price at which you buy and sell mutual fund shares if you deal directly with the company.

This is not to say bond funds don't work, because that's not correct, but they work overtime and are not generally good short-term investments. Bond funds should be considered long-term investments to give these problems time to work through. Bond funds are also a much cheaper way to build a diversified portfolio of bond investments.

Tax Consequences Different

You should know the tax consequences of investing in a bond fund before you send in a penny. What types of bonds does this fund look for in its portfolio? Most funds allow the managers great latitude in picking investments to meet the objectives of the fund. If tax consequences are important to you, individual bonds or bond funds that are very focused may be your only chance.

13.4 UNDERSTANDING YIELDS

Current Yield

Yield to Maturity

Determining what a bond is worth at any one time is an exercise in understanding yields. This section discusses the use of yields.

Current Yield

Bondholders measure the yield from their bond several ways. The simplest and most straightforward way is current yield. Current yield takes the annual **coupon** payment and divides it by the face value of the bond to arrive at the current yield. For example, a $5,000 bond that pays $300 in annual payments would have a current yield of 6 percent ($300 / $5,000 = .06 or 6%).

> **WORDS TO GO . . .** WORDS TO GO . . . WORDS TO GO
>
> The term **coupon** comes from the bond markets where years ago bond investors had to clip coupons off the actual paper bond and send them in to receive their interest payment. Thus, the term "coupon clippers" was given to bond investors.

Yield to Maturity

The current yield doesn't really tell you the whole story, especially if you bought the bond in the secondary market or wanted to buy a previously issued bond. The yield to maturity calculation takes into account the current yield, plus the gain or loss if you held the bond until its maturity and the reinvestment of coupon payments.

This is a complicated calculation that requires either a special financial calculator or an online yield to maturity calculator found on numerous websites. Your broker can also figure it for you. This is the only way to get a good picture of the effects of interest rates on bonds and yields.

◀ SEE ALSO 10.1, *"Defining Investment Options"* ▶

13.5 CREDIT RATINGS

Understanding Credit Ratings

Credit ratings by the major companies are your best protection against default. This section looks at those ratings.

Understanding Credit Ratings

One of the most important factors for investors is how creditworthy is the bond issuer. Fortunately, two services rate most bond issues for us. Bonds can add a measure of stability to your portfolio but, if you're not careful, investing in bonds can be as risky. Some bonds are more risky than others. You can rank the chance for default by bond type:

▶ U.S. Treasury/agency: No chance for default

▶ Municipal bonds: Investment grade bonds have a very slight chance of default (one analysis showed less than 0.05% over a 30-year period)

▶ Corporate bonds: Investment grade bonds have a higher risk, but still low

▶ Junk bonds: Below investment grade have much higher risk

▶ Foreign bonds: May have a high risk

▶ Unrated bonds: Highest risk of all

The interest rates paid by these bonds go up as the risk rises. The market always requires a higher return for a higher risk.

Another factor that correlates to default is the bond's years to maturity. The longer a bond issuer is exposed to market or economic factors, the greater the odds are that something may cause a default.

The most important indicator of a bond's potential to default is its rating by one or both of the two most recognized bond-rating services. Moody's Investors Service and Standard & Poor's are the two premiere bond-rating services. If one of these services does not rate a bond, you should pass on it.

13.5

The two companies study bond issuers and rate them on their creditworthiness. Here is an explanation of their rankings.

Investment Grade—Highest Grade:

Moody's—Aaa: These bonds are judged to be of the best quality. They carry the smallest degree of risk. Interest payments are protected by an exceptionally stable margin and principal is secure.

S&P—AAA: The issuer's capacity to meet its financial obligation on the bond is extremely strong.

Investment Grade—High Grade

Moody's—Aa1, Aa2, Aa3: These bonds are judged to be of high quality by all standards. Margins of protection may not be as large as in Aaa securities.

S&P—AA+, AA, AA–: The issuer's capacity to meet its financial obligation on the bond is very strong.

Upper Medium Grade

Moody's—A1, A2, A3: These bonds possess many favorable investment attributes. Factors giving security to principal and interest are considered adequate.

S&P—A+, A, A–: Although these bonds are somewhat more susceptible to the adverse effects of changing economic conditions, the issuer's capacity to meet its financial obligations is strong.

Medium Grade

Moody's—Baa1, Baa2, Baa3: These bonds lack outstanding investment characteristics and have speculative characteristics as well.

S&P—BBB+, BBB, BBB–: Adverse economic conditions are more likely to lead to a weakened capacity of the issuer to meet its financial commitment.

Both services continue their ratings for lower rated bonds, but unless you are into speculating, you should stick with issues that fall into one of the categories above. Remember, a bond's rating can change at any time if circumstances change. Just because the services rated a bond at one level when issued doesn't mean it can't lower the rating if some adverse condition arises.

Potential for Default

You can control the potential for default by following these guidelines:

▶ U.S. Treasury issues are your safest bet.

▶ Municipal bonds with an investment grade rating have a very low incidence of default.

▶ Corporate bonds with an investment grade rating have a good record but slightly higher risk of default.

▶ The higher the rating the less likely the bond will default.

▶ The risk of default grows with the length to maturity (except for U.S. Treasury issues).

▶ Nonrated bonds are highly speculative.

13.5

13.6 BUYING AND SELLING BONDS

U.S. Treasury Issues

Using a Broker for Corporate and Munis

Premium and Discount Bonds

Bond Ladders

Some bonds you buy directly from the issuer, while others require you to go through a broker. This section looks at the buying and selling of bonds.

U.S. Treasury Issues

The U.S. Treasury makes it easy for investors to buy new bonds by offering a service called Treasury Direct. You can buy bonds, notes, and bills once your account is open and pay no commission to buy or redeem matured issues. There may be small fees if you want to redeem some bonds before they mature. For most investors, U.S. Treasury issues are for **buy-and-hold** portfolios, so the no-commission aspect means all of your investment is working for you and not a broker. Treasury issues are easy to understand and come in small denominations, so you can build a portfolio without incurring a lot of trading costs.

> **WORDS TO GO . . . WORDS TO GO . . . WORDS TO GO**
>
> **Buy-and-hold** investing is a strategy that says investor success is a result of identifying quality investments and holding them rather than actively trading in and out of the market.

U.S. agency securities are sold through brokers that specialize in this type of bond. Because some of these securities come in large denominations, brokers and financial institutions have created a number of packaged issues that may make investing in mortgage-backed issues more affordable for the average investor.

Using a Broker for Corporate and Munis

Brokers that specialize in bonds carry an inventory of current corporate and municipal bonds or have access to them through their network of connections. There are thousands of bonds on the market, so it is usually best to tell your broker what maturity and/or yield you are looking for rather than naming an individual company or municipality.

This doesn't mean you should take anything that is offered—it should meet your rating requirements. Your broker can tell you what various rated bonds are currently yielding and you can decide how much risk you are willing to take for how much yield.

Premium and Discount Bonds

Investors who buy newly issued bonds and hold them until maturity don't worry about changes in interest rates. However, other bond investors who buy and sell bonds in the secondary market must understand how changes in interest rates affect the value of their bonds. This relationship is very important because it creates premium and discount bonds as interest rates change.

When you buy a bond, the interest rate is fixed for the life of the bond. For example, if you buy a $1,000 bond paying 6 percent for 10 years, you will receive $60 every year for 10 years, then your $1,000 back. If during that time, interest rates rise to 7 percent and you want to sell your bond, no one would buy it because new bonds are earning 1 percent more than your old bond. To sell your bond, you must discount it so that its current yield equals that of the new bonds at 7 percent.

If current interest rates rise to 7 percent, a bondholder will have to discount the $1,000 price to compensate for the 6 percent the bond is paying. By lowering the price, the bond's yield rises to the current interest rate. Here's how it works: The bond pays $60 per year in interest. To earn a current market rate of 7 percent, the bondholder has to discover what the price of the bond should be to yield 7 percent.

Bond Price = Annual interest / Current interest rate

Bond Price = $60 / 7%

Bond Price = $857.14

If the current interest rate dropped to 5½ percent, the bondholder could charge a premium because the bond is paying 6 percent. The price would be $1,090. ($60 / 5.5% = $1,090).

These two examples point out the relationship of price and interest rates. In the case of the bond that had a stated interest rate lower than the market rate, the bondholder had to discount the bond in order to make it competitive with newly issued bonds at the higher rate.

13.6

For the bond with the stated rate higher than the market rate, the bondholder could receive a premium price for the higher than market interest rate.

Bond Ladders

Bonds offer investors a measure of stability to their portfolios. However, rising and falling interest rates can sabotage your strategy. Investors are forced to guess the direction of interest rates and decide whether to buy long or short maturity bonds. A bond's yield is directly related to its maturity—the longer the maturity, the higher the yield. Should interest rates rise before maturity, the bondholder would be stuck with a below market rate for the term of the bond. The investor could sell at a loss or ride it out and hope to invest the principal at a higher rate when the bond matured but face the risk that rates could turn down.

For example, if you have a single $50,000 bond and interest rates go up, you are earning below market interest rates and your bond will lose value in the open market if you want to sell. On the other hand, if you wait until maturity, interest rates may fall and when you reinvest the $50,000, it may be at a lower rate.

A bond ladder addresses this problem. A bond ladder is a simple strategy that lets you minimize the interest risk associated with bond investing and manages the cash flow from your investment. Here's how it works.

Rather than buy one $50,000 ten-year bond, you buy ten $5,000 bonds with maturities beginning with one year and going up to ten years. Each year a bond matures and with these proceeds you buy a new 10-year bond. The previous two-year bond now has one year left—so you always have a bond maturing in one year.

This gives you a bond maturing every year for the next ten years. Here are some of the advantages of the bond ladder:

▶ You have a portfolio of short, mid, and long term bonds, which gives you an attractive current yield by taking advantage of the higher yields of long-term bonds without risking all your investment.

▶ If interest rates go up, you have a bond maturing every year that you can reinvest at a higher interest rate. You reinvest the maturing one-year bond at ten years to keep the ladder intact.

▶ If interest rates drop, only a small portion of your portfolio (the bond that matures that year) must be reinvested at the low rate.

▶ By choosing the type of bond for the ladder, you can match your cash needs for however long you build the ladder.

The bond ladder has advantages over investing a lump sum in one bond. You can build your own ladder to fit your particular needs, however, here are some guidelines to remember:

▶ A bond ladder doesn't have to follow the ten-year example. Five years is the minimum to take advantage of yield differences. The farther out it goes, the higher your yield will be and the greater the risk.

▶ Your ladder doesn't have to have bonds maturing every year. You could choose bonds that mature at two or three year increments, although this approach lacks the agility to respond to the market that yearly maturing bonds offer. The more bonds on your ladder, the more diversified it will be.

▶ This same approach works with bank certificates of deposit.

◀ *SEE ALSO 3.3, "Savings Accounts"* ▶

13.6

14

RETIREMENT PLANNING

14.1 SETTING RETIREMENT GOALS

Lifestyle After Retirement

Setting a Time Frame for Retirement

Setting financial goals for retirement depends in part on the lifestyle you envision. A quiet life tending a garden and puttering around the house will not require the resources of a person intent on seeing the world. This section looks at the process of setting retirement goals.

Lifestyle After Retirement

A few generations ago, retirement was considered a fixed point in time. You reached age 65 or some years of service for the military and other government jobs and you retired. While this may still be true for some people, it is not the case for many more. Companies **downsize** and employees take early retirement packages. Some voluntarily retire early to start a business. Others work many years past the standard retirement age.

WORDS TO GO . . .WORDS TO GO . . .WORDS TO GO

Downsize is a term used by companies to mean reducing the number of employees. One way this is done is to offer early retirement to some workers.

Part of planning for retirement is developing a vision of what your lifestyle will be after you leave full-time employment. If you haven't saved for an adequate retirement, your lifestyle options in retirement will be limited. The purpose of setting goals is to save for a specific lifestyle or to at least have the financial security to afford some choices.

You will need a certain amount of money just to maintain your living standard. If you plan a lifestyle that is significantly different from your current lifestyle, you need to account for those changes, too. For example, many retired people want to travel more than they were able to do while working. Where will the money come from to pay for these trips? What about a second home in a warm climate for the winter months? Consider how you want to spend your time after retirement, those hours you spent at work will need to be filled with some activity. Many hobbies can run into extra money.

Your retirement goals must provide for three major considerations:

▶ **Financial security:** You should have enough money to cover your living expenses and a cushion for emergencies.

▶ **Health care:** Health concerns should be covered by adequate insurance, including Medicare and supplements.

▶ **Options:** These are the financial resources beyond covering basic needs that give you the means to enjoy different lifestyle choices. This consideration comes last by design—the first two must be completed before this one is possible.

◀ *SEE ALSO 1.4, "Using a Financial Planner"* ▶

Setting a Time Frame for Retirement

When you retire is both a personal and a financial decision. If you are retiring from your current job to start a business or work part-time, that's different from retiring to not work at all. Retiring at age 55, which is possible with a number of corporations and government jobs, may mean you have 20–30 years of retirement in front of you.

Most **qualified retirement accounts** have penalties for beginning withdrawals before age $59^1/_2$, and Social Security reduces your benefit if you choose to take early retirement at age 62 or before your full retirement age.

WORDS TO GO . . .WORDS TO GO . . .WORDS TO GO

Qualified retirement accounts are designated by the IRS for special treatment, such as tax-deferred growth, while funds remain in the account. An example of a qualified retirement account is an IRA.

When setting a retirement age, you should consider these factors:

▶ Will you continue to work at another job?

▶ Will your employer's retirement plan pay full benefits immediately?

▶ Will you be past age $59^1/_2$ to avoid penalties on your qualified retirement accounts?

▶ Will you retire before, on, or after your full retirement age as defined by Social Security?

▶ Does your employer extend healthcare benefits to retirees? If not, will you retire before you are eligible for Medicare?

14.1

Even if you are 20 years or more away from retirement, you need to consider these factors in your planning. You may not know or have decided on the answers to all these questions, but you still must consider them. If you are several decades away from retiring and have no clear idea when you want to retire or what your lifestyle might be, choose the most costly option and plan for that.

14.2 DETERMINING FINANCIAL NEEDS

If You Retired Today

Expenses in Retirement

Factoring for Inflation

Working After Retirement

Determining a future need is the most difficult part of any financial planning process, and retirement planning is especially difficult because you don't know how long your money will need to last or what your health, economic, or financial circumstances will be. This section looks at planning for your financial needs in retirement.

If You Retired Today

Start figuring your financial needs in retirement by determining what your needs would be if you retired today. What regular expenses do you have that are associated with your employment? Transportation costs would likely drop, as would clothing costs and meals away from home. You may spend less at the dry cleaner and other services associated with your job.

As a rule, you should count on needing 80 percent of your current income to cover living expenses in retirement. Children still in college or a mortgage on a vacation home can change this, as could a chronic medical condition. If your home will be paid for and the kids will be on their own, you may get by with less than 80 percent.

◀ SEE ALSO 2.2, *"Tracking Expenses"* ▶

Expenses in Retirement

Although some expenses will drop or go away in retirement, others won't, and many will increase. You can count on taxes, insurance, and utilities to continue rising. Even if your home is paid for, these expenses don't go away. In addition to regular rate increases, if you are home more, your energy usage will be higher.

The biggest increased expense for many retirees is health care, including insurance and medications. Many of the health care advances that keep us active longer rely on expensive prescription medications. The new Medicare Part D program attempts to address this problem, but prescription drug costs remain a serious expense for many retirees who do not have adequate health care insurance.

14.2

One of your major expenses, for some the largest, will be income taxes. You may have retired from working, but the money you pull out of most retirement plans is taxed as **ordinary income.** There are exceptions, but you will be paying taxes and may not have that many deductions. If your house is paid for, you have lost the biggest single deduction for most taxpayers—the mortgage interest deduction.

WORDS TO GO . . .*WORDS TO GO* . . .*WORDS TO GO*

Ordinary income is the term the IRS uses to designate how money coming out of most retirement plans will be taxed. It means the funds will be taxed as if you earned them as salary, which in most cases is what happened, but the tax was deferred to this later date.

Don't overlook that some communities and states have higher tax rates than other states do. If the high taxes are buying good schools, you might ask yourself if that's how you want to spend your retirement dollars, with no more children in the education system. Many retirees move to states with no income tax to avoid this drag on their retirement income.

◀ *SEE ALSO 8.1, "Income Tax"* ▶

You have to meet your daily living expenses first. If you want an active lifestyle of travel or a second home in a resort area, your retirement expenses will be significantly higher. Adequate planning and saving can put these goals in reach, but you need a concrete plan to accumulate the assets necessary to fund an active retirement. A debilitating illness can derail the best of plans, so adequate insurance is necessary to protect your assets and your spouse.

A number of websites offer retirement expense calculators. You enter information such as your age, the age you plan to retire, the amount you have saved, and the amount you want to accumulate. The program projects out what you will need to save at what rate to reach your goal. Other programs estimate your expenses depending on how many years you are away from the retirement date.

Factoring for Inflation

There's no way to know exactly how much **inflation** will run during your retirement. It has been very low at times, while at other times quite high. The average is about 3 percent a year. Unfortunately, you can't count on retiring during a period when inflation is going to hit its average. You may find it cycling near record highs like recent years, in the low teens; or extremely low, near zero. Planning for retirement means your money can't retire when you do, it must continue to work and earn a return that is at least equal to an after-tax rate of inflation. This is the only way you can maintain your lifestyle.

WORDS TO GO . . .WORDS TO GO . . .WORDS TO GO

Inflation is a rise in the cost of goods and services with a corresponding decrease in the value of money.

A **diversified portfolio** of stocks and/or stock mutual funds is the way most investors protect their retirement assets from the effects of inflation. Stocks have the ability, over time, to adjust for the effects of inflation and provide investors long-term growth. A small portion of your portfolio in real estate makes use of that asset class's qualities as an inflation hedge. The temptation in retirement is to focus on preservation of capital, meaning very conservative investments that sacrifice return for safety. While this strategy has merit for a large portion of your assets, you should devote some resources to growth as a hedge against inflation.

WORDS TO GO . . .WORDS TO GO . . .WORDS TO GO

Diversified portfolios reduce the risk by spreading investment dollars over numerous stocks and or bonds to minimize the impact should one of the investments turn bad.

Even at 3 percent, your income needs will double in 20 years. The danger of outliving your money becomes real when its purchasing power is eroded by inflation. Unless you amass a huge amount of cash, you will need to keep growing your retirement fund and/or keep adding money to it through full or part-time work.

◀ SEE ALSO 10.4, "Asset Allocation" ▶

Working After Retirement

Working after retirement may be a choice or a necessity, depending on your personal and financial situation. Some people retire so they can work at another job or start a business. These people are only retiring from a job, not the job market or business world. They have plans to keep busy for much longer, and retirement from a former profession is a step toward something new.

14.2

If you have not adequately saved for retirement, working is a necessity. You may only work part-time or work at a job much different from your former career. Working during retirement means you need less income from your retirement fund so it can continue to grow and earn more because less is withdrawn. Social Security has rules about working and drawing benefits that are important to know and they are addressed in section 14.4.

If you don't have health care benefits from your former employer, you may consider working after retirement at a job that offers these benefits. The savings of a group plan are tremendous.

◀ *SEE ALSO 7.5, "Health Insurance"* ▶

14.3 CREATING A RETIREMENT PLAN

Assessing Your Current Status
Level of Saving
Calculating Funding Requirements
Committing Funds to Savings
Making Up for Lost Time

No matter how close or far away you are from retirement, it is never too late to take stock of your situation and create a plan of action. This section looks at creating your retirement plan.

Assessing Your Current Status

Creating a funding plan for your retirement starts with assessing your current financial status. What is your income and expenses? What obligations do you face between now and retirement? You'll probably face many obligations—new house, children, college, and such—before you get to retirement. However, retirement needs to move to the head of the list and here's why. All of your other obligations can be met out of current income, short-term savings, and borrowing. Your retirement obligation can only be met out of what you save *now*.

◀ SEE ALSO 1.3, *"Personal Finance Plan"* ▶

You borrow money to buy a house; you can borrow money to pay for part or all of college; you can finance a car; and so on. You can't finance your retirement. If you don't take care of yourself now by funding a retirement savings plan, your children or society will have to do it for you.

The urgency of your current status depends on your age. The younger you are, the less urgent it is to devote maximum resources to your retirement. If you have passed age 50 and do not have a sustained and aggressive retirement savings plan in place, you are in an urgent situation.

Level of Saving

There is not a correct level of savings that fits everyone. Many factors—age, income, other obligations, retirement goals—combine to create a funding requirement. At a minimum, however, you should be putting away 10 percent of your

14.3

gross income into a retirement fund or funds. You may have your contributions spread over several accounts such as a 401(k) plan at work, an IRA, an annuity, and so on. Many of these qualified accounts let you put your contribution in before withholding taxes are calculated, which reduces your current income tax burden. If you are at or past age 50 and you are not well on your way to an adequately funded retirement account, 10 percent of your gross will not be enough.

WORDS TO GO . . .WORDS TO GO . . .WORDS TO GO

Gross income is your pay or salary before any taxes, insurance payments or any other deductions are made.

Calculating Funding Requirements

Calculating funding requirements for the soon to be retired is not difficult if you know what your expenses will be. The math is simple and startling at the same time if you are not used to the numbers. For example, if you need $50,000 a year over what Social Security will provide, and you can earn 8 percent on your retirement fund, you will need $625,000 in your fund to meet your needs. To cover inflation, your nest egg needs to grow by 3 percent (assuming that's what inflation is that year) to produce the same **purchasing power** with an 8 percent return the next year.

WORDS TO GO . . .WORDS TO GO . . .WORDS TO GO

Purchasing power is what your dollars will buy relative to another point in time. Inflation reduces purchasing power by raising prices, thus your dollar is worth less this year than it was last year.

If your retirement is still many years away, this basic formula becomes more complicated, but the idea remains the same. Your retirement fund must be large enough to provide the cash you need each year, and grow by at least the rate of inflation.

This strategy assumes you don't know when you or your spouse will die and conserves your retirement fund so that the surviving spouse has enough cash for the rest of his or her life, however long that might be. Many people want to leave something for their children when they die and are concerned about spending the principal of their retirement fund.

Another approach is to spend down your retirement fund with no thought of leaving it intact for your heirs. You should approach this strategy carefully, probably with the help of a financial planner. You can withdraw interest and part of the principal each year of retirement to fund your living expenses. The danger is spending down your money too quickly and out-living your retirement fund. A financial planning professional can tell you how much you can withdraw from the principal each year and how long the fund will last. This approach does not necessarily require as large a retirement fund as living on interest only.

◀ SEE ALSO 1.4, "*Using a Financial Planner*" ▶

Committing Funds to Savings

The **time value of money** and the power of **compounding** work hardest when they have ample time. The earlier you start with your retirement savings plan, the easier it will be to reach your goal and the easier it will be to develop a savings habit. Always take advantage of employer-sponsored retirement plans, especially those that offer a match to part of your contribution. If you start with your earliest jobs, the retirement account will have the opportunity to grow over the years with your contributions, compounding to impressive numbers.

WORDS TO GO . . . WORDS TO GO . . . WORDS TO GO

The **time value of money** addresses the concept that a dollar today is better than a dollar tomorrow. You can invest a dollar today and it will earn interest. A dollar tomorrow is worth less than a dollar today thanks to inflation.

Compounding is the mathematical means by which interest earned during one period adds to the principal, then the next period interest is earned on the resulting principal plus interest in the first period. Another way to say this is interest earning interest.

However, if you are at mid-life and have not started or adequately funded a retirement fund, don't give up—you can still do much good in the remaining years before retirement.

◀ SEE ALSO 3.7, "*Time Value of Money*" ▶

Making Up for Lost Time

Having an inadequately funded retirement program is no excuse for taking risks with your investments hoping for a big gain to make up for earlier inaction. The

14.3

opposite is true: when you're starting a comprehensive retirement funding program late in life, you can't afford mistakes. You need to maximize your contributions to all possible retirement programs. Recognizing that many people have not adequately saved for retirement, many qualified retirement plans have special "catch-up" provisions for people age 50 and older that increase the maximum contribution.

If you need to have your college student children take out student loans so you can adequately fund your retirement, that is a viable consideration. Few parents want their children to start off in debt, but they have their whole working life to repay the debt. You have no way to finance your retirement other than what you are able to save now.

◄ *SEE ALSO 9.1, "Costs"* ▶

14.4 SOCIAL SECURITY AND MEDICARE

What to Expect from Social Security

What Medicare May Provide

Social Security and Medicare were designed to provide a safety net so elderly citizens could count on some income and health care. Much has changed since the original missions. This section looks at this social entitlement.

What to Expect from Social Security

Social Security provides a retirement benefit based on the number of years you have worked and contributed, through payroll taxes, to the system. The longer you have worked and the more you have paid in do not automatically mean you will receive a higher benefit. The formula is weighted so that lower paid workers actually receive a slightly higher benefit.

It is important to make sure your employer is reporting your wages every year and paying their share of the **withholding tax.** This record is found on your W-2 form each year. Another way to check that information (and much more) is to review the annual statement Social Security sends you. This statement usually arrives some time close to your birthday. It estimates what you can expect to receive in benefits depending on when you choose to retire. If you are many years away from retirement, the estimate won't mean much. However, if you are getting close to retirement, the estimate of monthly benefits can be helpful in planning.

WORDS TO GO . . . WORDS TO GO . . . WORDS TO GO

Withholding tax is the Social Security, Medicare, and income tax withheld each payday by your employer. Your employer matches your contribution to Social Security and Medicare.

You also need to know what date you will reach full retirement age. This is not the same date for everyone and it changes based on when you were born. This date is important because if you begin receiving benefits before this date, they will be reduced permanently. You can retire at age 62, but you will lose benefits if you do.

14.4

The first thing you need to know is what your full retirement age is, and that depends on your birth date. If you were born in 1937 or earlier, your retirement age is 65.

> 1938: 65 and 2 months
>
> 1939: 65 and 4 months
>
> 1940: 65 and 6 months
>
> 1941: 65 and 8 months
>
> 1942: 65 and 10 months
>
> 1943 to 1954: 66
>
> 1955: 66 and 2 months
>
> 1956: 66 and 4 months
>
> 1957: 66 and 6 months
>
> 1958: 66 and 8 months
>
> 1959: 66 and 10 months
>
> 1960 and later: 67

Use previous year if you were born on Jan. 1

This chart is the full retirement date chart as of 2006. However, it can be changed, and one of the ways to extend the life of the Social Security Trust Fund is to make people wait later before full benefits are available.

If you want to retire early, here's the bad news in terms of what you will receive in reduced benefits:

If your full retirement age is 65, benefits will be reduced:

> At age 62: 20 percent reduction
>
> At age 63: $13^1/_2$ percent reduction
>
> At age 64: $6^2/_3$ percent reduction

If your full retirement age is 66, benefits will be reduced:

> At age 62: 25 percent reduction
>
> At age 63: 20 percent reduction
>
> At age 64: $13^1/_2$ percent reduction
>
> At age 65: $6^2/_3$ percent reduction

You should weigh the costs carefully before choosing early retirement, especially if you want to work after you begin drawing Social Security retirement benefits.

Working after you begin receiving benefits makes financial sense only if you waited until reaching full retirement age. If you take early retirement, working will reduce your benefits. Here's how that works according to Social Security:

▶ In the years before you reach full retirement age, $1 in benefits will be deducted for every $2 you earn above the limit ($12,480 in 2006).

▶ In the year you reach full retirement age, $1 in benefits will be deducted for every $3 you earn above the annual limit ($33,240 in 2006) until the month you reach full retirement age. Once you reach your full retirement age, you can earn as much as you want and still draw full Social Security benefits.

What Medicare May Provide

Medicare is the federal health care program that provides basic services for people age 65 and older. If you collect Social Security, you are enrolled in Medicare Parts A and B. If you aren't collecting Social Security, you must apply for Medicare, usually three months before your 65th birthday to be eligible on that date. Those people who don't reach full retirement age until after age 65 still must apply at age 65.

There are four parts to Medicare insurance. Parts A and B are automatic if you sign up for Social Security. If you don't want Part B, you must opt out. If you are not eligible for Social Security at age 65, you must sign up for both parts when you turn 65. If you want this coverage, and most people do, you should make certain you sign up before the deadline. If you miss the deadline for Part B, you must pay a penalty in addition to the premium. The penalty never stops as long as you have the coverage. Part C is a provider plan that lets you receive all your services through provider organizations. The fourth major part of Medicare is prescription drug coverage (Part D), which rolled out a new program in the beginning of 2006.

All but Part A are voluntary and will cost you to participate, but the fees are very reasonable compared to private insurance.

Part A covers:

▶ Hospital costs

▶ Home health care

▶ Skilled nursing care (but not nursing home care)

▶ Hospice care

14.4

Part B covers:

- ▶ Doctor's services

- ▶ Outpatient hospital care

- ▶ Physical therapy and the use of medical equipment

- ▶ Ambulance expenses

- ▶ Other medical services not covered in Part A

The premium for Part B in 2006 was $88.50 per month.

Medicare parts A and B provide basic health care services, but many people who can afford it find that buying a Medigap insurance policy helps pay for those services that are not covered. Medigap insurance comes in numerous plans labeled A through L. These policies fill in the "gaps" of Medicare coverage and the amount of extra protection they provide determines the policy's cost.

Law standardizes these policies, so all A policies are identical no matter which insurance company is selling them. However, the premiums are not standardized, so it pays to shop. Insurance companies don't have to offer all 12 plans and each company may have different policies about **preexisting conditions.** Do not buy more than one policy; you'll just pay twice for the same coverage. The Medicare website has comprehensive information on these policies and you should familiarize yourself with them before talking to an agent. See the resource appendix for the Medicare website address.

WORDS TO GO . . . *WORDS TO GO . . . WORDS TO GO*

Preexisting condition is a medical situation that existed before you applied for any type of insurance. It is usually a chronic condition and may affect your ability to obtain insurance.

◀ *SEE ALSO 7.5, "Health Insurance"* ▶

Medicare began a new prescription drug plan on Jan. 1, 2006 amid great confusion because everyone on Medicare who wanted in the program had to enroll. Part D is an additional fee and private companies sell these policies. Each state has its own list of approved providers. The average cost (in 2006) was about $34 per month. The plans differ not only in price, but also in the drugs they cover. If you take a maintenance medication, make sure the company you choose covers your drugs. There is an enrollment period each year. If you miss the sign up, you face a premium penalty of one percent for each month you were eligible to enroll but didn't.

14.5 PENSION PLANS

Defined Benefit Plans

What to Expect

The defined benefit plan known to most as the pension operates on a formula that is mostly out of the employee's control. This section looks at expectations for defined benefit plans.

Defined Benefit Plans

Defined benefit plans have fallen out of favor due to their high cost to employers, which have been exaggerated by retirees living longer and requiring more pension dollars from the fund. Defined benefit plans, or pension plans, are entirely employer funded and based on a formula that considers your length of service and salary. The pension was seen as a way to retain employees and reduce turnover, because employees lost most if not all of their benefit if they switched jobs.

> **WORDS TO GO . . .** WORDS TO GO . . . WORDS TO GO
>
> **Defined benefit plans** calculate retirement benefits using a formula that applies a percentage to an average salary (usually the last five years or the best five years of compensation) and adds in a longevity bonus for the number of years worked. This gives employees a monthly benefit for the rest of their lives.

Until 30 years ago, this was the predominant retirement plan offered by employers. The switch to defined contribution plans focuses the responsibility for saving for retirement on the employee and not the employer.

Pension plans usually require you to work for a certain period before you are eligible for the pension benefits. This is called vesting, and it can take three to five years of service to complete.

A newer type of pension, the **cash balance pension**, is attracting some attention as companies are converting older, traditional pensions into the newer plans. Cash balance plans resemble traditional pensions with two major exceptions. First, the plans do not include a longevity factor in the formula. It is strictly based on salary. This plan hurts workers with lengthy tenure because they lose that extra bonus for length of service. Second, these pensions are portable. Once an employee is vested in the plan, the money belongs to them. If they leave the company, the money goes with them in the form of an IRA.

14.5

The many problems reported with traditional pensions prompted Congress to pass the Pension Protection Act of 2006, which gives companies with under-funded pensions seven years to get their act together or face stiff penalties. Some companies, including a couple of troubled airlines, get longer to fix their problems.

WORDS TO GO . . .WORDS TO GO . . .WORDS TO GO

Cash balance pensions are similar to defined benefit plans except there is no reward for longevity and employees can take the plan with them if they change jobs.

What to Expect

Each pension plan may have a different way of calculating your pension benefit, however most will be based on a formula that considers your income and length of service. Here is a sample formula:

▶ Highest average compensation, which is the highest 60 consecutive months of pay of the last 120 months before you retire (this considers your base salary only, no bonuses)

▶ Years of service

▶ A multiplier that goes up with years (1.3 percent for years 1–4; 1.4 percent for years 5–9; and 1.6 percent for years 10–35)

Here's how the formula would calculate the pension benefit for a person with a final average compensation of $60,000 who retired at age 65 with 30 years of service:

First 4 years: .013 × $60,000 = $780 × 4 = $3,120

Years 5–9: .014 × $60,000 = $840 × 4 = $3,360

Next 21 years: .016 × $60,000 = $960 × 21 = $20,160

Total: $3,120 + $3,360 + $20,160 = $26,640

This is the annual pension.

Your pension payout will often present a choice with your pension benefit, but not always; some plans have a single payout method. Your usual choices are to take a lump-sum payout and roll it into an IRA, or take a paid-up annuity that guarantees a monthly payment for life.

Rolling the lump sum into an IRA gives you a great deal of flexibility in where you can invest the funds to build and maintain your nest egg. However, you are responsible for keeping your retirement funds safe and growing enough to stay ahead of inflation unless you turn the job over to a paid financial advisor.

Your other choice may be a paid up **annuity** that guarantees a monthly income for the rest of your life. You may have the option of a single-pay annuity, which will give you higher monthly payments, but ends when you die. You can also choose a joint survivor annuity with your spouse, so if you die, your spouse will continue receiving the monthly checks. The monthly payment will be lower, but both of you will have income until you both die.

WORDS TO GO . . .WORDS TO GO . . .WORDS TO GO

Annuity is a contract with a life insurance company guaranteeing a certain payout over a period. It may contain a death benefit that would pay a survivor in the case of death.

14.5

14.6 PERSONAL CONTRIBUTIONS

Retirement Accounts
Other Savings Strategies

For those people not enrolled in a defined benefits plan, there are two options: a defined contribution plan, if available; or a personally directed retirement plan. This section looks at those options and other savings strategies.

Retirement Accounts

Personal contributions to your retirement take the form of either a **defined contribution plan** offered by your employer or a retirement plan you construct yourself using retirement products. In either case, you take the responsibility for funding the accounts and determining where your retirement dollars are invested. Your contribution is known, but the ultimate benefit will be determined by several factors including the performance of the investments you choose. This contrasts with the defined benefit plan, where it is possible to estimate your ultimate benefit at retirement.

> **WORDS TO GO** . . . *WORDS TO GO* . . . *WORDS TO GO*
>
> **Defined contribution plans** provide the employee an opportunity to invest pre-tax money deducted on a regular basis in a group of mutual funds and other investments. The employer may match part of the employee contribution, but is not required to by law. The employee will only know how much is contributed to the plan. The ultimate benefit at retirement will depend on how well the employee's choices of investments performed.

Of the two options, the defined contribution plan is usually the best alternative if your employer offers it. Known as **401(k)** or **403(b) plans,** they have the advantage of allowing you to contribute pre-tax dollars, which reduces your current income tax while funding your retirement at the same time. In addition, many employers will match part of your contribution up to a certain percentage. For example, your employer might match 50 cents for every dollar you contribute up to three percent of your salary. This is an automatic 50 percent return on this contribution before you even invest it. If your employer offers a match, you should contribute to the plan at least enough to take full advantage of the match.

401(k) plan is a qualified defined contribution plan offered by employers. It allows employees to have a certain percentage of their salary deducted and invested in the plan. The deduction is pre-tax, so employees experience a reduction in current income tax. The deposits and earnings are tax deferred until withdrawn in retirement.

403(b) plan is the retirement plan for religious, educational, and other non-profit groups. This plan may use tax-deferred annuities instead of mutual funds.

The defined contribution plans offer you the opportunity to invest your money in a variety of mutual funds, money market accounts, and annuities. You decide how much goes into each fund and can change the mix when you need to make adjustments. New reforms signed into law in 2006 will allow companies to begin providing more investment advice to employees.

If your employer doesn't offer a defined contribution plan or you are self-employed, you can use a number of retirement products to build your own plan. The Individual Retirement Account (IRA) is the workhorse of retirement funding for individuals. The traditional IRA lets you take a tax deduction for the annual contribution if you meet the guidelines, which are explained in Chapter 15. With the Roth IRA, you lose the tax deduction, but withdrawals during retirement are tax-free. IRAs have special provisions for people age 50 and over that let them contribute an amount over the normal annual limit as a "catch up" provision. IRAs also come in several other forms specifically designed for self-employed people and small business owners. These IRAs and retirement accounts have special funding limits that are much higher than traditional or Roth IRAs. All IRAs allow your contributions to grow tax-deferred until withdrawal. This feature helps make the most of compounding and the time value of money.

Other Savings Strategies

People who want to save more than is permitted under traditional retirement plans often look to alternative savings vehicles. One of the options is an annuity, which has the advantage of allowing your money to grow tax-deferred until you begin receiving benefits. Annuities have no limits on contributions or income qualifications like IRAs and other retirement plans do.

You can also use a regular, taxable investment account to save for retirement. The downside is that these accounts must pay a tax bill each year, which reduces the amount of gain from year to year. Another strategy is to invest in real estate

14.6

as a supplemental retirement account. Income-producing real estate can be an attractive investment to carry into retirement, but it should not be your primary or only retirement fund. Real estate is illiquid, and if you need funds for an emergency, it would be difficult to pull cash out in a hurry.

YOUR HOME EQUITY

Reverse Mortgages

Many people enter retirement with their house paid for and wonder how to use this equity without selling their home. For some people, a reverse mortgage is the answer. This section looks at reverse mortgages.

Reverse Mortgages

You can convert equity in your house to cash with a reverse mortgage. You must be age 62 and older to qualify for the products. Reverse mortgages are like regular mortgages, except instead of you paying off a note, the lender pays you for your equity. The value of your home is decided and, based on the factors discussed below, provides you with a sum of money. Here's how this works:

▶ **How much you can borrow:** Your age, the amount of equity in your home, and prevailing interest rates determine the amount you can borrow. The older you are, the more of your equity you can borrow.

▶ **How you are paid:** You can get any combination of a lump sum, a monthly check, a smaller sum and a monthly check, or a line of credit.

▶ **How you repay the loan:** You repay the loan when the house is sold or you no longer live there. In addition, if you do not properly maintain the home, the lender can force you out early. When the house sells, any remaining balance goes to you or your heirs. If you or your heirs want to keep the house, you will have to repay the note.

▶ **Nonrecourse loan:** Reverse mortgages are nonrecourse loans, meaning if what you owe is greater than the value of the house, the lender is stuck, not you. The lender must make up the difference.

▶ **What you can use the money for:** You are free to use the money for anything you wish, including paying off the first mortgage on the property.

▶ **What about taxes:** You don't pay taxes on proceeds from a reverse mortgage because it is a loan, not income. Likewise, it does not affect your Social Security benefits.

The most popular reverse mortgages are the Home Equity Conversion Mortgage and proprietary mortgages offered by financial institutions. Some state and local governments offer reverse mortgages, however they tend to be limited in scope and flexibility. The Home Equity Conversion Mortgage (HECM) is a federally insured mortgage backed by the Federal Housing Administration, which is part of the Department of Housing and Urban Development (HUD).

Reverse mortgages can provide cash to solve many problems, but the different choices also make them confusing. You cannot get a reverse mortgage without meeting with a reverse mortgage counselor. The counselor, who is approved by HUD, will discuss any questions you have and help you make the best decision for your particular circumstances. You can find a list of counselors at the website listed in Appendix B.

14.8 GETTING HELP

Professional Help

Planning 20 years or more of retirement is complicated, and many people find they need professional help to put the task in focus. In this section, we look at professional help for retirement planning.

Professional Help

Many people find retirement planning complicated and daunting, especially when it comes to projecting income and expense needs for the future. Professional assistance in drawing up a plan is often beneficial to help you focus on what needs to be done today to get to a goal in the future.

You can approach this at various stages, depending on your comfort level and how complicated you believe your retirement picture might be. Self-employed people and business owners may find it much more difficult to plan for the future with an uncertain income in front of them, while people who plan to work for a salary until retirement may find the future somewhat less uncertain in projecting future income.

If you are concerned about a clear path to retirement, a financial planner can help you construct a plan that incorporates your current financial reality with your retirement goals and tells you what has to happen to get from here to there. A systematic plan is helpful to many people in making a distant goal more real by accomplishing small current goals. A financial planner can also help prepare realistic income and expense projections that include the latest economic data on inflation and interest rates.

◀ *SEE ALSO 1.4, "Using a Financial Planner"* ▶

14.8

15

RETIREMENT ACCOUNTS

15.1 TYPES OF ACCOUNTS

Individual Retirement Accounts

401(k) and 403(b) Accounts

Annuities

The individuals have three main tools at their disposal to fund retirement accounts. These tools are, for the most part, funded and initiated by the individual. This section looks at these tools and how they fit into your retirement plan.

Individual Retirement Accounts

Individual Retirement Accounts (IRAs) are the workhorse of retirement accounts. Almost anyone qualifies for one, even people without earned income in certain circumstances. IRAs offer a flexible way to save for retirement. You can use a wide variety of investment products to fund your IRA. The IRA provides a **tax-deferred** vehicle for your investment. It grows without any tax liability until you begin withdrawing funds during retirement. There's even an IRA for which all withdrawals are tax-free. The traditional IRA reduces your current income tax liability while building a retirement fund.

> **WORDS TO GO . . .** WORDS TO GO . . . WORDS TO GO
>
> **Tax-deferred** refers to investment vehicles that allow principal and interest to grow without paying taxes on the earnings until sometime in the future. Qualified retirement accounts allow tax-deferred growth. Annuities, whether qualified or not, also allow tax-deferred growth.

The disadvantage of individual IRAs are the limits on the amount you can contribute each year and income restrictions that reduce or eliminate their benefits for people in higher income brackets.

401(k) and 403(b) Accounts

The 401(k) and 403(b) retirement plans are employer-sponsored programs that offer significant benefits. The difference between the 401(k) and 403(b) is the latter is offered to governmental, religious, and nonprofit organization, while the former is for private business. They are essentially the same in most other respects.

These plans are also known as salary reduction plans, but they are best known as defined benefit plans. They are called salary reduction plans because your contribution is taken before **withholding tax** is calculated. This reduces your current income tax liability. They are called defined contribution plans because only the contribution is defined or known. The ultimate benefit you will receive at retirement isn't known and depends on how much you contribute and how well your investment choices perform. Your employer may match part of your contribution, although that is not required.

WORDS TO GO . . .WORDS TO GO . . .WORDS TO GO

Withholding tax is the Social Security, Medicare, and income tax withheld each payday by your employer. Your employer matches your contribution to Social Security and Medicare.

You can choose to invest your contribution in a variety of mutual funds, fixed income accounts, and other choices in many plans. When you begin withdrawing funds at retirement, it is treated as ordinary income for tax purposes.

◀ *SEE ALSO 11.1, "Mutual Fund Basics"* ▶

There is a type of 401(k) that takes its contributions after taxes, but withdrawals during retirement are tax-free.

Annuities

Annuities are a **qualified retirement account,** meaning your earnings grow tax-deferred until withdrawn during retirement. Annuities require no employer or any other qualifying for the investor. You can invest as much as you want, which is not true with any other retirement product.

WORDS TO GO . . .WORDS TO GO . . .WORDS TO GO

Qualified retirement accounts are designated by the IRS for special treatment such as tax-deferred growth while funds remain in the account. An example of a qualified retirement account is the IRA.

Annuities have great flexibility on their payouts including a guaranteed income for life feature, which assures you won't outlive your money.

Some types of annuities carry very high expenses and may not be appropriate for every investor.

15.1

15.2 IRAs

IRA Overview

Traditional Deductible IRAs

Traditional Nondeductible IRAs

Roth IRAs

IRAs are the oldest retirement accounts available to individuals. Which IRA you qualify for depends on your income. This section looks at the three major types of IRAs.

IRA Overview

IRAs are very flexible retirement funding investments. You can use a number of investment products including from stocks, mutual funds, band CDs, bonds, real estate, and so on. Opening an IRA is a simple matter of filling out a short form at a bank, mutual fund, or brokerage firm. The firm you choose acts as the **custodian** of your account, but you make all the investment decisions. This means you are also responsible for knowing the rules governing contribution limits and approved investments. You must report your contributions to the IRS. Failure to follow the contribution limits can result in penalties and interest.

> **WORDS TO GO . . . WORDS TO GO . . . WORDS TO GO**
>
> The **custodian** of an account maintains the account and keeps records of deposits and withdrawals.

You have until your taxes are due to fund a traditional deductible IRA and claim the deduction for the previous tax year. Taxes are due on April 15, for income earned in the previous year. You have until April 15 to fund your IRA and take a deduction against income earned in the past year.

You should fund your IRA on the earliest date you can, which is the first business day of the year. This gives your IRA 15½ months to earn money for you rather than waiting until the last minute of April 15 when taxes are due.

Here's what it means to you if you could earn 8 percent compounded monthly:

	January 2, 2006	April 15, 2007
You contribute	$4,000	$4,000
Balance on Dec. 31, 2007	$4,433	$4,232
Difference	**+$433**	**+$232**

This investing pattern repeated every year will make a significant difference in your retirement fund.

◀ *SEE ALSO 3.7, "Time Value of Money"* ▶

If your spouse doesn't work, you can open a spousal IRA in their name and fund it to whatever limit you are eligible. This is in addition to your own contribution. It gives the nonworking spouse their own retirement account and contributes to the family's overall retirement fund.

The contribution limits for IRAs are:

▶ 2007: $4,000

▶ 2008: $5,000

▶ 2009: $5,000 plus an indexed amount to inflation

▶ 2010: $5,000 plus an indexed amount to inflation

People over age 50 can invest an extra $1,000 per year as a catch-up provision.

You can open as many IRA accounts as you want as long as you don't exceed the annual contribution limit. However, you may want to limit the number to save money. Each account will cost you a setup fee and an annual maintenance fee of some amount. These are usually not big sums, but there are other reasons for keeping the number of accounts to a minimum. Paperwork is reduced and confusion is lessened when it is time for withdrawals. If you are going to have more than one type of IRA, you will need more than one account. A Roth IRA must be in a separate account. You can't mix traditional IRA money and Roth IRA money in the same account.

You can move money from one IRA to another IRA or from a company-sponsored retirement plan to an IRA. This is called an IRA rollover and it is a way to keep the tax-deferred status of your account when you move it. The safest way to make the rollover is to have the custodian of the old IRA transfer the funds to the new IRA. This way you never touch the money and you avoid any potential withdrawal penalty. The IRS rule is that you have 60 days from the time the money

15.2

leaves the old IRA until it is deposited into the new IRA. If you ask for a check, 20 percent is automatically withheld to prepay the tax. You still have to deposit 100 percent in a new IRA within 60 days, which means you have to lend your IRA the missing 20 percent, if you have that much cash available. If you don't make up the missing 20 percent, the IRS considers it a withdrawal and you have to pay taxes and a penalty on it. These same rules apply if you receive a distribution from your company pension plan or change jobs and want to move funds out of your old 401(k) plan. They can all go in an IRA rollover.

Traditional Deductible IRAs

Of the three IRAs, the traditional deductible IRA has the strictest income requirements, but it is the only one that offers immediate tax benefits. Your contributions to a traditional deductible IRA are deductible from your income up to the current limits. Meaning you can deduct a $4,000 contribution to a traditional deductible IRA from your income before figuring income taxes for the year.

The income restrictions are such that you may not meet the requirements. If that is the case, your $4,000 deduction (assuming you made the maximum contribution in 2007) will not be allowed by the IRS. The rules are complicated by the catch-up provision for people age 50 and above who are allowed to make extra payments.

The **adjusted gross income** is the test for whether you qualify or not. There are different tests for single tax filers and for married filing jointly.

> **WORDS TO GO . . .**WORDS TO GO . . .WORDS TO GO
>
> **Adjusted gross income** (AGI) is the first cut at adjusting your gross reported income. It includes those adjustments that are allowed whether you itemized deductions or not.

For single taxpayers in 2006, the maximum contribution was $4,000. If your AGI was $50,000 or less, you were eligible to take the full deduction. If your AGI fell between $50,000 and $60,000, you could only take a partial deduction based on a formula from the IRS. An AGI over $60,000 means no deduction.

For married-filing-jointly taxpayers in 2006, an AGI of $75,000 qualified for a full deduction, while an AGI between $75,000 and $85,000 earned only a partial deduction. An AGI over $85,000 means no deduction. If neither of you have a retirement plan at work, you both can deduct if you meet the income requirement.

However, if your spouse has a retirement plan, you could see a reduced deduction if your income is over $150,000. If it is over $160,000, you lose your deduction.

Withdrawals

The IRS imposes strict restrictions on withdrawals from a traditional deductible IRA. If you make a withdrawal from your IRA prior to age 59½, you will pay ordinary income tax on the contributions and earnings, plus an additional 10 percent penalty.

The IRS recognizes two major exceptions to the rules covering early withdrawals. First-time homebuyers, meaning someone who has not owned a home in the past two years, can use withdrawals as can parents for their child's college education. Homebuyers can withdraw up to $10,000 from their IRA for a down payment. You will pay with ordinary income tax on any pre-tax contributions and earnings, but you don't have to pay a penalty.

◀ SEE ALSO 5.1, *"Buying vs. Renting"* ▷

Parents can also use IRA funds to pay a child's college expenses. You have the same rules about taxing contributions and earnings and the withdrawal is penalty-free.

◀ SEE ALSO 9.1, *"Costs"* ▷

There are also emergency exceptions for death, disability, and some medical conditions. Although the tax code allows these withdrawals, they may not be a good idea except as a last resort. You could be better off investing for a new home or your child's college education separately from your retirement accounts.

There are rigorous rules concerning mandatory distributions from traditional IRAs when you reach 70½ years old. You must begin taking distributions from a traditional IRA the year you turn 70½. There are several methods of calculating the minimum distribution that factor in your life expectancy and the life expectancy of your oldest beneficiary. You may face penalties of 50 percent of the amount under-withdrawn in addition to paying current income taxes. The IRS Form 590 has the details for minimum distribution.

Traditional Nondeductible IRAs

The traditional nondeductible IRA has no income limits, which is its only real benefit. If you can't qualify for a traditional deductible IRA or a Roth IRA, the nondeductible IRA may be an option. Your earnings still grow in a tax-deferred environment, however your contributions are not tax deductible so you will get no current income tax relief.

15.2

You are limited to the same contribution limits as a traditional deductible IRA and the same conditions for withdrawals, both premature and at age 70½ apply.

It is extremely important that you don't mix funds from a deductible IRA with funds from a nondeductible IRA. Because you have paid taxes on your contributions in the nondeductible IRA, you don't want to mix them with the deductible IRA funds that have not been taxed. If you can't clearly separate the two for the IRS—you do this by filing with the IRS every year—you will pay a penalty and may pay taxes on funds you have already paid taxes on.

Roth IRAs

Roth IRAs are the newest offering and may be the best option for most people. With the Roth IRA, you get no current deduction from your income taxes, however your contributions and earnings grow tax-free after five years. When you withdraw money in retirement, it is all tax-free, contributions and earnings. This makes the Roth IRA very attractive to people who expect to be in about the same or higher tax bracket when they retire. That's the gamble: whether it's worth giving up the tax deduction of a traditional deductible IRA for tax-free income in retirement. Most people answer that it is worth the gamble because of the additional advantages of the Roth.

With the Roth, you can withdraw your contributions at any time with no penalty or taxes to pay. After age 59½, you can make withdrawals of contributions and earnings tax-free. You can also choose to not take any distributions. Unlike traditional IRAs, there is no compulsory distribution age.

Roth IRAs do have AGI qualifications. For single taxpayers, an AGI below $95,000 is fully qualified; $95,000 to $110,000 is partially qualified; and an AGI over $110,000 does not qualify for a Roth IRA. Married-filing-jointly taxpayers with an AGI under $150,000 fully qualify; with $150,000—$160,000 partially qualify; and with an AGI over $160,000 do not qualify for a Roth IRA.

You can convert a traditional IRA to a Roth IRA. You'll owe taxes on any earnings and any contributions that were deducted from your income. There is an income limit of $100,000 in the year you make the switch and that's for single or married taxpayers. Whether it makes sense to convert depends on a number of factors, including your current tax rate, your age, when you expect to begin making withdrawals, how much you plan to transfer, and so on. There are online calculators that will help you with your decision, or a financial professional can work the numbers with you.

Roth IRA funds must be kept in a separate account and you can't commingle funds from traditional IRAs or you may lose the tax-free advantage of the Roth.

15.3 401(k) AND 403(b) PLANS

Employer Sponsored 401(k) Plan

Self-Employed 401(k) Plan

Roth 401(k) Plan

Nonprofit Organization 403(b) Plan

Defined contribution plans have overtaken traditional pension plans as the preferred retirement plan offered by companies. This section looks at the salary reduction plans, as they are also called.

Employer Sponsored 401(k) Plan

The 401(k) plan is a **defined contribution plan.** This means the plan defines how much is going into the plan, but not the amount of the eventual benefit, which will depend on the performance of your investment choices. The 401(k) plan is the most popular retirement plan offered by companies today. It has replaced the old pension plan because, for the most part, it is funded by the employee, not the employer.

The traditional 401(k) plan is a **salary-reduction plan,** which means it deducts contributions from your paycheck before withholding taxes are calculated. This reduces your current income taxes and puts your contribution to work in a tax-deferred environment.

WORDS TO GO . . . WORDS TO GO . . . WORDS TO GO

Defined contribution plans provide the employee an opportunity to invest pre-tax money deducted on a regular basis in a group of mutual funds and other investments. The employer may match part of the employee contribution, but is not required to by law. The employee will only know how much is contributed to the plan. The ultimate benefit at retirement will depend on how well the employee's choices of investments performed.

A **salary-reduction plan** is another name for any retirement plan that takes its contribution before withholding taxes are calculated. Your salary is reduced and taxes are lower after the contribution is taken.

Employers contract with a provider to offer a 401(k) to their employees. The provider is usually an investment company that has a family of mutual funds and other investment opportunities for the 401(k) plan. These mutual funds may range from very conservative to more aggressive. Many plans offer at least 10

15.3

and some offer up to 20 funds for participants to pick from, in addition to fixed income accounts, money market accounts, and so on. Many companies also make their stock available to the 401(k) plan often at a discount.

Participants can divide their contribution to the plan among the different mutual funds and accounts as they see fit and change the allocation as necessary. Although frequent switching is not a good idea and your plan may put limits on the number of times you can make changes in a year.

Many plans include lifecycle funds. These funds have a maturity date and investors pick the fund whose maturity date is close to their anticipated retirement date. The lifecycle fund automatically adjusts the fund's holdings according to how near or far away you are from retirement. As the maturity (retirement) date approaches, the fund adjusts its holdings to become more conservative, holding back aggressive moves to protect capital that you'll need in retirement.

◀ *SEE ALSO 11.2, "Types of Mutual Funds"* ▶

If you don't use a lifecycle fund, you'll need to adjust your investment in the funds about once a year. Rebalancing is the process of bringing your allocations to the various funds into alignment. If one of your funds had a large increase during the year, it may be out of the balance you originally set for your investments. Rebalancing usually means selling off some of your big winners to bring the ratios back to where you want them.

◀ *SEE ALSO 10.4, "Asset Allocation"* ▶

Congress sets your contribution maximum, although your employer may also set a percentage of your salary that results in a lower limit. In 2006, the limit is $15,000, with people over the age of 50 able to kick in another $5,000 as a catch up provision.

Some employers match all or part of their employees' contributions up to a maximum. This is an important benefit because it is free money, yours just for participating in the 401(k) plan. A typical offer might be to match $0.50 of every dollar you contribute up to six percent of your salary. This gives you an automatic 50 percent return on those dollars before they are invested in any mutual fund. If your employer offers a match, you should definitely be contributing at least up to the limit of the match.

Some companies match with cash, while other companies match with company stock. This may seem like an attractive offer, but be careful of having too much company (or any single) stock in your portfolio. If something bad happens to that stock, it could seriously jeopardize your retirement fund.

If you practice good asset allocation, you will avoid most of the dangers of investing for the long term.

Your company's 401(k) plan may or may not allow loans. You may think you are simply borrowing from yourself, but it's not that simple and it's not a good idea in most cases. You are actually making a partial withdrawal up to the limits set by your plan. You avoid the penalties and interest when you agree to repay the money. Of course, while your money's not invested, it's not earning for you. The interest you pay may equal what it would have earned if you left it in the account, but you also could miss a big swing in the market.

You must pay a market interest rate (usually a **prime interest rate** plus 1 percent) on the loan and may have only five years to repay, although you can get a longer term if the money is used to buy a house. However, if you lose your job or something else happens and you can't or don't repay the loan, the IRS considers it a premature distribution and hits you with a 10 percent penalty and interest.

WORDS TO GO . . .WORDS TO GO . . .WORDS TO GO

Prime interest rate is the rate banks charge their very best customers. It is also the rate other loan rates are pegged to.

Here are the major rules concerning withdrawals from 401(k) plans:

Except as noted later, withdrawals from a traditional 401(k) before age 59½, incur ordinary income taxes on your contributions, any matching funds from your employer, and any earnings in the account. In addition, the IRS would impose a 10 percent penalty on the previously untaxed amount.

The IRS requires you to withdraw a specific minimum amount beginning no later than April 1 the year after you turn age 70½. The IRS bases withdrawals, called "minimum required distributions," on your life expectancy and account balance.

You can get your life expectancy from IRS publication 590 at www.irs.gov/formspubs/index.html.

If you don't begin withdrawals, the IRS may impose a 50 percent tax on the amount you should have taken out. For example, if IRS publication 590 says you have a life expectancy of 15 years and your account balance is $150,000, your minimum required distribution is $10,000. Check the IRS publication for specific instructions.

15.3

An easier option than poring through IRS publications is using an online calculator.

The National Association of Securities Dealers has one for calculating minimum required distributions for 401(k) plans and IRAs. (You can navigate to it at www. nasd.com under Investor Information / Tools & Calculators.)

You cannot roll the minimum required distribution into an IRA or other qualified retirement plan. (Different rules apply to employees of the sponsoring company age 70½ or above and part owners of the company. You should consult a tax professional for advice.)

You can withdraw funds before age 59½ under certain hardship conditions. Your plan will describe what constitutes "financial hardship" conditions, although many plans use the IRS definition of hardship as:

▶ Extraordinary medical expenses

▶ The purchase of a home

▶ Payment of college expenses for the next year

▶ Emergency payments to stop eviction or foreclosure

Consult your plan for specifics. You still have to pay ordinary income taxes on the withdrawal and a 10 percent penalty. Under other circumstances, such as permanent disability, death, extreme medical costs, separation from service at age 55 and above, you (or your heirs) can take a distribution without the 10 percent penalty. However, you will still have to pay applicable income taxes.

Recent reforms have sought to bring more workers into the 401(k) pool by allowing employers to automatically enroll employees into the program. If an employee did not want to participate, they would have to opt out. The reforms also opened the way for companies to provide more investment advice for employees without the liability issue of being sued for bad recommendations. The hope is that better informed workers will make better investment decisions with their 401(k) money.

Unlike traditional pensions, if you leave your job, you can either take your 401(k) money with you or, in some cases, leave it at your old employer. You may have several choices if you take a new job. Your new employer may let you roll over your old 401(k) money into its 401(k) plan. This is done with a transfer between the two plans. Your old employer may let you keep your 401(k) where it is even if you are working somewhere else. A third option is to roll your 401(k) into an IRA.

No matter which option you choose, let the old plan transfer the money to avoid the 20 percent withholding and potential penalty problems.

Self-Employed 401(k) Plan

For some self-employed people, an individual 401(k) is an alternative. You must own an incorporated business and be the only employee to set up a solo 401(k). For individuals who generate high incomes, the individual 401(k) has some advantages over other retirement plans. You can defer the annual maximum of $15,000 in salary, plus another $5,000 if you are over age 50. Your business can add in up to 25 percent of your earnings. The combination of your deferred salary and the company's contribution can't exceed $44,000 a year (as of 2006) plus the catch up provision if you are age 50 or over.

Roth 401(k) Plan

In 2006, companies began offering a Roth 401(k). The new Roth 401(k) has many of the same characteristics as a Roth IRA. It is funded with after-tax dollars and withdrawals of your contributions and earnings at retirement are tax-free. It has the same contribution limits as regular 401(k) plans, which means you may have two accounts (a traditional 401[k] and a Roth 401[k]), but you still have just one contribution limit. Employer matches to Roth 401(k) accounts are held in a separate account and taxed as income when withdrawn during retirement.

Because you are giving up a current tax reduction for tax-free withdrawals, you should feel confident you will be in the same or higher income tax bracket when you retire. If you "know" you will be in a lower income tax bracket than you are now, it might not make sense to give up the current tax break of a traditional 401(k).

Unlike a traditional 401(k), there is no mandatory distribution at age 70½.

Nonprofit Organization 403(b) Plan

The 403(b) retirement plan is for employees of public schools, religious organizations, and some nonprofit corporations. In many ways, the 403(b) is virtually identical to the 401(k) retirement program. Early withdrawals, contribution limits, loans, and other administrative matters are the same.

One area that differs is the funding mechanisms. The 403(b) grew out of a program called Tax Sheltered Annuities, which was the retirement program for many teachers for years. As the program evolved along with the growth in popularity of the 401(k) plans, other funding vehicles were added. Now there are three basic funding types for 403(b) accounts.

15.3

▶ Annuity contracts provided by life insurance companies

▶ Custodial accounts, which invest in mutual funds

▶ Retirement income funds, which invest in either annuities or mutual funds—available only to church employees

Older 403(b) plans may have some restrictions on investments that are not present on 401(k) plans.

15.4 SMALL BUSINESS RETIREMENT PLANS

Simplified Employee Pension Plans (SEPs)

Saving Incentive Match Plans for Employees (SIMPLE)

Keogh Plans

Retirement plans can be complicated and expensive to administer, but some let small businesses offer benefits to their employees. This section discusses the three most popular small business retirement plans.

Simplified Employee Pension Plans (SEPs)

Simplified Employee Pension Plans (SEPs) are a form of IRA that small businesses can use to offer a retirement plan to their employees. Because they are IRAs, the employees set up the accounts themselves, even though the business provides the funds. This means less administration for the employer. For the employee, it means they are immediately vested in the account and, if they leave the company, the account and money go with them.

The employer must treat all employees the same, including the owner or president. Everyone in the plan gets the same benefit. The usual qualifications for participating are: that you must be at least 21 years old; have worked three of the last five years; not be a nonresident alien; and make the required annual minimum wage. All employees meeting these requirements must be included.

The employer funds the program up to 25 percent of the employee's earnings or $44,000, whichever is less. Employers can change the amount they contribute each year or skip a year if business is bad. To end the plan, or if an employee leaves the company, the assets are rolled into an IRA to maintain the tax-deferred status.

Saving Incentive Match Plans for Employees (SIMPLE)

The Saving Incentive Match Plans for Employees (SIMPLE) plan is more like a 401(k) plan in that employees may contribute up to $10,000 in 2006. Employers are required to contribute either 2 percent of their compensation for all eligible workers or match dollar-for-dollar up to 3 percent of a contributing employees' compensation. Employees eligible to participate must make $5,000 a year or more.

15.4

Like the SEP, a SIMPLE is set up so that each employee has an IRA in his or her name. The employees are immediately vested and can take the assets with them if they change jobs.

Keogh Plans

Keogh plans offer a way for self-employed workers and business owners to save for retirement. The plan can take several forms depending on whether you have employees or not and whether you want a simple or sophisticated plan. Because of the complicated nature of Keogh plans, you should consult a tax accountant or attorney familiar with setting up these types of plans before you commit yourself to a plan that may be hard to maintain.

If you have no employees and qualify for a Keogh, you also qualify for a SEP retirement plan. The Keogh will probably let you shelter more money in your retirement account, but it is more complex to set up and expensive to maintain.

15.5 GETTING HELP

Professional Assistance

Deciding which retirement products to use and when can be a daunting task. Many people find a professional financial planner can provide clarity to the process. This section discusses the professional assistance that's available.

Professional Assistance

Funding your retirement usually doesn't mean picking one product and putting all your money in that effort. The best strategy is using the strengths of several products working together to reach your goal. Your employment situation may limit your choices to some extent, but there are enough different retirement plans that you can find solutions to almost any funding dilemma.

Many people find it productive and cost-beneficial to work with a financial planning professional to fashion an investment plan using the retirement tools available. A financial planning professional will know which retirement products you qualify for and which ones make the most sense for your personal situation.

You can find professional financial planners working in a variety of settings—either in pure planning practices or with investment companies or life insurance firms. You should look for professional designations to determine their qualifications and adherence to ethical standards. Those designations are:

▶ **Certified Financial Planner (CFP):** This is the top professional designation for financial planners. CFPs have knowledge of investments, estate and retirement planning, insurance and taxes, and must complete extensive course work and pass qualifying exams.

▶ **Chartered Financial Consultant (ChFC):** These planners must complete course work and pass exams on financial planning, investing, insurance, taxes, and estate planning in addition to completing three years of work experience in financial planning.

▶ **Certified Public Accountant and Personal Financial Specialist (CPA and PFS):** These are CPAs who have taken additional course work that is specialized in financial planning.

▶ **Charter Life Underwriter (CLU):** These professionals work for life insurance companies and take the same financial planning topics as the ChFC designation.

15.5

Professional financial planners will assess your current savings level, your retirement needs and goals, and which retirement products will work best in reaching the funding level you need to accomplish your goal.

◀ *SEE ALSO 1.4, "Using a Financial Planner"* ▶

16
ESTATE PLANNING

16.1 ESTATE TYPES

Taxable Estate

Probate Estate

When you die, you leave behind two major types of estates: a taxable estate and a probate estate. The two do not contain the same assets. This section discusses those two types of estates.

Taxable Estate

You may not escape taxes even in death. Federal and state governments have several different taxes that may apply to your estate depending on its size and the state where you live.

The **federal estate tax,** sometimes called the inheritance tax or the death tax, has an exclusion of $2 million, which means if your estate is valued at less than that, your estate owes no federal estate tax. However, if your estate must pay federal estate tax, the rate is 46 percent. The federal estate tax is controversial and politically sensitive.

WORDS TO GO . . .WORDS TO GO . . .WORDS TO GO

The **federal estate tax** is paid on estates valued at over $2 million in 2006. The tax rate is 46 percent.

The federal estate tax liability is determined by computing the value of the gross estate, which is the value of the property the deceased had an interest in (one-half of community property) no matter where it is located. Types of property included in a taxable estate include:

- ▶ **All assets privately owned:** Stocks, bonds, real estate, vehicles, ownership of a business, collections, and so on.

- ▶ **Deceased interest in jointly owned property:** If someone other than a spouse owns property with the deceased, the full value of the property is included in the estate, unless the person surviving can prove their contribution.

- ▶ **Jointly owned property with spouse:** Property owned with a spouse is only counted at 50 percent of its value to the taxable estate.

▶ **Property where deceased retained control:** Trusts and life estates for example, are counted at full value in your taxable estate.

▶ **Retirement accounts:** The value of all retirement accounts are counted in the federal taxable estate.

If the deceased owned a farm or business, special conditions may apply and professional help is needed. Once the gross value of the estate is established by the executor, certain deductions, including funeral expenses, other taxes, mortgages and loans, and other claims can be deducted.

State taxes, which may be called inheritance, transfer, or pick-up taxes, vary greatly and may or may not follow federal guidelines. Check with a qualified accountant or estate attorney familiar with your state's laws.

Probate Estate

Your **probate** estate includes those assets in your will that are filed for probate with the court. Some assets will pass to your spouse without going through probate or the court, while others must be processed by the court. There are strategies to minimize the amount of assets that must go through probate, which speeds the process some and will get the assets into the hands of the people you want to have them.

WORDS TO GO . . . WORDS TO GO . . . WORDS TO GO

Probate is a judicial process where a special court determines the validity of a will, appoints an executor to carry out the will's instructions, and oversees the disposition of the deceased's assets.

The probate process is greatly aided by a well-written will that clearly describes your wishes. The more complicated your financial life, the more important it is to prepare your estate so that your heirs fully understand your wishes and have the means to carry them out.

16.2 PROBATE

What Happens

Executor's Role

Complications

When you die, a special court system handles your estate. The role of the court is to follow the law in regards to executing your will and dispersing your assets. This section discusses the probate process.

What Happens

Your will enters the probate or surrogate court system in the county where you resided when you died. There it is administered by the court to ensure that state law and your wishes are followed to the extent they coincide. The court will resolve any disputes. If you died without a will, the court will work to resolve your estate according to guidelines in state law. This could include custody of your children if both parents are dead. If you die without a will, the state must decide who will raise your children; it may not be the relative you would have picked, and it may be an institution if no one steps forward.

The court works with the **executor** (or appoints an administrator if there is no will) to pay all the outstanding debts and satisfy all the necessary loose ends so the estate can be concluded. If there are complications such as business owner-ship, the executor can arrange for an appraisal of the interest's value if it does not pass to the surviving spouse.

> **WORDS TO GO . . .** *WORDS TO GO . . . WORDS TO GO*
>
> The **executor** of a will is the person named in the will and appointed by the court to administer the estate through the probate process.

Executor's Role

The executor's role is to wrap up all the loose ends so the estate can pay its bills, file tax returns, arrange for valuations of business interests, or handle other com-plicated business matters. The executor also has to find all named and potential heirs. Because the process may take several months, investment decisions may need to be made and the executor is responsible for profits or losses.

The executor is obligated to the estate and heirs as a fiduciary, meaning they must act in their best interest at all times and do what they can to preserve the value of the estate. Investing estate assets in risky ventures would be inappropriate.

If the estate is very large and complex, some people may consider hiring a professional executor. This step may also be necessary if there is conflict in the family and choosing an executor from among family members would make matters worse.

Specific duties of the executor include:

- ▶ Inventory all the assets in the estate; find and document bank accounts, life insurance policies, benefits from work, retirement benefits, and so on.

- ▶ The executor can hire accountants, attorneys, or other professionals to help evaluate a complicated estate.

- ▶ The executor preserves the estate's assets. This may mean paying insurance bills on time or placing idle funds in a safe investment until the estate is settled. The court will issue special letters that authorize the executor to access bank accounts and other financial holdings.

- ▶ If the decedent provided the funds, the executor might be directed to pay off the mortgage or be directed by the will to use his discretion—it may make more sense to not pay off the mortgage and use the proceeds for living expenses. The executor will have to pay the regular bills such as utilities, credit cards, and such. In addition, any remaining medical bills and funeral expenses must be paid. All attorneys' fees are priority, also.

- ▶ The executor, with professional tax help, will figure out how to file federal and state inheritance forms and pay any taxes due out of estate funds.

- ▶ Claims against the estate by creditors are processed. In some states, notices must be published in newspapers at specific times to alert creditors. At some point, the court will authorize the executor to proceed, and all remaining claims against the estate will be paid.

- ▶ After taxes and claims are settled, the executor distributes what's left of the estate's assets according to the directions in the will. If there is no will, the administrator follows state law on distribution.

- ▶ Accounts and assets held as joint tenancy with rights of survivorship, and those that have a named beneficiary, are not part of the estate and cannot be sold to pay estate bills or debts.

The executor is entitled to compensation for their time and effort in settling the estate, because the process can involve considerable effort. For simple probates, many family members decline the fees.

Complications

Complications to probate arise primarily from no will or a poorly written one. In either case, the court has to sort out what the law says will happen in certain situations rather than trying to guess what your intentions were.

If you die without a will, the laws in your state have specific ways that the assets are divided. Any property not held in joint tenancy with rights of survivorship is divided by the court according to a formula. Although the formula may be different in your state, here's what it will probably look like depending on your status at death:

▶ **Married/children:** It seems logical that the surviving spouse would get everything, but in most states it doesn't work that way. The surviving spouse gets one-half to one-third of the estate and the children get the rest.

▶ **Married/no children:** Again, everything should go to the surviving spouse, but the court in most states will award only one-half to one-third while the balance goes to your parents if they are alive. If your parents aren't alive, your siblings may get the balance.

▶ **Single/children:** In this case, the state will give everything to the children. If the children are minors, a guardian will be appointed until they reach age 18 (or 21).

▶ **Single/no children:** In most cases, states will award the estate to your parents. If your parents are dead, it may be divided among your siblings.

The major complication is no will for the court to honor your wishes. The court will not consider what your spouse or friends say were your wishes. If you want to direct how your estate is divided and protect your spouse and children, a well-written will is your best defense.

Heirs can challenge the validity of a will, especially if there has been a recent change in heirs, such as a new wife or husband. In some cases, a new spouse is accused of undue influence to exclude children from a previous marriage.

People may have several wills during their lifetime and it is important that only the most current be available. You should retain the original and make sure it contains a clause voiding all earlier wills.

16.3 WILLS

Types of Wills

Living Wills

Community Property States

Power of Attorney

Medical Power of Attorney

A well-written will is your best method of assuring yourself that your wishes will be honored following your death. This section looks at wills and other legal documents that capture our intentions at death.

Types of Wills

Professional estate planners insist that a well-written will is the best way you can direct the disposition of your estate. Without a will, those **assets** that are part of your estate will be distributed by a formula devised by state law. There are several different types of wills. Each accomplishes a specific task.

> **WORDS TO GO . . .WORDS TO GO . . .WORDS TO GO**
>
> **Assets** are physical items and financial accounts you own that can be converted to cash.

▶ **Simple will:** With an uncomplicated estate, the simple will provides for the distribution of your assets. When couples have wills drawn up, they often are reciprocal, which means each will gives everything to the other. If there is something that one person wants to go to another member of the family or someone or something else, it is spelled out as an exception. An example might be passing a specific family heirloom from a father to a son.

For some families, the picture becomes complicated by previous marriages, stepchildren, children you've had together, and property you owned before you married this spouse.

▶ **Pour-over will:** A pour-over will is used in connection with a trust where you place your assets to avoid probate. The pour-over will addresses any assets you forgot to put in the trust and custody of the children.

▶ **Testamentary trust will:** These wills are used to establish trusts for some of your assets after you die.

▶ **Holographic will:** A handwritten will that is not witnessed. Fewer than 20 states recognize these wills.

▶ **Joint will:** A single will covers both a husband and wife (or any two people)—usually not a good idea because what may work for the husband if the wife dies may not work for the wife if the husband dies.

▶ **Oral will:** A will that is spoken to witnesses. Few states recognize this type of will.

Living Wills

Living wills are not wills at all, but directives to medical personnel regarding your wishes about life support in the event of a major illness or accident. You can direct medical personnel to perform or not perform the level of emergency life sustaining treatment you desire in certain circumstances.

The key to the effectiveness of these documents is communication. Communicate your desires with your family and your physician. Make sure they have copies of the living will so they can vouch for your decision if necessary.

Community Property States

Nine states are community property states, which means property and other assets acquired during a marriage are considered to be owned equally by the two spouses. All income, real estate, and other assets acquired during the marriage are owned equally. The remaining states divide property under common law, which considers contribution more strongly.

The community property states are Arizona, California, Idaho, Louisiana, Nevada, New Mexico, Texas, Washington, and Wisconsin

Power of Attorney

Power of attorney is a legal step that grants a person the right to act on another's behalf. There are very narrow powers of attorney that focus on just one area, and a broad power of attorney that lets an individual make all the decisions in another person's life. Frequently, an elderly person will give an adult child their power of attorney to manage their affairs. This allows the adult child to write checks, pay bills, manage bank accounts, and act in the parent's behalf as her legal representative. Other times a limited power of attorney will address a specific activity and grant the person the authority to act for another person in this specific matter only.

In either case, make sure you completely understand the consequences and what will be done on your behalf.

Medical Power of Attorney

A medical power of attorney (also called a health care power of attorney) authorizes someone to make health care decisions if you are unable to do so yourself. This person, called your agent, is involved and follows your wishes as expressed in the document regarding treatment and your care. If you make clear your wishes regarding certain levels of sustaining care, it can relieve stress on those close to you, who may not want to make such a decision, or prevent a medical professional from making the decision without regards to your wishes. For example, if you do not wish to be put on a respirator to be kept alive, your agent can make that decision knowing that is your wish.

16.4 TRUSTS

Types of Trusts

Expenses

Trusts can be used to avoid probate of your estate. The advantages are that you bypass much of the time and expense of transferring assets. This section looks at trusts.

Types of Trusts

Estate planners often recommend living trusts to help avoid probate. The reasons to avoid probate are the expense and time involved to process your will through the probate court system. Additional expenses drain resources from the estate, so heirs receive less in a probated estate.

In addition to the living trust, the other main type of trust is the testamentary trust, which is created upon the **trustmaker's** death and the terms of the trust are immediately executed.

Here's how they generally work together. The trustmaker creates a revocable living trust, a written contract that puts legal title of property in the name of the trust managed by the **trustee,** while retaining the economic benefits of the property. In other words, the trust owns the property, but you still receive any benefits just as before. If you want to change the terms of the trust, you can. If one of the assets in the trust is a mutual fund, you would receive any income you wanted and could buy and sell shares as you wished.

WORDS TO GO . . .WORDS TO GO . . .WORDS TO GO

The **trustmaker** is the person who creates the trust and is the economic beneficiary of the assets in the trust.

The **trustee** manages the assets in the trust. The trustee and the trustmaker can be the same person.

When you die, the living trust becomes irrevocable, which means the terms can no longer be changed. Provisions of the trust agreement govern the disposition of the assets upon your death and it is the trustee's responsibility to carry out the terms immediately, or by whatever schedule the trust sets. The trust and the assets held in the trust do not go through probate.

Trusts do not avoid taxes, so don't presume that this is a tax-saving strategy. Your assets will still be counted in your taxable estate, whether they are in a trust or not.

Living trusts work when there are assets that are not held in common with your spouse, as in joint survivorship with rights of survivorship. If most of your holdings have a named beneficiary, you may not need a trust.

While trusts can transfer assets and avoid probate, they can be costly to set up and maintain. Living trusts are not inexpensive, so consider whether you have a sufficiently large enough estate to justify the expense.

Even with the living trust, you will need a will. Called a pour-over will, it captures any assets you forgot to put in the trust and "pours them in" upon your death. More importantly, if you have children, you should make it very clear who you want to be their guardian in the event both parents are dead. A trust will not accomplish this for you.

Expenses

Drafting and setting up a revocable living trust is more expensive than a typical will. You will need an attorney and perhaps an accountant to make it solid. The other expense is transferring all of your assets to the trust. Assets such as real estate and vehicles will need to be retitled in the trust's name in most states. This can be expensive in administrative time and money. It may also trigger a reassessment of real estate in some jurisdictions, which could mean a higher tax bill.

If you have significant assets to transfer on your death, living trusts are worth considering.

16.5 ESTATE PLANNERS AND ATTORNEYS

Directing the Team

Self-Prepared Estate Plans

How much help you need preparing your estate will depend on its size and complicating factors. This section looks at working with professional estate planners.

Directing the Team

Planning your estate is an important exercise that requires your involvement even if you leave the technical details to the professionals. It begins with you deciding how you want your estate divided. If your spouse dies first, how would that plan change? What about the family business or farm? There are many questions to answer when you orient your thinking toward a world without you.

If you have a large and/or complicated estate, you will definitely want to begin working before you retire with an estate planner to design a strategy. If your estate is of more modest means, your most important task is to get a will for you and your spouse and determine if you face any potential estate tax liability.

Many financial planners do estate planning also and can help you prepare a one-shot plan to alert you to tax problems with your state or federal authorities. Their input will be very helpful in working with an attorney to prepare your wills. If there are complications such as business interests in closely-held corporations or farm ownership, the estate planner will have worked that out or given you a strategy to find the right solutions.

Self-Prepared Estate Plans

There are a number of good self-prepared estate plan books and software on the market. Their main benefit is raising many questions that you might not have thought of on your own. Some contain fill-in-the-blank wills and trust forms. These are good starting points, but have them reviewed by competent professionals before you rely on them.

A
WORDS TO GO
GLOSSARY

401(k) plan is a qualified defined contribution plan offered by employers. It allows employees to have a certain percentage of their salary deducted and invested in the plan. The deduction is pre-tax, so employees experience a reduction in current income tax. The deposits and earnings are tax deferred until withdrawn in retirement.

403(b) plan is the retirement plan for religious, educational, and other nonprofit groups. This plan may use tax-deferred annuities instead of mutual funds.

Actively managed mutual funds are open-end funds that employ a portfolio manger who buys and sells stocks and bonds in an attempt to post a better return than the market, usually represented by some stock index, such as the S&P 500.

Actual cash value is what the insurance company determines your car was worth just before the accident. This value is not what you paid for the car, but factors in depreciation, resale value, and other factors. It is also used by property insurance companies to compensate you for items damaged or stolen. It is the least expensive form of coverage because it provides the least coverage. The actual cash value considers depreciation, market value, condition, and so on.

Actual dealer invoice price, often quoted in dealer ads when they say "One percent over dealer invoice!" is not the dealer's true cost. Do your homework and find out what their real cost is (or close to it) and you'll get a better price on your new car.

Adjustable rate mortgages (ARMs) are a home mortgage option that lets the lender adjust the interest rate at predetermined intervals. The advantage to the borrower is that these loans often let people qualify for larger loan amounts than conventional fixed rate loans. The downside is that, when interest rates rise, borrowers may find they can no longer afford the payments. ARMs come with adjustment periods from one to seven years.

Adjusted Gross Income (AGI) is the first cut at adjusting your gross reported income. It includes those adjustments that are allowed whether you itemized deductions or not.

Alternative Minimum Tax is a parallel tax system that eliminates many common deductions to recalculate your taxes. The AMT was supposed to only catch the very wealthy who claim so many deductions they never paid any taxes. Instead, thanks to inflation, many upper middle class taxpayers are caught by AMT and forced to figure their taxes the traditional way and by the more stringent AMT method. Taxpayers must pay whichever tax bill is the highest.

Anchor tenant is a major company, often a national or regional leader in their business, who will attract traffic to a shopping center. They often are on the ends of shopping centers—anchoring the development.

Annuitant is the person the life insurance company uses to base the annuity payments. In most cases, the owner and the annuitant are the same person, however it doesn't have to be.

Annuitizing is the process of taking the value of the annuity and calculating the monthly payment based on the payout option selected by the owner.

Annuity is a contract with a life insurance company guaranteeing a certain payout over a period. It may contain a death benefit that would pay a survivor in the case of death.

Appreciation is the increase in value of an asset over time. Not all assets appreciate, however in normal market conditions, real estate shows a historical pattern of appreciation.

Assets are physical items and financial accounts you own that can be converted to cash.

Asset allocation is the allocating of major asset classes (stocks, bonds, cash) based on your life circumstances. Typically, younger investors can afford to be more aggressive in their allocation because time is on their side, while older investors need to be more conservative.

Asset classes are tangible assets such as stocks, bonds, cash, real estate, and other types of assets. These different classes form the basis of active diversification.

Associates Degree requires a two-year course of study, usually at a community college, that often is in a vocational discipline rather than preparatory to advancing to a four-year program.

ATM or automatic teller machine networks are large systems of machines, many privately owned by entrepreneurs that provide access for customers in many locations around the country and even in many foreign countries. The network recognizes cards issued on its system and will offer certain services depending on the machine and location. There is usually a fee to use the ATM.

Boilerplate format is the use of standard legal terms for the bulk of a lease or other legal documents. These terms and phrases have stood the test of time and courts, so attorneys reuse them rather than create something new and take the chance it may be challenged in court.

Builder's liens are a legal document filed by contractors against the title of a house to ensure they are paid for their work. With a lien on the title, a house cannot be sold or the title clearly conveyed to the new owner until the lien is cleared. There are other types of liens, including tax liens that prevent a clean sale also.

Buy-and-hold investing is a strategy that says investor success is a result of identifying quality investments and holding them rather than actively trading in and out of the market.

Callable CDs allow the financial institution to call or redeem the CDs after a certain period, typically six months. This means you bear the interest rate risk. If rates fall, the bank can call your CDs once the protection period ends. You get your principal and interest to-date, but lose the higher paying CDs and must reinvest your money at the now lower rate.

Capital gains result when an asset is sold for a profit. In the case of a mutual fund, that asset may be a stock, bond, or a fixed-income security. If the asset has been held for less than one year, it is a short-term capital gain. If it was held more than a year, it is a long-term gain.

Cash-balance pensions are similar to defined benefit plans except there is no reward for longevity and employees can take the plan with them if they change jobs.

Cash flow in the context of a personal budget refers to when and how often money is received in your bank account. This will not be the same for every worker, as some are on a paycheck and paid every week or two, while others may be on commission and paid some time after orders are booked, for example.

Charge cards differ from credit cards in that they don't offer a true line of credit. You are expected to pay the balance each month. How much you can charge during the month depends on previous spending patterns and other financial factors.

Closed-end mutual funds are funds that trade on stock exchanges like common stock. A fixed number of shares are issued and the value of the fund is more a function of supply and demand, unlike an open-end fund, which can issue more shares to accommodate new investors.

Compounding is the mathematical means by which interest earned during one period adds to the principal, then the next period's interest is earned on the resulting principal plus interest in the first period. Another way to say this is interest earning interest.

Consumable in the context of consumer finance means any good or service that is used immediately and provides no lasting value. Financing consumables is a poor personal finance decision because you have used and/or disposed of the goods or service, but continue to pay interest on the charges.

Consumer Price Index is a basket of goods and services tracked by the Bureau of Labor Statistics that measures the relative price change from month to month. This change is the rate of inflation.

Consumer Price Index for Urban consumers is a variation of the consumer price index that focuses in on those items that urban dwellers would buy to measure how inflation impacts them.

Core holding is a mutual fund or exchange traded fund that is broad based and central to an investor's investment strategy. The investor will plan an investment to hold and not trade.

Cost of living is a generic phrase used to describe the general increase in the cost of goods and services. It comes from the Labor Department's Consumer Price Index, which is also known as the rate of inflation.

Coupon comes from the bond markets where years ago bond investors had to clip coupons off the actual paper bond and send them in to receive their interest payment. Thus the term "coupon clippers" was given to bond investors.

Custodian of an account maintains the account and keeps records of deposits and withdrawals.

Debentures are unsecured bonds that are offered on the credit of the corporation. For a well-known, established company, this may not be a very risky bond, but these are very risky investments for less financially secure companies because they are unsecured by any corporate asset.

Debt-to-income ratio is a measurement of how much consumer debt you are carrying relative to your income. It is an important ratio to judge your financial health and used by lenders to decide if you are financially strong enough to take on more debt.

Deflation is a marked decline in the prices of goods and services, usually accompanying high unemployment and a drop in the output of a nation's economy.

Default in the context of a loan means the person owning the money fails to make payments. A mortgage loan in default may lead to foreclosure if the responsible person does not make back payments.

Defined benefit plans calculate retirement benefits using a formula that applies a percentage to an average salary (usually the last five years or the best five years of compensation) and adds in a longevity bonus for the number of years worked. This gives the employee a monthly benefit for the rest of their life.

Defined contribution plans provide the employee an opportunity to invest pre-tax money deducted on a regular basis in a group of mutual funds and other investments. The employer may match part of the employee contribution, but is not required to by law. The employee will only know how much is contributed to the plan. The ultimate benefit at retirement will depend on how well the employee's choices of investments performed.

Demand deposit account is an account at a financial institution with no strings attached that has no penalties for early withdrawal or minimum wait for withdrawals. It's your money and you can have it when you want it. You will usually pay for this convenience with a low rate of interest.

Depreciation is the amount of money an asset drops in value over time. It is an expense that is deducted from income but does not represent an actual outlay of cash. It is also the loss in value an asset experiences over time. In the case of cars, depreciation is a function of not only mechanical wear, but the fact that each year cars are different in design (some more so than others) rendering last year's model out of fashion and so worth less because it is no longer "new."

Discharging a bankruptcy is the final act by the bankruptcy court that completes the process of finally eliminating the debts from your responsibility.

Discount brokers focus on quick trades and straight-forward execution. They offer their services for much less than full service brokers, but don't provide personal advice or research.

Discretionary expenses cover the costs of items and services you buy that are not necessary for maintaining your home or life. They may include items or services that are important to your career, such as haircuts and clothes, but are matters of personal choice.

Diversification is the reduction of risk by spreading investment dollars over numerous stocks and or bonds to minimize the impact should one of the investments turn bad.

Dividends are cash payments (usually, but not always) to shareholders by companies. Dividends are a distribution of profits to the owners. Companies that pay regular dividends are valued for that extra return they provide shareholders.

Dollar cost averaging is investing a fixed amount on a regular basis in a mutual fund, usually monthly and through an automatic debit to your bank account. This investment method means you buy fewer shares when prices are high and more share when prices are lower resulting in an overall lower average cost.

Downsize is a term used by companies who are reducing the number of employees. One of the ways this is done is to offer early retirement to some workers.

Earnest money is a check that accompanies your offer to buy a house. It may be known by different names in different markets, but the purpose is to show the seller that you are serious about your offer and willing to tie up your personal funds to demonstrate your interest.

Earnings is a word that can have several meanings when used to describe accounting activity, however it generally means profits when used without a modifying term to describe some other function.

Earnings per share (EPS) is a way of reporting earnings or profits on a per share of stock. The number is found by dividing the annual earnings by the number of shares.

Emergency cash reserve is a ready supply of cash in bank products or a money market mutual fund that you can tap in a hurry in the event of an emergency such as the loss of a job, a big uninsured medical expense, or some other financial crisis. You should have enough to keep your household running for six months.

Equity in a loan context is the difference between an asset's value and what you owe on the asset. If you sold the asset and paid off the loan, what remains for you to keep is the equity.

Escrow accounts are often set up to hold earnest money while the seller considers your offer. In some states, the real estate company may have an escrow account for holding the funds, while other markets may use a title company, bank, or other financial institution. If the offer to purchase is accepted, the earnest money becomes part of the cash down payment and is conveyed to the seller at closing.

Escrow agents serve as disinterested third parties to the real estate transaction and their role is to hold funds (often down payments) until all matters in the real estate transaction have been resolved. When the seller is satisfied, the buyer is satisfied, and the lender is satisfied that everything is in order, the escrow agent will disperse funds to the appropriate parties (usually the seller).

Exchange Traded Funds (ETFs) are similar to mutual funds in that they are baskets of stocks or bonds, but they are traded on the open market like stocks.

Executor of a will is the person named in the will and appointed by the court to administer the estate through the probate process.

Expected Family Contribution (EFC) is the amount of money the college expects you to pay toward the total cost. The difference between that number and the actual cost of all college expenses for the year is your "need" and that is what the financial aid tries to cover.

Expense ratio is the percentage of assets used to cover the expenses of the mutual fund. These expenses are deducted from the fund's assets, which lowers the shareholders' return. The expenses include the management fee, operating expenses, investing fees, and other fees.

Face value is the amount the bond pays at maturity. It is usually the amount the investor pays for a newly issued bond, but may not be the price an investor pays on the open market.

Federal estate tax is paid on estates valued at over $2 million in 2006. The tax rate is 46 percent.

Financial aid officer (FAO) is the key officer at each school who decides who is eligible for how much financial aid and what kind of aid they are to receive.

Financial independence is a goal that may mean different things to different people, but is a valid goal nevertheless. If you can visualize what financial independence means and put it into a financial perspective (debt-free, own your on business, and so on), you can plan for it.

Financing is to borrow money to purchase goods or services. If you charge something on a credit card and don't pay the balance in full when the bill arrives, you are incurring a debt and paying interest on the money you borrowed.

Fixed annuity is a contract with an insurance company that pays a fixed amount, usually monthly, for a stated period. The insurance company guarantees the principal and interest.

Fixed expenses remain the same regardless of any activity during the month. These expenses include such items as the mortgage or rent, fixed-rate auto loans, and so on.

Foreclosure is the legal process of seizing your house for not paying your mortgage or your taxes. The property is sold and the proceeds go to paying off the note or taxes.

Free Application for Federal Student Aid (FAFSA) is the main federal form used to qualify for financial aid. It is a detailed questionnaire about your family's income and assets.

Full service brokerage firms provide account representatives to handle your business, along with research and other services. Many are converting from charging commissions to charging a fee based on assets under management.

Gross income is your pay or salary before any taxes, insurance payments, or any other deductions are made.

Growth stocks represent companies that are growing at a faster pace than the market in general. They often plow profits, if any, back into the company to finance more growth. Investors count on continued growth to keep stock prices increasing. If the company stops growing, even for a quarter, the stock market may lose confidence in the company and the stock's price can plummet.

Holistic approach an approach to financial planning that looks at every aspect of your life and considers what will work and won't work based on your lifestyle.

Increasing term policies raise the premium on the anniversary date annually. These policies tend to be less expensive than level billing in the early years when you are younger and more expensive if you hold the policy until your older years.

Inflation is a rise in the cost of goods and services with a corresponding decrease in the value of money.

Investment banking firms are large financial institutions that handle the initial distribution of shares during an IPO. They sell shares to national and regional brokerage firms who in turn sell them to their best client.

Itemizing deductions is the process of calculating individual allowable deductions that exceed the amount available under the standard deduction. Not every taxpayer can itemize.

Level billing policies look at the term of the policy (10 years, for example) and determine a premium that is appropriate for the whole period. The premium will fall in the middle, but remain constant for the term of the policy. These policies are convenient for planning purposes, since you'll know what the premium will be.

Leverage is the use of borrowed money to increase your purchasing power. If the value of the asset rises, your return on investment increases dramatically. If the asset loses value, the borrowed money that must be repaid magnifies your loss.

Liabilities are ongoing debts you owe. They are not monthly bills for services, but obligations that will follow you even if you move to another location.

Liquidity refers to how easily and quickly an asset can be converted to cash. Stocks and mutual funds are liquid because you can sell and get cash easily. Bank accounts, such as savings and checking, are liquid. Real estate is not liquid at all, because it could take some time to find a buyer and close the deal to get your money.

Managed care insurance plans attempt to control costs by managing the care patients receive and the providers that dispense the services. By negotiating discounts with providers and driving patients to them, insurance companies can lower overall health care costs.

Margin is an investment strategy that uses borrowed money to increase buying power. Investors, with good credit, can borrow up to 50 percent of the value of their assets from their broker. Usually the money is used to buy more stock. The investor must maintain the value of the account at a certain level. If the price of the stock begins to fall, the investor will be asked to put more money into the account or sell the stock and pay off the margin loan. This is known as a margin call.

Marginal tax rate is the tax rate you pay on the last dollar of income. It is useful in determining what additional income will mean from a tax perspective.

Market capitalization or market cap, as it is known, is calculated by multiplying all of a companies outstanding shares (those shares available for trade on the stock exchanges), by the current per share price.

Market makers on the Nasdaq make a market for a stock they cover by providing a quote at which they would buy or sell the stock. They enter customer's orders and the computer system places the best buy order and the best sell order at the top of their respective quote lists.

Maturity is when a bond reaches the end of its financial life and the face value or principal is returned to the owner. Bonds may have maturities of just a few years or may stretch out for many years.

Meal tickets allow college students to eat at campus dining facilities even if they live off campus. They are often a bargain compared to fast food and may be more convenient than eating all the meals at a distant apartment.

Medicare taxes are collected on all wages. Employees pay 1.45 percent and employers pay 1.45 percent for 2.90 percent on all wages—there is no upper limit. Self-employed people pay the full amount.

Need in college financial aid is the difference between what you can afford and what the college cost. The FAO is responsible for presenting you with an aid package that address some or all of your need.

Needs based financial assistance is driven by the financial circumstances of the family. This assistance specifically targets lower income households.

Negative amortization is a loan situation where your payment does not cover all of the interest or any of the equity. You make payments, but the balance of the loan keeps going up because you pay interest on the interest you did not cover in your payment.

Net asset value is the daily value of a mutual fund that includes all the assets minus the fund's liabilities converted to a per share price. This is the price you buy and sell mutual fund shares at if you deal directly with the company.

Net worth statement is a listing of all you own and all you owe—your assets and liabilities. When you subtract your liabilities from your assets, the remainder is your net worth.

Nonfixed expenses, or variable expenses, change from one month to the next, often because of some action on your part. A credit card bill will change based on any payment or additional charges you make during the month.

Open-end mutual funds make up the largest number of funds on the market. Open-end funds simply issue new shares when someone wants to buy into the fund, rather than matching an existing shareholder who wants to sell.

Ordinary income is the term the IRS uses to designate how money coming out of most retirement plans will be taxed. It means the funds will be taxed as if you earned them as salary, which in most cases is what happened, but the tax was deferred to this later date.

Passive loss results from depreciation, which is not a direct loss due to economic circumstances. Usually, tax laws do not allow you to mix active gains and losses with passive gains and losses.

Passively managed mutual funds are funds that track specific stock or market indexes such as the S&P 500 or the Dow. The funds are passive because there are no investment decisions. The fund mirrors the index by investing in the stocks that comprise the index. This keeps expenses extremely low.

Payday loans are personal loans that let you borrow against your next paycheck. There are fees for the service and, if you don't pay back the loan in a short period, it renews with additional fees and interest. Some of these loans can result in consumers paying well over 100 percent interest on an annual basis.

Personal exemption is a dollar amount the IRS allows for you, your spouse, and every dependent in your household. The amount changes each year. There is a specific definition of dependent, which is in the instructions for completing the forms. You can claim personal exemptions on all three tax forms.

Points are equal to 1 percent of the loan amount and are charged by the lender at closing to reduce the interest rate.

Preexisting condition is a medical situation that existed before you applied for any type of insurance. It is usually a chronic condition and may affect your ability to obtain insurance.

Preferred stocks are a special type of stock that companies issue. They grant limited rights when it comes to voting on company business, but they pay a steady dividend and that's what attracts investors. The stock's price may not rise (or fall) nearly as fast or as far as the common stock. Income investors like preferred stock from solid companies for its dependability.

Private mortgage insurance is required by lenders when the buyer does not present at least 20 percent down payment. The insurance protects the lender against default. When the homeowner's equity passes 20 percent, the policy can be canceled; however, the lender may need to be prompted.

Probate is a judicial process where a special court determines the validity of a will, appoints an executor to carry out the will's instructions, and oversees the disposition of the deceased's assets.

Prospectus is a legal document required by the Securities and Exchange Commission that details all the information investors need to know about an investment, including the risk of losing your money.

Purchasing power is what your dollars will buy relative to another point in time. Inflation reduces purchasing power by raising prices, thus your dollar is worth less this year than it was last year.

Qualified retirement accounts are designated by the IRS for special treatment such as tax-deferred growth while funds remain in the account. An example of a qualified retirement account is an IRA.

Real estate investment trusts are closed-end funds that invest in real estate and mortgages. They must pass 90 percent of all profits onto the shareholders, which makes them well-suited for people looking for current income.

Redeem, in bond parlance, means for the issuer to pay the owner the full face value of the bond. Bonds are usually redeemed at maturity, but can be redeemed earlier through a call provision.

Reinvesting earnings from a mutual fund account automatically buys more shares of the fund. This is a way to build your stake in the fund by using profits. You still must pay taxes on the earnings in most cases.

Revolving credit is a form of consumer credit that renews the amount of credit available (up to a limit) by the amount of payment you make. You don't have to reapply—the credit line renews automatically.

Risk pool is the number of people who share the risk for a particular group insurance policy. A basic principle of insurance is the larger the risk pool, the less risk there is to the insurer and the lower the premium.

Salary reduction plan is another name for any retirement plan that takes its contribution before withholding taxes are calculated. Your salary is reduced and taxes are lower after the contribution is taken.

Schedule A is found on your IRS form 1040, also known as the long form, and it is where you list your itemized deductions such as unreimbursed medical expenses, charitable contributions, and so on.

Schedule B is also found on your IRS form 1040 and it is for reporting ordinary dividends (from stocks or mutual funds, for example) and interest income.

Schedule D is attached to your IRS form 1040 and it is for reporting short and long-term capital gains or losses.

Secondary market is any market for a security after the initial issue. In the secondary market, securities are bought and sold among investors rather than from the company or agency that issued the stock or bond initially. Stock exchanges are secondary markets. For bonds, most trades are done through brokers matching buyers and sellers.

Secured bonds are issued by corporations and are tied to a physical asset such as real estate or equipment. These bonds are typically more secure because of the collateral of the asset linked to the bond.

Securities and Exchange Commission is the main regulatory agency responsible for monitoring the stock markets and securities industry. It must approve all IPOs and requires frequent and regular filings from publicly traded companies. It is a watchdog for investors to protect them against unethical investing practices.

Social Security taxes are collected on all wages up to a limit. Employees pay 6.2 percent and employers pay 6.2 percent for 12.4 percent on wages up to $94,200 (2006). Self-employed people pay the full amount.

Specialists are employees of a member firm of the NYSE. These investment professionals are responsible for maintaining a market in a particular stock. The specialist matches buy and sell orders, but if the market gets out of balance may step in and buy or sell out of the company's account to regain balance.

Spread is a financial term that describes the difference between two interest rates—one the bank pays and the other the bank collects. It is also used to describe other financial arrangements where there is a difference in price or interest rates. The difference or gap is the spread. Sports betting enthusiasts will also recognize the term as the difference in points between what one team is expected to score over another.

Standard deduction is an amount allotted by the IRS for taxpayers who do not itemize deductions. It is a lump-sum deduction that comes off the taxpayer's income to lower the amount that will eventually be taxed.

Stock options give the owner the right, but not the obligation, to buy a certain number of shares of stock at a fixed price on or before a certain date regardless of the current market price of the stock. Employers often use stock options as incentives for employees.

Stocks-to-bonds ratio is the percentage of your portfolio occupied by stocks and bonds. Since bonds are considered more conservative, investors use a higher ratio of bonds for a less aggressive market position and a higher ratio of stocks for a more aggressive position.

Stop-loss orders tell your stockbroker to execute a sell order when the price of a stock drops to a specific level. When the price falls to this level, the broker sells the stock at the current market price. This strategy prevents you from losing more than a specific amount.

Strike price is the price specified in the option that the owner can pay for shares of stock. If the market price is higher than the strike price, the options are valuable; however, if the market price is lower, the options are worthless.

Sub-accounts are another name for mutual funds. They reside in the separate account of a variable annuity. Variable annuity investors split their money among the various sub-accounts. The money manager frequently takes an existing mutual fund and clones it into a sub-account for the variable annuity.

Surrender for cash value of an annuity is what the account is worth at any point in time. That may be the invested premium, plus interest, less fees and withdrawals. If you withdraw early, there would be penalties and surrender charges deducted.

Term life is a life insurance policy that offers a death benefit for a defined period (the term). The policy may be guaranteed renewable, but at a different premium. Terms can run from 1 year to 20 years. When the term ends, so does your coverage. Most term life insurance products have no cash value nor do they build any residual value. Term policies are popular because they are cheaper than other forms of life insurance, such as whole life insurance.

Tax audit is an examination by agents of the IRS of your current and, possibly past, tax returns to ensure they are in compliance with tax law.

Tax credits are dollar-for-dollar reductions in your tax bill and are more desirable than tax deductions.

Tax deductions reduce the income that is ultimately taxed. Deductions reduce your tax bill, but only by your tax rate.

Tax-deferred refers to investment vehicles that allow principal and interest to grow without paying taxes on the earnings until sometime in the future. Qualified retirement accounts allow tax-deferred growth. Annuities, whether qualified or not, also allow tax-deferred growth.

Tax-free money market funds invest in securities that generate tax-free income. In most cases, only investors in the highest income tax brackets should invest in these funds because the return is very low.

Time value of money addresses the concept that a dollar today is better than a dollar tomorrow. You can invest a dollar today and it will earn interest. A dollar tomorrow is worth less than a dollar today thanks to inflation.

Total return of an investment in a mutual fund includes any dividends, capital gains distributions, and interest income. This is the appropriate number to consider. It should be noted that this is also a pre-tax return.

Trailing stops are similar to stop-loss orders, but they are used by investors to protect a profit. Investors place a trailing stop behind a profitable stock so that if the price begins to fall, the broker will sell while the price will still produce a profit. If the stock continues to rise, the trailing stop rises with the stock's price, usually following by a percentage.

Trustees manage the assets in the trust. The trustee and the trustmaker can be the same person.

Trustmaker is the person who creates the trust and is the economic beneficiary of the assets in the trust.

Tuition credits are a way to prepay college costs by paying a set price for tuition credits today that can be used in the future by your children. However, with college costs rising at a rate faster than many state university systems anticipated, many have stopped selling the credits or capped their future value.

Umbrella policies are liability protection that begins after your automobile or homeowners liability protection has been exhausted. They cover a variety of liability issues including libel and slander cases.

Upside down in a loan, whether it's for a home or a vehicle, means you owe more than the asset is worth. This can happen because the asset depreciates in price or you paid too much in the first place. In either case, you may have to pay down the note to get out of it.

Usual and customary charges are a list of fees that the insurance company says it will pay for health care services. Doctors in the company's network have agreed to these charges; however, if you go outside the network, a provider may charge more and not agree to the insurance company's fee schedule.

Value stocks represent companies that investors believe the market has under priced. The stock price may be depressed because the company's business is out of favor or for some other reason. Investors believe the stock will eventually be repriced at a higher price that more accurately reflects the true value of the company.

Variable annuity is a contract with an insurance company that pays a minimum interest rate, usually very low, and the rest of the payments vary depending on the market performance of the investments, which are mutual funds.

Vesting schedule is a period set by management for the options to become valid. For example, 20 percent of the options might become valid after one year; 40 percent after two years; and so on. This is known as stepped or phased vesting. Another type of vesting is cliff vesting and that declares 100 percent of the options valid after three years, for example.

Withholding tax is the Social Security, Medicare, and income tax withheld each payday by your employer. Your employer matches your contribution to Social Security and Medicare.

B

RESOURCES

Chapter 1, "Personal Finance Planning"

Certified Financial Planner—www.cfp.net

Certified Public Accountant and Personal Financial Specialist—pfp.aicpa.org

Chartered Financial Consultant—www.chfc-clu.com

Charter Life Underwriter—www.chfc-clu.com

Chapter 2, "Budgeting"

About.com Financial Software—financialsoft.about.com/About_Financial_Software.htm

Quicken Intuit.com—quicken.intuit.com

Microsoft Money.com—www.microsoft.com/money/default.mspx

Chapter 3, "Banking"

AARP: Preventing Identity Theft—www.aarp.org/money/wise_consumer

Bankrate.com—www.bankrate.com

Yahoo! Finance—finance.yahoo.com/banking

Chapter 4, "Credit and Debt"

About.com Debt/Credit Management—credit.about.com/About_Credit_Debt_Management.htm

Bankrate.com—www.bankrate.com

Insurance rating companies:

    A. M. Best—www.ambest.com

    Standard & Poor's—www.standardandpoors.com

    Moody's—www.moodys.com

My Fico.com—www.myfico.com/Default.aspx

Chapter 5, "Housing"

Bankrate.com—www.bankrate.com

E-Loan.com—www.eloan.com

Quicken Loans—www.quickenloans.com

Chapter 6, "Automobiles"

Bankrate.com—www.bankrate.com

Cars.com—www.cars.com/go/index.jsp

Carfax.com—www.carfax.com/cfm/general_check.cfm?vin=

Chapter 7, "Insurance"

About.com Personal Insurance—
personalinsure.about.com/About_Personal_Insurance.htm

Bankrate.com—www.bankrate.com

Insurance Institute for Highway Safety—www.iihs.org

Life and Health Insurance Foundation—www.life-line.org

Chapter 8, "Taxes"

About.com Tax Planning—taxes.about.com

Personal Tax Preparation Software:

> TurboTax—turbotax.intuit.com

> TaxACT—www.taxact.com

> TaxCut—www.taxcut.com

Internal Revenue Service—www.irs.gov

Chapter 9, "College Financing"

Federal student aid website—www.studentaid.ed.gov

Free Application for Federal Student Aid (FAFSA)—www.fafsa.ed.gov

T. Rowe Price College Cost Estimator—www.troweprice.com

Chapter 10, "Investment Planning and Management"

Investment Company Institute: Risk and Reward—
www.ici.org/i4s/bro_i4s_risk.html

Investopedia: Introduction to Investing—
www.investopedia.com/university/beginner

Securities & Exchange Commission: Asset Allocation—
www.sec.gov/investor/pubs/assetallocation.htm

Chapter 11, "Investing in Mutual Funds and Exchange Traded Funds"

Reuters.com Mutual Funds based on Lipper research—
funds.reuters.com/lipper/retail/reuters/overview.asp?type=f

Morningstar.com—
www.morningstar.com

MSN Money: Exchange Traded Funds—
moneycentral.msn.com/investor/research/etfwelcome.asp?ETF=true

Chapter 12, "Investing in Stocks"

About.com Stocks—stocks.about.com/About_Stocks.htm

Bloomberg.com—www.bloomberg.com/welcome.html

Marketwatch.com—www.marketwatch.com/default.aspx?siteid=mktw

Chapter 13, "Investing in Bonds"

Investing in Bonds.com—www.investinginbonds.com

Treasury Direct: U.S. Treasury Bonds—
www.savingsbonds.gov/indiv/indiv.htm

Yahoo! Finance: Bonds—finance.yahoo.com/bonds

Chapter 14, "Retirement Planning"

About.com Retirement planning—
retireplan.about.com/About_Retirement_Planning.htm

Federal Trade Commission: Reverse Mortgages—
www.ftc.gov/bcp/conline/pubs/homes/rms.htm

Social Security and Medicare—www.ssa.gov

Chapter 15, "Retirement Accounts"

Investopedia: Retirement Plans—
www.investopedia.com/university/retirementplans

MsMoney.com: Retirement accounts—
www.msmoney.com/mm/planning/retirement/retirement_accounts.htm

Smart Money.com: Small Business Retirement Plans—
www.smartmoney.com/tax/workbusiness/index.cfm?story=smallbiz

Chapter 16 "Estate Planning"

AARP.com Financial and retirement planning—www.aarp.org/money

CNN Money.com: Estate planning—money.cnn.com/pf/101/lessons/21

Smart Money.com: Estate planning—www.smartmoney.com/estate

INDEX

E

Earned Income Credit Assistant, 181
earnest money, 121
earnings,
  mutual funds, 241, 245
  stocks, 276
earnings per share (EPS), 288
earthquake insurance, purchasing, 151
education. *See* college tuition
EFC (expected family contribution),
  194-195
electronic processing, banks, 65
emergency cash reserves, 39, 220-221
  budgeting for, 39-41
employee stock options, 294-297
employer sponsored 401(k) plans,
  357-361
employer-sponsored loans, college
  tuition, 212
enrolled agents, tax preparations, 176
EPS (earnings per share), 288
equities, 218-219, 276. *See also* mutual
funds
  active traders, 277
  ADRs (American Depository
   Receipts), 285-286
  AMEX (American Stock
   Exchange), 280
  buy-and-hold investors, 277
  buying, 291-292
  cap stocks, 284-285
  choosing, 287-288
  deflation, 285
  dividends, 283-284, 289-290
  Dow Jones Industrial Average, 281
  employee stock options, 294-297
  growth investors, 287
  growth stocks, 283
  income investors, 288
  income stocks, 283
  indexes, 281
  IPOs (initial public offerings),
   277-278
  market prices, 278

  Nasdaq, 279-282
  NYSE (New York Stock Exchange),
   279
  preferred stock, 283-284
  returns on investment, 298-299
  S&P 500, 281-282
  selling, 291-292
  stocks-to-bonds ratio, 250-251
  stop-loss orders, 292-293
  trailing stops, 292-293
  value investors, 287-288
  value stocks, 284
equity, loans, 73
escrow accounts, 121
estates, 368
  estate planners, 378
  probate estates, 369-372
  self-prepared estate plans, 378
  taxable estates, 368-369
  trusts, 376-377
  wills, 373-374
ETFs (Exchange Traded Funds), 217,
  267, 280
  buying, 268
  choosing, 271-272
  fundamentals, 267-268
  market ETFs, 270
  market index ETFs, 270
  sector ETFs, 270
  selling, 268
  tax consequences, 268
executors, estates, 370
exemptions, income taxes, calculating,
  174
expected family contribution (EFC),
  194-195
expected returns, investments, 229-230
expected risks, investments, 229-230
expense ratios, mutual funds, 216-217,
  255
expenses, 22-23
  capturing, 28
  discretionary expenses, 27
  fixed expenses, 27
  payment plans, 29

retirement, 327
seasonal distribution of expenses, 29
spending plans, 30-31
tracking, 28-29
variable expenses, 27
extended theft protection, homeowners
insurance, 152

F

face values, bonds, 219-220, 302
FAFSA (Free Application for Federal
Student Aid), 194
Fannie Mae, 308
FAOs (financial aid officers), colleges,
192
federal aid, college tuition, 199-201
applying for, 201-202
Federal Supplemental Education
Opportunity Grants, 200
Pell Grants, 200
Perkins loans, 200
PLUS (Parents Loan for
Undergraduate Students), 201
Stafford loans, 200
work-study programs, 201
federal estate taxes, 368
Federal Home Mortgage Corporation,
308
federal income tax, 170-173
AMT (Alternative Minimum Tax),
184-185
audits, 186-187
basic structure, 170-171
calculating, 173-174
forms, 178-179
itemized deductions, 171
record keeping, 172
standard deductions, 171
tax credits, 171-172
tax deductions, 171-172
tax savings strategies, 182-183
Federal National Mortgage Association,
308
Federal Supplemental Education

Opportunity Grants, college tuition,
200
fee-based financial planners, 18
fees, banking
account maintenance fees, 62
minimum balance fees, 62-63
transaction fees, 63
fees, credit cards, 79-80
FHA (Federal Housing Authority)
loans, 110
financial aid, college tuition, 195-202
financial aid officers (FAOs), colleges,
192
financial assessments, financial
planning, 3-4
financial independence, financial
planning, 7-9
financial institutions, choosing, 44-47
financial needs, retirement,
determining, 327-330
financial planners, 17-18
commission-based financial
planners, 18-19
fee-based financial planners, 18
financial planning, 2-3
annual reviews, 11-12
calculations, 14-16
college funding, 7
cost of living, 3
financial assessments, 3-4
financial independence, 7-9
financial planners, 18-19
goals, setting, 4-5
holistic approach, 2
net worth statements, 12
personal financial software, 12
questions, 9-11
retirement, 5-7
time value of money, 10-11
financial software, 34-38
choosing, 37-38
financial planning, 12
Microsoft Money, 37-38
Quicken, 37
tax preparation, 36-37